The Book of Truth

Second Volume

www.thewarningsecondcoming.com

The Book of Truth

Second Volume

The Second Coming

Coma Books

Coma Books

Published by Coma Books

www.comabooks.com

First published 2012
1 3 5 7 9 10 8 6 4 2

A CIP catalogue record for this book is available from
the British Library

ISBN 978-1-909448-01-8

Production by **author**_ization!_
E: martin-west@btconnect.com

Printed in Poland

Dedicated to
Mother of God, Mother of Salvation

CONTENTS

The Seal of the Living God
Book of Revelation 7.2

"After this I saw four angels standing at the four corners of the earth holding back the four winds of the earth so that no wind could blow on land or sea or against any tree. Then I saw another angel come up from the East, holding the seal of the living God. He cried out in a loud voice to the four angels who were given power to damage the land and the sea, "Do not damage the land or the sea or the trees until we put the seal on the foreheads of the servants of our God.

The Seal featured on the cover of this book was created as a result of a divine message received by Maria Divine Mercy from God the Father at 12.20am on 20th February 2012 in which He told her he was giving the world the "Seal of the Living God" to protect everyone from the antichrist.

Extract from this message
My daughter tell My children that I do not relish the thoughts of punishing My children for I love them.

They are mine, my cherished creation. To see how the evil one has corrupted their souls is a constant torment to Me, their beloved Father. I desire to take all of you loving children who know and understand My love for you, into My beautiful New Paradise on earth.

I promise you that the persecution will be swift and that you will be protected.

For I now bequeath the Seal of My Love and Protection.

With this you will **escape the notice of those who will cause hardship** in your countries.

My Seal is My promise of Salvation. My power will surge through you with this seal and no harm will come to you.

This is a miracle children, and only those who bow before Me, their Lord and Creator of all things, as little children with love in their hearts for Me, can be blessed with this divine gift.

Rise now and accept My Seal, the Seal of the Living God.

Recite this Crusade Prayer (33) to acknowledge My Seal and accept it with love, joy and gratitude.

O My God, My loving Father
I accept with love and gratitude
Your Divine Seal of Protection

Your Divinity encompasses my body and soul for eternity
I bow in humble thanksgiving and offer you my deep love and loyalty
To you my Beloved Father

I beg you to protect me and my loved ones with this special Seal
And I pledge my life to your service forever and ever
I love you Dear Father
I console you in these times Dear Father

I offer you the Body, Blood, Soul and Divinity of your dearly beloved Son
In atonement for the sins of the world and for the salvation of all your children.

Amen.

Your loving Father in Heaven
God of the Most High

To download this Seal free of charge log onto **www.thewarningsecondcoming.com**

ABOUT THE BOOK OF TRUTH

The Book of Truth is mentioned in Daniel 10:21. This is where a mysterious Book of Truth is referred to. Gabriel explains to Daniel that everything that has been revealed to him about the future and the end times is to be found in the Book of Truth. Daniel is told to seal it up as it is to be left to another time called "The Time Of The End."

Second Volume

Saturday 07 January 2012 – Tuesday 4 September 2012

Judge and curse another in My Name and you spit in My Face
Saturday, January 7, 2012 15:40 hours

My dearly beloved daughter, while My followers continue to fight amongst themselves as to the authenticity of these, My Holy Messages to the world, more and more souls continue to be separated from Me

To those of you who claim to know Me, be assured that your love for Me must be proven.

It is not enough to say you love Me. You must love your neighbour first. How do you love your neighbour? By treating them with love and respect no matter how they offend you.

Woe to those of you who slander another in My Name. You are lost to Me. Without humility in your heart, you, when you judge and curse another in My Name, spit in My Face.

Remember you do not represent Me when you slander and show public hatred for others.

Yet many of those, who project themselves as holy apostles of Mine, fall into this trap, laid down for them by Satan, in order to trip them up.

Go away I say. Pray for forgiveness, far better that you spend more time in prayer for the salvation of your brothers and sisters.

Oh how I wish those followers, who say they come in My Name, would behave in the way I have taught them. How they hurt those poor souls who try their utmost to remain humble in My Eyes.

There is a great need for discernment with regard to these Holy Messages from My Divine Lips, the last such Messages of their kind in these, the end times.

Never create your own opinion based on a flawed understanding of Who I Am and My Teachings.

I Am, above all, a God of Mercy first before I come as Judge.

I love all of you, but, I suffer the same pain today as that I experienced during My time in the Garden of Gethsemane. I will never rest until I save you from the evil one.

Any man who says that I do not suffer does not know Me. Any man who thinks he has been given authority to judge others in My Name, does not truly love Me. Instead, he loves himself and is stuffed with pride.

Any man who wags his finger at others, in order to bully them into believing in Me, has also misunderstood My Teachings of love, humility and patience.

Many well meaning Christians believe that their role is to analyse and re-evaluate My Teachings. Yet much of their analysis is based on human and logical reasoning, which is of little substance in My Kingdom.

When I urge you to become little in My Eyes I mean as a child who does not question. I mean as a child who trusts completely in his father without fear in his heart.

Until you become little in My Eyes you are not fit to speak in My Name.

When you find the humility I seek out, only then can you help me to save souls.

Your Teacher
Redeemer of Mankind
Jesus Christ`

God the Father – You My beloved children have a glorious future ahead of you
Sunday, January 8, 2012 14:04 hours

I am the King of all Creation. I am the Alpha and the Omega. All Mankind will honour Me.

My dearest daughter, the time for humanity to honour Me, their heavenly Father, in all My Glory, is at last drawing very close.

The prayers of My beloved children, those humble servants of Mine, are saving souls and much of humanity against the forces of darkness, which cover the earth.

Behold, I say onto all of you, My humble followers and those who believe in Me, the Creator of all mankind, unite. You must join as one force to honour Me, your Father.

Pray in unity now for global conversion. The Holy Spirit was poured out, by Me, upon the whole world on the 10th May 2011. Already, it has beckoned so many good souls to proclaim My Word.

Now that the power of Satan is diminishing, he will attack as many souls as possible. The worst attacks will be inflicted on My Churches and all those who honour Me, their Heavenly Father.

The faith of My Church will continue to weaken, but, the faith of those who bow before Me will sway the minds of good Christians everywhere and bring them closer to Me.

Much confusion is evolving among My children. To all those who are distracted from praying to Me, God of the Most High, hear My plea to humanity now.

Never allow anyone to distract you from the Truth of My Holy word given to mankind to salvage souls.

Never allow anyone to deter you from praying for those poor tormented souls who have been seized by Satan.

Unite as one, children, and pray for Mercy one last time. Your prayers offer Me the help required to save most of humanity.

You, My daughter, are the end time prophet, who will suffer the most. Because of this Mission you will receive the last such Messages of their kind for the world and will be the primary target of Satan and his minions.

There are now many prophets who have been given a holy mission sanctioned by Me to help guide humanity.

After your Mission I will not be sending anyone else to impart My Messages because the world, as you know it, will have been changed forever.

As the end time prophet, your voice will be rejected, by believers first most, for they will oppose these Divine Message, aggressively, in a way which will startle and frighten you, My daughter.

Satan will attack those poor holy souls as a means to hurt Me. He has already blinded the hearts of believers to the Truth. He will twist the Truth in the minds of those who pay homage to Me, their Heavenly Father and My beloved Son, Jesus Christ.

Be joyful, however, because much conversion has already been achieved with the help of other visionaries and prophets in the world. So many catastrophic events have already been averted because of their work. However, a certain number of chastisements will continue to befall humanity in order to purify nations.

My daughter, the serpent's power will be crushed, and soon. This is why My children must not fear the future. You, My beloved children, have a glorious future ahead of you. All you need to do is to pray for your brothers and sisters and trust in Me completely.

While The Warning, which will take place soon and unexpectedly, will save souls, much prayer is still needed. The prayers I ask of you now are especially for young people in every part of the world.

These are the children entrapped by the wicked lies perpetrated by Satan. These are the children who spend much of their time living in false idolatry and in a make-believe world. They need your prayers the most. Unite, children. Put your differences aside. Shed your coat of pride. Drop down, in love and humility, to ask Me for the graces you need. These graces will flood your soul with the Holy Spirit. Only then will your prayers be heard and answered.

Your beloved Heavenly Father
God the Most High

Jesus calls to children all over the world
Sunday, January 8, 2012 15:30 hours

My dearest beloved daughter, I call out today to all children over the age of seven and to every single child of Mine in the world. You, My little children, are like jewels in My Eyes. You bring Me such tender love and I delight in your company. Know that I love you very much. Some of you know Me already and that is good.

I invite you to chat with Me more, in your own words, as a friend. Never feel you must learn or recite prayers, which you may find difficult. Instead, come to Me and share all of your thoughts, fears, news or problems. I am always at your side even when you ignore Me. I am always hopeful.

To those poor young people, whose lives are filled with falsities, or who are involved with drink or drugs, you must know this. Although you may feel emptiness inside, you must give Me your hand and I will grasp it. I will save you from drowning in a sea of confusion.

Many of you feel worthless and of no significance. You are so overwhelmed by those you idolize in the world of music and celebrity that you feel completely inadequate. Never feel like this, my little children because, in My Eyes, you are very special. Each of you holds a unique place in My Heart. Allow Me to take you on a journey to a wonderful new future.

I will, shortly, introduce a new wonderful Era of Peace and Glory on earth.

You must keep strong. Never give up when you feel down. Never despair when you feel worthless.

You, remember, were born for a reason. No matter what your circumstances are, the reason for your birth is this. You were born to join with Me as part of My New Glorious Kingdom.

I know it is hard for you to hear My Voice as there are so many false gods trying to get your attention.

My promise to you is this. Live your life in hope and love for Me, your Jesus, and I will give you the Gift of Paradise. This Paradise is what is waiting for you if you would only ask Me to help you on your journey towards Me.

I am the love that is missing from your life.

I am the peace you look for.

I am the help you need to feel love in your heart again.

I am Love.

I am the Light.

Without Me you will remain in darkness.

I love you no matter how you may hurt Me or offend Me.

Say this little prayer and I will come running to you immediately.

(Open my eyes Prayer for the young)

Jesus, if you can hear me, then listen to my call for help.
Please help me deal with those who cause me pain.
Help me to stop envy taking over my life and to stop me wishing for things I cannot have.
Instead open my heart to You, dear Jesus.
Help me to feel real love – Your Love and to feel true peace in my heart.

Amen.

Rejoice, My children, because I now speak to your heart from the Heavens.

I am real. I exist. I love you and I will never give up My fight to save you so that I can take you, your family and friends to the New Paradise on Earth.

This Paradise was created for Adam and Eve and will now return to earth.

I want you to be part of this new Glorious life, which is beyond your dreams.

I bless you now.

Your Beloved Friend
Jesus

After The Global Confession I will prepare for My Second Coming
Monday, January 9, 2012 08:10 hours

My dearest beloved daughter, the times are moving swiftly and The Warning will herald the preparation for My Second Coming.

After the Global Confession, when most of humanity will be given special graces and blessings, I will prepare the way for My Second Coming.

Mankind must accept that the time for this great event is almost upon them. Waste no time in preparing your souls and those of your family for My Glorious Return.

My Second Coming will bring to an end the torment you have endured for thousands of years on earth.

So great is this Glorious Event that no man will fail to gasp in wonder and astonishment as I appear in the skies.

You, of this generation, have been chosen to benefit from this journey with Me into My New Paradise, during the Era of Peace, over which I will reign.

No one must be excluded. Not one soul must be allowed to fall through the net. It is My greatest desire to bring you all with Me into My Kingdom.

This is the glory which mankind has waited for since My death on the Cross.

For those of you who turn a blind eye to My pleas, I urge you to begin preparing now.

My time is drawing close. I have now sent My final messenger into the world to help you prepare your souls. This has been prophesised.

Do not ignore My Warning, because if you do, you are not awake and you will fail to prepare adequately.

I will impart many Messages from now on, so that the world is ready to accept Me, as their Ruler.

Your beloved Jesus
Redeemer of all Mankind

Virgin Mary - So many souls choose to ignore the signs I give
Tuesday, January 10, 2012 20:30 hours

My child, you must tell the world of the importance of prayer at this time.

My children are suffering everywhere in every country.

It is important that all God's children unite at this time in order for the darkness to be finally lifted from the earth.

How I weep with sorrow when those souls choose to ignore my visitations to visionaries on earth. So many choose to ignore the signs I give to ensure that faith can be restored.

So cold are their hearts, including those of priests and clergy, who are blind to the Truth, that much time has been wasted.

If they had only opened their hearts to the Messages I have given the world, then more souls would have been given the nourishment they needed.

These are the final days when my words of encouragement must be heeded.

Pray, pray, pray that my Son's Voice will be heard in the way it was meant to be.

Did you not think, children, that He would not prepare mankind for His Great Mercy?

This, He now sets out to achieve, through the conversion of as many souls as possible.

His plans are complete with one exception. He needs more prayers for without such prayers souls will be lost to the deceiver.

My child, my Son will bring much needed relief to His beloved children soon.

In His Mercy, He will now also prepare the world for His Second Coming.

Pray that all those, who believe in my Son, will open their hearts to the Truth of His Holy Messages.

If they listen and follow His instructions all will be well.

If they ignore The Warning, given to them out of Pure Love, they will deny others the chance of salvation.

I plead for the generosity of souls to pledge their allegiance to my beloved Son by marching with Him towards the Glorious Reign in the New Paradise.

The messengers have been sent into the world for some time to help prepare the world for this great event.

The final stages are now in place.

Hear now the Voice of my Son as He speaks with you. Do not reject Him.

Your loving Mother
Queen of Heaven
Mother of Salvation

The biggest abomination since the Holocaust is being plotted against the Jews
Wednesday, January 11, 2012 15:00 hours

My dearly beloved daughter, watch now the efforts being made by the Global Power, not of the Light, which attempts to mount a campaign against My people. I refer to Christians and My chosen people the Jews.

Wicked plans are being plotted to wipe out the practice of Christianity in a devious, but, subtle way. It will start with a change in the constitutions of countries everywhere in the western world.

Every attempt will be made to cast scurrilous claims against My Christian Churches. My sacred servants will slowly withdraw, leaving My people with little spiritual support. All these laws will have a cunning exterior of tolerance.

Your faith, My children, is being put to the test like never before

Christianity, and any attempts to publicly proclaim My Name, will be thwarted. In its place, an empty doctrine will emerge, and people will be confused. They will think that this doctrine is a good and fair replacement for the Truth, when, in fact, it will be a lie. This wicked group is so powerful that very few know they exist. Yet they are everywhere pulling the strings.

My children are like puppets. My chosen people, the Jews are facing, yet again, a terrible persecution. Plans to overthrow them are under way.

Those, they believe to be their friends, are their enemies. They will suffer such hardship. I call on all mankind to pray for Israel. The biggest abomination since the Holocaust is being plotted against My people.

Pray, pray that the antichrist's group are stopped from committing these evil acts. These dark souls need your prayers so that, during The Warning, they will recognise their offences. Pray that they drop their armour and beg for My Mercy. If they do, then the wars and unrest in Israel can be diluted.

Many prophecies will now unfold before your eyes. Those blind to My Promises must be given the Light of My Mercy in order to see again.

Do not be deceived, children. What seems good on the outside is not always as it seems. Peacekeeping forces, many of them innocent pawns, are being lied to.

Never fear, because My Mercy will have an important influence over this sect, who have been plotting against My Church for centuries.

They cannot and will not win. But, they will cause tremendous terror, unless prayer can mitigate their wicked dominance. Pray the New Crusade of Prayer to help stop the antichrist and his group, about whom I speak.

Crusade Prayer (18) Help stop the antichrist

O dear Jesus, save the world from the antichrist.
Protect us from the wicked snares of Satan.
Save the last remnants of Your Church from evil.

Give all Your Churches the strength and graces needed to defend ourselves against wars and persecution planned by Satan and his army of terrorists.

Amen.

Your beloved Jesus
Saviour and Redeemer of all mankind

Pray for souls in mortal sin, who may not get the chance to seek redemption
Thursday, January 12, 2012 15.30 hours

My dearest beloved daughter, there is a need for everyone to pray with all their hearts now for the souls who may not survive the shock when they witness The Warning and My Great Mercy.

Some of these poor souls in mortal sin may not get the chance to seek redemption, so please ensure that your prayers are offered up for such souls.

Prayer is urgently needed for those souls in darkness. So intent are they in their wickedness to destroy humanity, through monetary and other controls, that they will find The Warning to be a terrible shock.

I need them to be given the chance to repent, but many will resist Me. Please pray for these tortured souls.

Finally I would like to ask all My followers to recite the Divine Mercy at every opportunity as the times gets closer now for My Great Warning.

To all those believers who refuse to accept that it is I, Jesus Christ, their Saviour speaking to them through these Messages, hear Me now.

Do not be like those poor souls, who lived in the time of Noah, when he was sneered at.

Open your minds and give generously of your time in prayer. That is all I ask of you at this time. You, My children, will cry tears of remorse when you realise your mistake. And yes, I will forgive you even though you have hurt Me deeply.

Your insults wound Me.

Your taunts are like a knife twisting Me inside out because you think that you know Me, but, you don't.

Your minds are closed to My True Voice, which is like a cry in the wilderness.

Your loftiness offends Me.

You must accept that the way is now being planned for My Second Coming.

You may not listen to Me now, as I plead with you to pray for souls who will be lost to Me. But, you will when this is proven to you, after this great event.

For then I will expect you to follow Me and form the remnants of My Church. It will be then that we will all unite to pick up the pieces left, as we walk towards My New Paradise.

Your beloved Jesus Christ
Saviour and Redeemer of all Mankind

Virgin Mary: Crusade Prayer (19) Prayer for young people
Friday, January 13, 2012 08:00 hours

My child, I am sorrowful today because I suffer much as I think of those poor souls who will die during The Warning.

You must ask for urgent prayer for these souls, who anger my Father. Their behaviour is an abomination in His eyes.

Please pray, pray, pray for these children of the dark, many of whom do not know what they are doing.

Their wickedness causes my Son to weep and His Wounds to fester. It is important that as many souls as possible are enveloped into the Arms of my Son at His Divine Mercy. Please ask for this **Crusade of Prayer to be said to me, the Mother of Salvation, to save these poor children.**

Crusade of Prayer (19) Prayer for young people

Mother of Salvation, I ask you to pray for the Mercy of young souls who are in terrible darkness so that they recognise your Beloved Son when He comes to redeem the whole of mankind.

Let not one soul fall by the wayside. Let not one soul reject His Great Mercy. I pray, Mother, that all are saved and ask you to cover these souls with your Holy Mantle. To provide them the protection they need from the deceiver.

Amen.

My child, all souls are important to my Son. But, it is the young souls in mortal sin, who hurt Him the most.

Pray that the Light of Mercy shines through the darkness of their minds and souls. Pray that they will reject the terrible lives of depravity and emptiness that they lead. Pray that they will reach up and beg for Mercy. Otherwise, they will never receive the graces they need to enter the New Paradise.

What a loss these young people will be to the rest of you, who will accept the Gift of the Warning and enter the New Era of Paradise on earth. It will break My Son's Heart if they cannot be saved.

Your beloved Mother
Mary Queen of Heaven
Mother of Salvation

Virgin Mary – My child, peace will reign on earth soon.
Friday, January 13, 2012 20:15 hours

My child, peace will reign on earth soon.

There will be turbulence and strife, but it is necessary in order to weed out the final wickedness on earth.

My Father's Hand will fall swiftly on those who ignore my Son's Mercy. He will not tolerate their disobedience once the Truth has been revealed to them.

Those who turn their backs on my Son, after The Warning, will be accorded a certain period of time in which to show remorse for their sins, but, this will not last long. Pray for those souls whose obstinateness will be their downfall.

My child, the changes are already underway and much will happen quickly. Watch the skies, children, for the first signs of my Son's Mercy. For those with humble and contrite hearts have no fear because this is the time you have been waiting for.

Those souls, who do not recognise my Son's Existence, will be surprised and sorrowful when the Truth is finally presented to them.

Those tormented souls who have pledged allegiance to the evil one will be overwhelmed with grief, while others will hide from the Truth, because they will not be able to withstand the Light.

Pray that all such souls, through the prayers of others, can and will be redeemed, in the Eyes of my Precious Son.

Conversion will avert Chastisement and ease the wicked plans underway by the antichrist to destroy humanity.

Pray that the battle between Heaven and the evil one will result in that all of God's children can be saved and spared from the fires of Hell.

Your beloved Mother
Queen of the Roses
Mother of Salvation

Scientists will publicly deny this Miracle has taken place
Friday, January 13, 2012 21:35 hours

My dearest beloved daughter, My Divine Mercy will be finally realised and understood at last.

My Rays of Mercy, which will commence with the pink skies, will flood the earth to save mankind.

Not one person will be excluded. Presidents, kings, queens, princes, paupers, celebrities, beggars, thieves, murderers, atheists and believers in God, the Father and Me, His beloved Son, will all be touched by My Gift.

The arrogant will fall in humility when they see their grievous sins, as they appear before My Eyes.

The wicked will see the Light of My Divine Existence, and will have to make a choice. They will accept My Love and Mercy, or they will slap Me in the Face. Either way, all of God's children will see My Rays of Mercy, and will find it hard to ignore this Miracle.

I urge all of you to pray that My Mercy will be welcomed and accepted like a hungry man who grasps the bread of life. Without this bread he will die.

There are only two paths. Come with Me, your Divine Saviour, or face the fires of Hell.

I am ever merciful, but there will be so little time for you to show remorse after The Warning.

Many scientists, and those in Satan's army, will be used to publicly deny that this Great Miracle will have taken place. Pray for them, so that this deceit does not seduce those lukewarm souls who may be tempted to turn their backs on Me, yet again.

Prepare, children. Remember this intervention from Heaven is the only way I can save most of humanity.

Were I not to pour out My Mercy over the whole world, very few souls could enter My New Paradise on earth.

I love you all and welcome you into the bosom of My Love and Mercy.

Have no fear, your souls will be flooded with My Holy Spirit. For believers, this will make you even stronger in your love for Me, and then you will join in My army to convert those who need more time to turn to Me.

Your Saviour and King of Mercy
Jesus Christ

God the Father: Final messenger to herald the Second Coming
Monday, January 16, 2012 13.20 hours

My daughter, when I send prophets into the world, they will usually be those whom you least expect.

Never will you find them in the highest echelons of My Church. Nor will they be the most outwardly holy souls.

In many cases, they will not be worthy of this special gift. Yet, I chose imperfect souls from unusual, but simple, walks of life, so that I can mould them into the creatures I so desire.

My prophets for the end times are no different. They will not be accepted easily. As in the beginning, when I first sent My prophets to prepare mankind for the arrival of My beloved Son, Jesus Christ, the Messiah, they found it difficult for their voices to be heard.

The voices of My genuine end time messengers will not be listened to at the start of their mission. Yet, in time, they will be recognised, for it will be My Voice that will become easily identifiable. You, My daughter, are the final messenger sent to herald the arrival of My beloved Son, Jesus Christ, for His much-anticipated Second Coming.

This is frightening for you and, at times, very difficult to digest. Yet it is the Truth.

This Work, when you will be given Divine Messages to prepare the remnants of My Church on earth for The Second Coming, will be difficult.

While I have selected many chosen souls up to now and will continue to communicate with them for the good of all mankind, their lot will be easier.

Your lot will be difficult in the extreme and you will be persecuted because of it.

I bless you with every grace from My Heavenly Kingdom.

You will move forward, as the chosen instrument, to impart My Most Holy Word to the world. This Work will be protected at all times.

Yes, you will be attacked, almost daily, but know this. If this Work were not so important, do you think that it could escape the notice of Satan and his dominion of fallen angels?

They, My daughter, have infiltrated the earth and have crawled, in many cases, unsuspectingly, into the hearts and souls of many of My children.

The Holy Path of your work, you the final messenger, sent to earth to help save humanity from the final grip of Satan, has been foretold in the Scriptures.

The world has been awaiting these instructions, by My Holy Command.

Many false prophets will try to block this, My Holy Word, through the spread of lies and confusion.

These Messages will be questioned and examined by My Church for errors. Yet they impart only the Truth.

Much of the Truth, ignored by My Churches down through the centuries, will emerge again.

More revelations as to the Truth of your Eternal Life, children, will be revealed to you.

This work will cause outrage, My daughter. You will be spat upon, ridiculed, looked down upon and blocked in every way imaginable.

To those who find difficulty with the Truth given to you, the final end time prophet, hear now My pleas.

You must ask Me for the Gift of the Holy Spirit, before you can open your ears to hear My Voice, to the Truth of My Holy Word, and to the instructions that I will give you all, so that you can have Eternal Life.

My Words will be made simple so that every man, woman and child can follow My Holy Word. But, you must know this. While there will be much Love and Light shining through My Word, there will also be an Air of Divine Authority, which you will find impossible to ignore.

That is how you will know that it is I, your God, your Eternal Father, who speaks. My Love will invade your souls and lift your hearts in union with Mine.

All preparations are in place. After My beloved Son's Great Mercy, the time will be set aside to prepare the world for His Second Coming.

Yes, children, I am now arranging to save My children from the darkness. I am reclaiming My Creation, My children, and I am taking you to your rightful home, your inheritance, The New Paradise.

Be patient, children. Just remember I love you. Trust in Me and in My Holy Word given to you through My end time prophet, Maria Divine Mercy.

Your Eternal Father
God of the Most High
Creator of all things

Sacred Servants, you will be led towards the false prophet
Tuesday, January 17, 2012 14:00 hours

My dearest beloved daughter, the time has come to tell the world to prepare their souls for My return to earth as foretold.

My people will rise and welcome Me, when I come again, this time, to reclaim My Rightful Throne, as the King of Mankind.

For those who recognise My Voice, you must trust in Me completely.

I will direct you on the path of Truth so that each of you will be made worthy to enter the New Paradise on earth.

Reject the voice of darkness, which will, at every opportunity, blind you and tempt you to turn your back on Me.

I am your beloved Saviour, who died cruelly on the Cross. Yet My suffering will continue, until I have salvaged the remnant of My Church on earth.

I am coming to save you, yet again. Allow Me to do this, without hindrance.

So many of you are already turning a deaf ear to My pleas to humanity to prepare your souls for this Glorious Era of Peace. Don't you know that I love you?

It is because of the compassionate love I hold for each of you, that I come, not just to warn you, but, to help to prepare you for this great moment.

I realise that those of you who love Me, especially My sacred servants, watch guardedly, for false prophets, who may emerge. This is very important. Come now and ask Me to fill you with the Holy Spirit, so that the Truth can and will be revealed to you.

Should you not turn to Me, then you will fail to understand what it is I expect of you.

Come to Me. Hear Me, now. Your suffering will be difficult, for Satan will not give you a moment's rest.

He knows that I am making myself known, not just through My end time prophet, Maria, but, through many souls. Those souls of mine, chosen to be the end time messengers, will be the ones who will be blocked by My sacred servants, the most.

You will, sadly, be led by the deceiver towards the false prophet instead, and his minions who spew lies and untruths everywhere.

For those of you quick to condemn My messengers, be very careful. You, My sacred servants, will be the main target of the deceiver.

It will be your minds, which will be turned the other way first. For when you turn your back on Me, your Divine Saviour, you will then steer My people in the wrong direction.

Unwittingly, you will prevent them from hearing the Truth from My Divine Lips.

You will starve My children of the nourishment essential to their spiritual growth.

Know now, that the end times are upon you. Do not squander the time you have left living in a vacuum of lies and confusion.

The battle has begun and My remnant Church will be saved as it marches with Me to My Glorious New Reign.

Pray that not one soul is left behind.

Pray also that you, holy servants of Mine, are not responsible for drawing My children away, from the Truth, from the Light, from the Salvation, that is their right.

Follow me, now, and help me save souls.

Your beloved Saviour
Jesus Christ

Virgin Mary: Wicked plan, within The Vatican, to destroy the Catholic Church
Wednesday, January 18, 2012 09:50 hours

My child, perseverance is needed by all God's children, during this time of apostasy in the world.

So few believe in their Divine Creator, my Father, God the Most High.

They will see the Truth shortly, but many will still argue that there is no God. Much prayer is needed now, children.

Pope Benedict XVI is being plotted against, within his own corridors, by an evil sect.

This sect is known to exist among those sacred servants within The Vatican, yet they are powerless against this evil group, which has infiltrated the Catholic Church for centuries.

They are responsible for twisting the Truth of my Son's Teachings. So little is known about them or their vile works.

They have driven the True Doctrine from the Catholic Church, and, in its place, a lukewarm, watered down version has been force fed to Catholics over the last forty years.

So much confusion has been spread by this wicked, but, hidden sect, that my children have wandered away from the True Church.

Pray that they do not drive the Pope away.

Pray that the false prophet will not take the Seat of the Holy Father so that he can spread lies.

Pray that those sacred servants in the Vatican are strong enough to withstand this evil plot, designed to destroy the Catholic Church.

They plan to replace the Holy Vicar, Pope Benedict XVI, with a dictator of lies. He will create a new church in league with the antichrist, and his group, in order to deceive the world.

Sadly, many of my children will, in their allegiance to the Catholic faith, follow blindly this new false doctrine like lambs to the slaughter.

Wake up, children, to the Truth. This wicked plan has changed the fundamental authenticity of the Catholic Doctrine over the years.

You insult my Son when you receive the Holy Eucharist in the hand.

This was their doing.

You insult my Son when you do not seek the regular Sacraments. Yet, those whom you rely on for these do not ensure your spiritual well being, because they do not make the Sacraments available to all.

My child, a great evil, hidden for centuries in the corridors of the Holy See, will shortly emerge for the world to see. Those of my children, who are covered with the Holy Spirit, will see the Truth, when the wicked lie is presented to the world.

Others will follow blindly down a dark alley. Great division will emerge within the ranks of priests, bishops, archbishops and cardinals, one side against the other.

Those true disciples will have to hide and preach privately, or else be killed. So hidden will the True Church be, that the true faithful will have to bind together, in order to practice their allegiance to my Eternal Father.

The earth will shake in every corner, caused by the wrath of my Heavenly Father, against this travesty.

My child, they cannot win. It will be by the faith and courage of the remnants of the Christian Faith, that will result in these wicked imposters being destroyed forever.

Await now and prepare for the Catholic Church to announce these changes.

Then you will know the Truth of what I tell you.

Pray, pray, pray for Pope Benedict and his true disciples.

Your beloved Mother
Mother of Salvation

Antichrist who is hidden in the wings will soon appear in the world
Thursday, January 19, 2012 20:30 hours

My dearly beloved daughter, rise now with strength in order to continue to proclaim My most Holy Word.

To those, who listen and believe in My most Holy Word, great graces can be obtained through the recital of My Crusade Prayers.

The Purgatory on earth, soon to be experienced by souls who show true remorse for their sins, after The Warning, will be difficult.

This penance is important children. Do not fight it. Accept it.

To those who believe in Me, you must listen now. You will grow in numbers, after My Great Mercy is shown to the world, and your voices will echo from the wilderness.

It will be through your strength and fighting spirit, that My Church will be able to survive the persecution.

You, children, have nothing to fear when you walk humbly by My side.

Your humble obedience is essential if you are to be given the graces, in order to stay strong, to keep your nerve, and fight in My army, against the antichrist.

He, My children, is hidden in the wings, but will soon appear before the world.

He has no shame and will boast of his humanitarian efforts. Many will fall for his charm, while he will appeal to their goodness of heart. Here is the Crusade of Prayer to help stop the antichrist from destroying My children

Crusade of Prayer (20) Stop the antichrist from destroying the world

O God the Father, in the Name of Your precious Son, I call on you to prevent the antichrist from ensnaring the souls of Your children.

I beg You, Almighty Father, to stop him from inflicting terror on Your children.

I beg You to stop him from contaminating Your Creation, and ask You to have Mercy on those poor souls who will be powerless against him. Hear my prayer, dear Father, and save all Your children from this terrible evil.

Amen.

Your beloved Jesus Christ

The Sealed Book of Truth will be opened in preparation for My Second Coming
Friday, January 20, 2012 20.15 hours

My dearly beloved daughter, it is not necessary to worry about human opinion.

The views of mankind are nothing, when compared to My Holy Words, given to you.

My Word comes first. No other views against My Word should concern you.

Time, My daughter, is very short now for Me to save humanity.

My daughter, so much will now be expected of you, so quickly, that you will not be able to draw your breath.

There are many revelations now being imparted to you, so that My children know how to prepare themselves properly.

Should you allow distractions, such as people's opinions or views, to take up your time, unnecessarily, then this will take you away from the Work, which is truly important.

Allow Me to fill you with love and comfort at this time, My daughter.

The Warning is very close. As soon as My Rays of Mercy envelop the whole world, anyone who believes in Me, will repent.

Those who denounce My Messages, given to you, and who love Me, will turn back to My Sacred Heart, with love and joy in their souls.

No sooner will The Warning have taken place, than a number of events will occur.

The antichrist and his group, although weakened as a result of the Global Confession, will begin to plan his seizure of My Holy Church from within.

My army will take position, and begin to fight, to save the Holy Catholic Church, from ruination. They, the false prophet and his followers, will not win, My daughter, but, how I cry for those sacred servants of mine who will fall by the wayside.

So deluded will they be, that they will think they are following the orthodox Catholic Church.

In fact. they will be siding with the false prophet, who will rule over My Holy See, with pride and contempt in his heart.

You, My daughter, must ask My children to pray hard, in order to mitigate this abomination.

I need prayer to save the souls of My poor misguided priests, bishops and cardinals, blind to the Truth.

The Holy Seat of Peter will be desecrated by Satan's fallen angels, in league with the antichrist and his various organisations.

All are one, My daughter, spawned from Satan.

I know that this is frightening, but it will not last long. Prayer, and much of it, will ease and help avert these events.

Prepare your souls now, children, by going to Confession, if you are Catholic, as soon as you can. Otherwise I urge all of you to seek redemption for your sins with a purity of heart.

This will ease your suffering of penance at The Warning. Afterwards, you must pray for peace on earth.

Preparations for My Second Coming will commence immediately after The Warning takes place.

The sealed Book of Truth will be opened, and the secrets revealed through you, My daughter, for the whole world to see.

My Book of Truth will be given to the world, so that your souls are purified, in union with Me.

Only then, will you be ready to come with Me, into the Era of My Father's Divine Will, the Era of Peace, My New Paradise on earth.

Your beloved Jesus
Saviour of Mankind

False prophet will be treated like a living saint. Those who oppose him will be considered heretics.
Saturday, January 21, 2012 13:15 hours

My dearly beloved daughter, My messengers in the world, appointed to spread My Holy Word, have each been given a different role. No two the same.

This is why My messengers must never confuse each Message by comparing them with one another.

You, My daughter, as the 7th messenger, have been chosen, to inform My children of the Truth. Much of My Truth has been given to you already, but much more is to come now.

Because of the secrets contained within these, you will, when they are revealed, be ridiculed, sneered at and made to look like a fool.

These Messages are to help purify My people, including those who accept the calling to follow Me, as well as those souls, empty of love, and cold of heart.

Without this cleansing, the earth cannot be purified. It needs to be purified, in order for it to be made worthy, for Me to walk it again.

My children must rejoice. Fear is not something, which comes from Me.

Fear comes from evil. Yet, you would be forgiven and justified when you fear for those souls who walk in blindness. Not because they cannot see, but, because they choose not to see.

You duty to Me, My beloved army of followers, is to help Me prepare the way for My forthcoming Divine Reign on earth.

I need your help. I need your prayers. Your prayers will weaken the work of the antichrist, as well as the false prophet, who will take up position in the Holy See of Rome.

To all My children, you must know that I am all forgiving. Even those who are involved with satanic groups, about whom I speak, can be saved from descending any further, downwards to the gates of Hell.

Sin can be diluted, because of prayer. You do not have to go into battle and fight with your fists raised; all you have to do is to pray.

My New Paradise is magnificent, children. So much preparation has been completed, with the same wonders as presented to Adam and Eve, which they rejected, through sin. All is ready.

You, My followers, will benefit from the beautiful New Paradise on earth, over which I will reign.

Because you, of this generation, have been selected to enjoy this

Paradise, you must not stop in your work to help Me take all of My children, with Me, into My Glorious Kingdom.

My children, be aware, however, that the false prophet will have you believe he is also preparing you for a similar place of paradise.

His lies will enthrall a naïve group of Catholic followers. He will present a wonderful and loving external charisma, and all of My children, in the Catholic Church, will be confused.

One sign to look out for will be his pride and arrogance, hidden behind an exterior, false humility. So fooled will My children be, that they will think he is an exceptional and pure soul.

He will be treated like a living saint. Not one word out of his mouth will be questioned.

He will also appear to have supernatural gifts and people will instantly believe he can perform miracles.

Anyone, who opposes him, will be criticised and considered a heretic.

All such souls, accused of being heretics, will be cast aside and fed to the dogs.

All Truth, regarding My Teachings, will be twisted. Everything will be a lie. Persecution will evolve slowly and be subtle at first.

My true sacred servants will have to say Mass privately, and in many cases, not in a Catholic Church. They will have to offer Masses in refuges. Children when this happens, you must not lose hope. This will be over within a short period of time.

Just pray for those souls, who will, in their pledge to the False Prophet, forget about the Blessed Trinity which is the very foundation upon the Church is built.

Many religions follow just one entity of the Blessed Trinity. Some honour the Father, others the Son, but, all are one, My daughter.

There is only One True God. That is the Father, the Son and the Holy Ghost, three distinct persons all in One Divine Essence. All religions will be given the Truth, soon, and many will accept this Holy Mystery.

Follow Me towards the path of salvation, for you My followers have a glorious future ahead, but, you must remain strong.

This is the chosen generation, for My New Paradise on Earth.

Don't reject this glorious Gift of Life, which glitters in all its magnificence. Not one soul will want for anything. My New Paradise on earth will be an Era of Peace and happiness, without sin.

This is the Divine Will of My Father and has been His promise to mankind, right from the start.

Be joyful and happy, for you have much to look forward to, children.

The trials ahead will pale into insignificance, when you will witness the Glorious Kingdom, which is waiting for you.

I love you, children. I know that you love Me. Because of this, I ask you to show love to those who are blind to My Holy Spirit.

Pray for them at every opportunity, so that they can see again the Truth of My Promise, made to mankind when I died, to secure your eternal salvation.

Your beloved Jesus
Saviour of all Mankind

Hear my urgent plea to pray for the souls of atheists
Monday, January 23, 2012 15:20 hours

My dearly beloved daughter, the world is about to change beyond recognition.

For My time is almost here now.

I urge all those believers in Me, their Divine Saviour, and My Eternal Father, to stop what you are doing and listen.

Whether or not you believe in these, My Messages to the world for these times, hear now My urgent plea.

Pray, pray and pray with all the love you hold in your heart for Me, for the souls of atheists.

Many will die during The Warning.

Many will not get a chance to repent in time.

I urge you to offer up all your suffering and prayers for those souls so that I can save them from the fires of Hell.

Pray for those who will not turn back to Me, even when the Truth is presented to them. Pray also for those who will find the Purgatory on earth, the penance, which will be accepted by them with good heart, to be very difficult. Many will find it very painful. Pray that they receive the strength they need to persevere.

Go, children, and do everything I have asked of you, for there is little time left.

I love you. Remember there is nothing to fear, if you love Me.

Just pray for those who reject Me, now today, and those will turn their backs on the Truth.

Your beloved Saviour
Jesus Christ

Good News – God, My Eternal Father, has sanctioned the salvation of much of mankind.
Tuesday, January 24, 2012 16:55 hours

My dearly beloved daughter, it is I, your Jesus, who comes to you today to give you the good news for the world.

Much prayer and suffering, offered up by My many chosen souls on earth, has meant that many more of God's children can now be saved.

If you understood the power of sacrifice and prayer, children, you would never stop praying.

God, My Eternal Father, has sanctioned the salvation of much of mankind.

This means that many will convert during The Warning, and those who don't, may be saved because of the power of prayer.

It does not mean that all will be saved, because, sadly, they won't.

Those hardened people, whose first allegiance is to Satan and the evil sects he controls in the world, will not want to be saved.

Instead, they will choose a different paradise. A paradise they are led to believe exists, outside of the one promised to mankind by My Father.

This false paradise, which satanic followers of the beast believe in, does not exist.

It has been created, by Satan, in the minds of his disciples, and is simply an illusion. So much is promised.

Dark souls believe in a different universe, a different entity, where God does not exist.

They believe in other life forms, other creatures and a peaceful regime, all of which is based on a lie.

None of this is real children. It does not, nor cannot exist, because, it was not created by My Father.

God the Almighty Father, created the entire universe – the stars, the planets and the earth as well as all the spaces in between.

Pray for those who follow such cults.

Pray that more of My children, who, because they are in pain, do not seek out these spiritual outlets, which are not from God

Pray now, in thanksgiving for this special gift, which is now being offered to mankind, by My Father, in this the Crusade Prayer.

Crusade Prayer (21) Thanksgiving to God the Father, for the salvation of mankind

We praise You and thank You, O Holy God, the Almighty Creator of mankind, for the Love and Compassion You have for humanity.

We thank You, for the Gift of Salvation You bestow on Your poor children.

We beg You, O Lord, to save those who follow the evil one and that their hearts will be opened to the Truth of their Eternal Life.

Amen.

Rejoice, children, for this great Gift. But, you have still much work to do to help souls, as many of your brothers and sister will remain stubbornly opposed to the Truth of My Holy Word.

Your Beloved Jesus
Saviour of all Mankind

Virgin Mary: Nuclear war involving Iran being plotted
Wednesday, January 25, 2012 13:50 hours

My child, much is happening right now in the world, as Satan's army continues to spread havoc everywhere.

They are trying to take control of all financial institutions, so they can inflict a terrible atrocity on my children.

They, the evil group, driven by lust and power, are also trying to create a nuclear war in Iran.

You, my child, must pray that God the Father will, in His great Mercy, open their hearts to stop these things from happening.

Never lose faith, children, because your prayers are working.

Great evils including abortion, euthanasia, prostitution and sexual perversities, are beginning to weaken in the world now.

Pray, pray, pray my Most Holy Rosary, children, in groups, if possible everywhere.

Satan is losing his power quickly as my heel begins to squash the serpent's head.

It won't be long now for my Son's arrival on earth.

First, He will give you this last chance to convert.

Then, He will prepare the world quickly for His Second Coming.

Time is short now.

Prayer is the weapon, children, to keep Satan's army from the final persecution they are planning against humanity.

Remember that my Eternal Father will, through His Love and Compassion, protect all of you who believe in Him.

For those who will continue to disobey Him, and deny the Truth of the Existence of my beloved Son, pray, pray, pray for their salvation.

The time is ready. Open your hearts to the Divine Mercy of my Son.

The skies will start to change now and then all will see this great miracle unfold before them.

Be ready.

Prepare your homes and pray my Holy Rosary at every opportunity to loosen the grip of the evil one.

Your beloved Mother
Mother of Salvation

The final secret of Fatima reveals the Truth of Satan's evil sect entering the Vatican
Thursday, January 26, 2012 09:40 hours

My dearly beloved daughter, it is time for the full Truth of the Mysteries of the Divine Realm to be revealed to the world. The Truth has been hidden for some time.

Acknowledgement of My Divine intervention in the world through the miracles, apparitions and Divine Communications to chosen souls, has been pushed to one side by My Church, for many years.

Why My Church felt the need to dampen the Truth, when it was needed to strengthen the faith of My children everywhere, is known only to them.

Every true visionary of Mine and My Blessed Mother was ignored in the beginning, and treated with contempt by My Church.

My daughter even the final secret of Fatima was not given to the world, because it revealed the truth of Satan's evil sect entering the Vatican.

The last part of secret has not been revealed, in order to protect the wicked sect who entered the Vatican in great numbers since My Mother's appearance at the Holy Shrine of Fatima.

My daughter Lucia was silenced by the powers, which control part of the Vatican, over which My poor beloved Popes have little control. Watch how they have, not only twisted the Truth of My Teachings, but, introduced new methods of Catholic worship, which insult Me, and My Eternal Father. The Catholic Church is the One True Church, and as such is a primary target of Satan, and his wicked sect. The Truth comes from Me.

The Truth makes mankind uncomfortable, because it can involve personal sacrifice.

The Truth causes outrage, in some instances and, in many cases, is treated as heresy.

Yet only the Truth can set you free from lies, the lies, which come from Satan and, which create a heavy burden on your soul.

The time has come for the Truth to be unveiled in a world, which is full of lies.

So many lies, My daughter, have been presented to My children by false religions, false gods, false church leaders, false political leaders and organisations as well as a false media.

So much of the Truth is hidden. Yet, if the Truth of what is happening in the world were revealed today, very few people would accept it.

The same applies to My Father's Ten Commandments. These are the Rules laid down by My Eternal Father, and given to His prophet, Moses.

The Truth never changes, no matter how much mankind tries to change it.

My Father's Commandments are no longer accepted, even amongst Christian Churches.

Thou shalt not kill means you cannot kill another human being. It does not refer to self-defense, but in every other circumstance.

No man can justify murder – abortion, execution or euthanasia. No one. This is a mortal sin and the punishment is an eternal life in Hell.

Do My children accept this My daughter? No. They even pass laws, which make it not only acceptable, but excusable, in the Eyes of God. But, it is not.

Every one of My Father's Ten Commandments are broken every day.

Yet My Church never preaches about the seriousness of sin. They never tell people that they will go to Hell should they commit a mortal sin, if they do not show remorse.

My Heart is deeply wounded. They, My Churches, all over the world, do not preach the Truth. Many of My sacred servants no longer believe in the state of Hell, or Purgatory.

They do not accept My Father's Commandments. They excuse every sin. They talk about My Father's Mercy, but fail to explain the consequences of dying in a state of mortal sin. By not carrying out their duties, for which they have been assigned, they offend Me greatly.

They are, in many cases, responsible for the loss of so many souls. Wake up to the Truth, all of you who profess to be a believer in God the Almighty Father, Creator of all things, and know this.

There is only One Truth. There cannot be more than One Truth. Anything other than the Truth, is a lie, and does not come from My Heavenly Father, God the Almighty, Creator of all things.

Your beloved Saviour
Jesus Christ

Note: it should be pointed out that in a previous Message Jesus told Maria that even the sin of murder can be forgiven in a person who truly repents.

Call to Clergy: Prepare My flock for My long awaited Second Coming on earth.
Friday, January 27, 2012 23:50 hours

My dearly beloved daughter, never forget that when you work for Me you will be persecuted, for mankind will not like to hear the Truth, as I reveal it to you, in these, the end times.

My Holy Word has been quashed for so long, but this will no longer be the case.

My Voice will be heard all over the world. My Love will be revealed in all My Glory, and man will be able, finally, to free himself from the shackles of evil, placed around his ankles, by Satan.

As the Truth will penetrate the souls of My children, and bring them the freedom, which they have been awaiting, for such a long time it will, unfortunately, cause division.

My beloved sacred servants, priests and all religious clergy, within the Holy Catholic Church, know that I love all of you.

So many of you have given up your lives for Me, with generousity of heart. You will need to lean on Me now.

You must pray for guidance to remain strong in your faith and for discernment at all times.

Never take your eyes off Me, for one moment.

I need you to prepare My flock, in order to welcome Me, during My long awaited Second Coming on earth.

You will need to persevere and not allow your love for Me to be dissuaded, no matter how much pressure you are put under.

You are my true disciples, and I must urge you to take up your weapons to save My Church. This very Church, founded on the Rock, by My beloved disciple, Peter, will never fail.

The enemy may believe it to be destroyed, but that would be a foolish assumption.

No one will, or can, destroy My Church. Out of the ashes it will rise to proclaim My Glory, as I come back to salvage My Kingdom on earth. You must never desert Me, your beloved Saviour, ever.

For without Me, there is no Light. Without Light, there is no future.

My daughter, I give the world this Crusade of Prayer, for the Catholic Clergy to recite.

Crusade of Prayer (22) Catholic Church to uphold the Teachings of the Church

O My beloved Jesus, keep me strong and the flame of my love for You alight, every moment of my day.

Never allow this flame of love for You to flicker or die.

Never allow me to weaken in the presence of temptation.

Give me the graces needed to honour my vocation, my devotion, my loyalty and to uphold the Teachings of the Orthodox Catholic Church. I offer you my allegiance, at all times.

I pledge my commitment to fight in Your army, so that the Catholic Church can rise again in glory, to welcome You, dear Jesus, when You come again.

Amen.

Your beloved Saviour
Jesus Christ
King of all Mankind

Virgin Mary: Pray for Pope Benedict with all your heart
Saturday, January 28, 2012 21:00 hours

My child, Satan's power is getting weaker by the day, as the Holy Spirit continues to spread His wings over all of God's children.

Faith and love of God is growing everywhere, because of prayer, and the special graces given to my children, by my Father, God the Most

High. Conversion is increasing. Many of my children may not be aware of this, but you will see this, if you open your eyes.

Please, my child, you must pray for Pope Benedict, with all your heart. He suffers so much and in many ways is alone in his grief for the apostasy he sees both outside of and inside the Holy Vatican.

His days in the Holy See have been extended and because of this, much of the havoc caused by the evil one, has been averted.

Prayer, my children, is like a roll of thunder in the heavens. Your prayers are being heard and answered in Heaven, children.

This is good. Continue to pray the Crusades of Prayer given to you, my child. Here is a special prayer for Pope Benedict's safety.

Crusade Prayer (23) for Pope Benedict's safety

O My Eternal Father, on behalf of Your beloved Son, Jesus Christ, and the suffering He endured to save the world from sin, I pray now that You protect Your Holy Vicar, Pope Benedict, Head of Your Church on earth, so that he too can help save Your children, and all Your sacred servants, from the scourge of Satan, and his dominion of fallen angels who walk the earth, stealing souls.

O Father, protect Your Pope so that Your children can be guided on the True Path towards Your New Paradise on earth. Amen.

Your heavenly Queen of the Earth
Mother of Salvation

My Divine Mercy is to be realised as revealed to St Faustina
Sunday, January 29, 2012 21:18 hours

I, your Jesus, wish to inform the world that My Divine Mercy is to be realised, as revealed to My daughter, Helena, Saint Faustina.

This mystery will be revealed, as all will witness the final manifestation of My Rays of Mercy, for the salvation of mankind.

For those who mock you, My daughter, and say that this mystery has already been revealed to the world, they must know this.

How many people in the world today know about My promise of Divine Mercy? Very few, including you, My daughter.

Did My followers not know that I would come back to prepare the world for this Great Event?

I always prepare My children for such events. My Eternal Father sends prophets into the world, with one goal, to give you adequate warning so that souls are not taken unawares. Relish this Gift of Prophecy. Don't reject it.

Never think you know all about My Ways because, while you may love Me, you do not always know Me, or understand My Ways.

For each one of you who mocks My prophets, remember it is not they you mock, but, Me. They are simply the instruments.

You, My children, must never assume you really know Me for if you did you would not deny Me. Yet today, just as My disciples did, when I walked among them, you still deny that it is I who beckons you to Me.

You hold one hand out to Me with your left and you slap Me with your right.

Don't you hear Me speak to you now? If not, then sit quietly and pray to Me, so I can fill your weary heart, with the Fire of My Holy Spirit.

I love you, and if you will allow Me into your heart, without your armour of steel, which blocks Me, I will make you free.

When you open your eyes and see that it is I, your Divine Saviour, speaking with you, then follow Me on the road to the New Paradise, with love and joy in your heart.

Do not allow the evil one to plant doubts in your mind. Pray that you will be strong enough, humble in mind and spirit, to run into My Arms.

Only when you come to Me, as a child, will you truly find peace in your soul. This is the only way to allow Me into your heart.

Your beloved Jesus

Virgin Mary Calls for day of prayer and fasting to prepare for The Warning
Monday, January 30, 2012 13:00 hours

This Message was received by Maria Divine Mercy, after two separate apparitions of the Virgin Mary – one, which took place at midnight, January 29 and the second at 13:00 hours, on Monday January 30, 2012, during which, the Virgin Mother appeared very sorrowful throughout.

My child, while my Son comes now to cover the whole world with His Rays of Mercy, it is with a heavy Heart that I must tell you that many people will die during The Warning.

Pray, pray, pray for their souls.

You, my child, must ask all of the followers of these Divine Messages to allocate tomorrow, Tuesday, January 31st 2012, as a special day of prayer. On this day, you must recite the Most Holy Rosary and the Divine Mercy Prayer.

Where possible, everyone must try and fast during this day. In this way more souls, especially those in mortal sin at the time of death, can be saved by the Mercy of my beloved Son Jesus Christ.

I cry tears of sorrow for those poor people who have no idea how much pain and anguish their sins cause my Son.

The joy of the Gift, that my Son now brings the world, is tinged with sadness for those who cannot be saved, by their own choice. The lies, which will spring and spread all over the world, by dark souls, after The Warning takes place, must be stopped through your prayers.

Pray that no one will deny my Son's Divine Mercy during or after The Warning. For every soul lost to such lies, is a soul that will be seized by the evil one. Spread conversion everywhere, children. Accept that I am the Co-Redemptrix and Mediatrix, working closely with my beloved Son, Jesus Christ, to save all souls from eternal ruination.

My love for you, children, is very strong. I plead for mercy for each soul, every second of the day, by begging my Father for clemency.

But, children, you must help by joining with me in prayer and sacrifice to help all of God's children enter the gates of the New Paradise.

Your Heavenly Mother
Mother of Salvation

Jesus reveals Plenary Indulgence, for Total Absolution
Tuesday, January 31, 2012 09:30 hours

This Message was given to Maria Divine Mercy after one and a half hours, during the Eucharist Adoration.

My dearly beloved daughter, how I rejoice at the love shown to Me, by My precious followers, whose love is so closely entwined with My Sacred Heart.

I delight in My loyal children, whose love for Me brings Me such joy amidst My pain. They are the light who bring Me the strength needed to lead My army. These, My chosen children, believe that it has been their faith alone that has brought them to Me. What they do not realise, is that My Holy Spirit descended upon them, especially on those with open hearts, so that they could join My remnant Church on earth.

They, My beloved followers, who show obedience, determination of will and pure love in their souls, will be the foundation, upon which I will now rebuild My Church on earth. My army, through their love for Me, will be given very special graces now.

I grant them this Plenary Indulgence, to enable them carry My Torch of Fire, so that they can spread conversion. This Gift from Me will enable them to spread the Truth of My Holy Word, so that it will touch hearts everywhere they go.

They must say this prayer for seven consecutive days and they will be given the Gift of Total Absolution and the Power of the Holy Spirit.

Crusade Prayer (24) Plenary Indulgence for Absolution

O My Jesus, You are the Light of the earth.
You are the Flame that touches all souls.
Your Mercy and Love knows no bounds.
We are not worthy of the Sacrifice You made by Your death on the Cross.

Yet we know that Your Love for us is greater than the love we hold for You.

Grant us, O Lord, the gift of humility so that we are deserving of Your New Kingdom.

Fill us with the Holy Spirit so we can march forth and lead Your army to proclaim the Truth of Your Holy Word and prepare our brothers and sisters for the Glory of Your Second Coming on earth.

We honour You. We Praise You.

We offer ourselves, our sorrows, our sufferings, as a gift to You, to save souls. We love You, Jesus.

Have Mercy on all Your children, wherever they may be.

Amen.

Go forth in peace, My beloved followers, and remember that your love for Me enkindles My Heart and brings great joy to My Eternal Father, My Blessed Mother, the angels and all the saints in Heaven.

I love you all. I await the moment, when I will embrace each and every one of you, in My Arms, so that you will find the peace, love and joy, that you have been awaiting for all your lives on earth.

Your Beloved Jesus Christ

Virgin Mary: No one will prevent the Book of Truth being revealed to the world
Wednesday, February 01, 2012 20:15 hours

My child, when you work for my beloved Son, Jesus Christ, you must show obedience at all times.

Never question His Holy Word, because He speaks the Truth, and only the Truth.

So many of my children question every Word He says, since the beginning. For every one who obeys His Holy Word, as contained in my Father's Book, there is always another who interprets His Word, in a different way.

You must do everything that is asked of you under the direction of my Son. Never succumb to those who demand that His Words be adapted to their interpretation.

Move now, my child, with speed to carry the Messages given to the world by my Son to save sinners who are lost. My Son has one intention and that is to save souls. Have no fear, my child, because everything my Son tells you does not contradict the Teachings of His Most Holy Church on earth.

His Gifts to my children are very special, and are being given in these, the end times, for all souls.

So generous and merciful is my Son, that He wants to shower sinners with special graces, to ensure their salvation.

Anyone, who tries to stop my Son in His Mission to prepare the world for His Second Coming, will be stopped by the Hand of my Eternal Father.

This Work, to unveil the Book of Truth, as the Seals are broken, is one of the most important Missions on earth for my Father.

The world has been promised the Truth, at this time.

All souls, believers and non-believers, must be told the Truth, because they are so far removed from the Church, that it must be given to them in this way.

All the angels have been sent to earth to protect humanity against the deceiver, and the lies he spreads about the Truth of eternal salvation.

Mankind may not want to hear the Truth, and many obstacles will be placed before you, my child, but, it will be useless.

No one will prevent the Book of Truth from being revealed to the world, for should they attempt to do this, the Power of my Father will be unleashed, like Flames of Fire, poured from the Heavens. My child, never doubt these Messages as they are being given to you.

Never change one word to suit those who try to make you amend the Word of God.

There can be only one Master and that is God, in the Name of the Father, the Son and the Holy Spirit.

Go now with the assurances you need.

Remember these Messages, from my Son, are for all God's children, and are not just for His Catholic Church, or for His chosen people the Jews. They are for everyone.

Each soul is loved by my Father, equally. No soul is deemed more important than the other.

Your Heavenly Mother
Mother of Salvation

Did you think I would ignore you until the Day of Judgment?
Thursday, February 02, 2012 15:30 hours

My dearly beloved daughter, how joyful I am at the response of My followers, to My Great Gift of a Plenary Indulgence, for Total

Absolution. But, how sad I am for those ungrateful hearts who reject My Gift.

These souls fail to understand that only God the Father can sanction this Gift of a Plenary Indulgence. Whether it is given to the world through My Holy Vicar or Me, your Divine Saviour, is not important. What is important is that there is little time left in which to save the souls of mankind.

To those who question My Word know that I am your Divine Saviour speaking to you from Heaven. Don't you accept that I exist? That I wish to send you a Message in these the end times? Did you think I would ignore you until the Day of Judgment? That I would not prepare your souls by communicating with you in this way?

If you believe in Me, then you must believe in Divine Intervention. And if you don't, then you have not opened your hearts. How do you know it is I? I ask you to sit now and speak to Me privately. Ask Me for the Grace of the Holy Spirit and I will respond immediately to open and pure souls.

Put down your armour and allow Me to give you this special Gift. Know you offend Me, when you reject My Gifts. Does this mean, too, that you will reject My Mercy? Bow your heads and ask for forgiveness. When you come to Me in humble gratitude, I will enlighten you to the Truth.

When you open your eyes to the Truth, your tears of understanding will pour forth and you will thank Me, finally, for My Great Gift of Absolution.

Your Divine Saviour
Jesus Christ

Virgin Mary: Hatred is hatred. There are no two types. They are the same.

Saturday, February 04, 2012 10:09 hours

My child, evil is spreading in certain quarters of the world rapidly.

While wars are being orchestrated with hatred in souls, the Holy Spirit, at the same time, floods the souls of others in different parts of the world.

The Battle of souls has begun. Good against evil.

My child, never assume that those hardened of soul are those with no belief or with lukewarm faith. Many compassionate believers in my Son, Jesus Christ, will now be turned by temptation. Their minds will be filled with doubts that will make them blind to the Word of my beloved Son as He speaks to the world through you, my child. Their hatred, as they turn on His Holy Word will be just as powerful as the hatred shown by murderers towards their victims. Hatred comes from the deceiver.

Lies are spread by the evil one, who uses weak souls to undermine the Truth. Hatred is hatred. There are no two types. They are the same.

The pride of those loyal souls will now be stirred as a final attempt is made by the evil one, to prevent these most urgent Messages for the world, from being spread.

My Son needs the support of His beloved followers to form His army on earth. This army will stem from His loyal followers. Be assured that it will be this group whose hearts will be hardened first.

You cannot harden a soul that is already in the dark. And so it will be the souls who are in the Light, who will be tempted by the deceiver. They will then spread lies to hurt my Son and delay this Work. They will not understand that this is happening to them because they think it will be their duty to defend the True Word of my Son.

By finding fault with these Messages He gives to you, my child, my Son will be tormented.

The very foundation of His Church will turn their backs on Him shortly. They will deny Him and then they will crucify Him again.

Pride prevents them from opening their eyes when He stands before them now with loving and open Arms. My child, I urge that all of God's children unite as one and fight for the salvation of all souls.

So many are not listening, my child, to these Messages now, but after The Warning takes place they will. Pray, pray, pray for those souls who inflict hurt, slander and spread untruths about you. I will now give you a Crusade Prayer to ask for protection for all my visionaries and those chosen by God the Father to spread His Most Holy Word on earth in these times.

Crusade Prayer (25) For protection of visionaries around the world

O God of the Most High, I plead with You to offer protection to all Your holy messengers in the world.

I pray that they are protected from the hatred of others.
I ask that Your most Holy Word is spread quickly all over the world.
Protect Your messengers from slander, abuse, lies and every kind of danger.

Protect their families and cover them with the Holy Spirit, at all times, so that the Messages they give to the world are heeded with contrite and humble hearts.

Amen.

My child, pride is a trait, which is most displeasing in the Eyes of my Father. It is more painful for Him when the sins of pride invades the souls of devout and holy souls when they refuse to accept the Truth of His Holy Word given to the world today, through His messengers.

They must ask for the gift of true discernment, which will only be granted, by the Power of the Holy Spirit, to humble souls, with a pure heart, empty of pride and arrogance.

Your beloved Mother
Mother of Salvation

Wars involving Iran, Israel, Egypt and Syria interlinked
Saturday, February 04, 2012 10:55 hours

My dearest beloved daughter, your loyalty to Me is tested every day. So many try to stop you in your work for Me, yet they cannot do this because of the holy protection afforded you, from the Heavens. Those who try to inflict pain, suffering and abuse on you will be punished. I will not tolerate such action.

Remember it has been foretold that no man can stop the Fire of the Holy Spirit, which will pour forth from My Most Holy Messages, for the whole of mankind.

I ask, therefore, that you continue to ignore the obstacles placed before you and ignore the hatred, for it comes from Satan.

Engage with hatred and it spreads.

Ignore it and it will die, because it cannot find the nourishment it needs to grow and fester.

Now I want you to tell My children that the events foretold in the Book of Revelation are now unfolding in the world.

My children must not be frightened because their faith and their prayers will help dilute the effects of war, genocide, famine and apostasy.

Wars will emerge which involve Iran, Israel, Egypt and Syria. All will become interlinked.

So too, will Italy suffer the fallout, which is connected to the rise of the false prophet and his partner the antichrist.

Pray hard that all countries are not drawn into a global power, which will control your money, for should they succeed, it will be very difficult.

Pray to God the Father, so that He can stave off such atrocities.

Prayer for the souls of others will save your own souls. That is all I ask. Prayer. Pray too, for conversion. It is not long now for all things to make sense, My daughter.

All will be well, once conversion takes place, after The Warning. Go now and tell my children never to fear when they proclaim My Word. I will be standing beside them. If they are mocked they can be sure of the Truth of this, My Most Holy Word.

Your beloved Jesus

God the Father: World to undergo a Chastisement – My intervention is necessary
Saturday, February 04, 2012 15:00 hours

My daughter, the world is about to undergo a chastisement as a result of the terrible sin being waged by mankind.

While much of this chastisement has been averted, My Hand will fall now on the wickedness, which is being perpetrated in every corner.

So much hatred for Me, God the Father, must be stopped, or My children will suffer an even greater horror.

I now prepare the world for the changes required to purify the earth, so that it is according to My plan to save humanity.

So many souls are tormented by sin.

I Am the God of all Creation and I will not sit back and watch My children destroy each other.

My daughter, there is a wicked plan to destroy much of humanity through war. These wars are not accidental. Have you seen how many are taking place, in so many nations, everywhere? This is by the hand of the antichrist, who awaits his moment of glory on earth, patiently. He, when nations are on their knees, will march in and create a false peace of his own devious making. This will be a mask of deceit.

My punishment will be unleashed on those nations who partake in this great deception to control the world through the seizure of nations. Be strong, My daughter, for this period, when the earth will shake, will not last long. It is necessary in order to wake up My children.

They, My children, have been warned, but My Voice is detested. My poor children who live good lives and who watch in dismay at the evil in their world must understand that My intervention is necessary.

If I do not stop what is happening then much of mankind will be destroyed. Pray that My children will pray for peace in your countries. Never be afraid to proclaim My Word even if you are persecuted. For just one soul, who professes their faith aloud, is enough for hundreds of conversions.

Go in peace. The time has come for Me, God the Father, to sanction the breaking open of the Seals. Only then will humanity accept that they are powerless.

They do not control the world for it cannot be so.

Only the Creator of all Mankind has the Power over Satan, and now I will unleash a punishment on those cold hearts and dark souls, who have pledged their allegiance to him.

The final stages of Purification will now commence.

God the Father

Virgin Mary: When you say my Rosary you can help save your nation
Sunday, February 05, 2012 13:15 hours

My child, I call on all of my children to pray for unity in the world at this time.

Belief in my Son is disappearing, and my children are being left with barren souls.

I am your Immaculate Heart and through the love I have for my precious Son, Jesus Christ, will work with Him closely to save humanity.

By praying for me to intercede I will beg my Father, God the Most High, to keep His Hand of Justice from the severe punishment He will pour down on the earth, to stop wickedness from spreading.

I will help you, children, to become closer to my Son's Heart. When we work together, my children, we can avert disasters worldwide.

Never forget the importance of my Most Holy Rosary, because when you say it every day, you can help save your nation. Satan's power is weakened when you say my Rosary. He runs away in great pain and becomes powerless. It is most important, no matter what Christian faith you belong to, to say this at least once a day.

So many people do not accept me, their Blessed Mother.

Like my Son, I am rejected, scorned, insulted and demeaned. Yet, by asking for my help, I can bring souls right to the Sacred Heart of my Son, Jesus Christ.

My Son, Jesus Christ, is your Saviour, children, and He will never reject sinners no matter how blackened your souls are.

If you feel sorry for having offended Him, just call out to me, your loving Mother, and I will take you by the hand to Him.

My Son is preparing to come to bring all His children together so you can all join with Him in the New Paradise on earth. Only pure and humble souls can enter.

You must start your preparations now. Start by reciting my Holy Rosary.

So important is this Prayer that it must now become a Crusade Prayer, in its own right.

Crusade Prayer (26) – Pray the Rosary to save your nation

Feel the peace, children, when you meditate on my Rosary.

As the graces are poured over you, after reciting it, you will then know that the deceiver has moved away from you and, in its place, will come love. Love comes from my Eternal Father.

When you feel love in your hearts, you will know that you are winning the battle to defeat the evil one.

Your beloved Queen of the Angels
Mother of Salvation

Pray that a nuclear war, which would wipe out one third of humanity, can be averted
Monday, February 06, 2012 20:15 hours

My dearly beloved daughter, My followers must unite together as one family, and stay strong.

I afford all My beloved and trusting followers the graces to keep calm amidst the storm.

While the earth continues to shake in every way your prayers are comforting to Me during this time.

How it breaks My Heart to see the innocent being killed in the wars in the Middle East. These poor souls are scourged and suffer just as I did.

The wickedness I see will be diluted and My Father's Hand will delay, but will not stop these countries from killing each other.

The Seals have been broken, My daughter, and wars will emerge quickly.

Pray that the global atrocity of a nuclear war, which would wipe out one third of humanity, can be averted.

I need more prayer, children. I realise how hard you pray, but, please, I implore you, invite as many prayer groups, friends and families to pray for peace.

I give you now a new **Crusade Prayer (27) Prayer for Peace in the World**

O My Jesus, I beg for Mercy for those afflicted by terrible wars.

I plead for peace to be instilled in those tortured nations who are blind to the Truth of Your Existence.

Please cover these nations with the Power of the Holy Spirit so that they will stop their pursuit of power over innocent souls.

Have Mercy on all Your countries, who are powerless against the evil atrocities, which cover the whole world.

Amen.

My daughter, I urge you to be patient, for it will not be long before the Confession. Once it takes place, everything will become calmer.

Go in peace and love. Above all, place all your trust in your beloved Jesus.

Your Saviour
Jesus Christ

The Mysteries for so long hidden in the archives of the Divine Realm.
Tuesday, February 07, 2012 20:00 hours

I am your beloved Jesus, Son of God the Most High, born of the Immaculate Heart of Mary. I come in the Name of the Holy Trinity.

These are the days, My dearly beloved daughter, which you will find to be the most difficult. Your suffering, handed over to Me, with joy and surrender in your heart, will save many souls. You must be brave when you do this and not be worried about your health. For this is just another trial, which will not last too long, but, which will go a long way in bringing Me lost souls.

My Book of Truth is being given so that believers will bear witness to My proclamation of the Mysteries, for so long hidden, in the archives of the Divine Realm.

Now that the Truth is being unraveled, mankind must accept that this, My Most Holy Word, will now be presented for everyone to digest.

This will provide sweet relief for your souls, but, which, for those who are removed from Me, will become very hard to accept.

The bitterness of the Truth is hard to swallow, but, if accepted, will bring comfort to those who will accept that it is, indeed, I your precious Jesus, who comes to embrace you in these times.

I, the Lamb of God, come now to bring you towards your salvation.

Without My help this would not be possible.

I bring you the Light now and you must walk behind Me as I lead you to the New Paradise.

I call on all of you to be brave, strong and fearless in the awful wilderness you now find yourselves.

It will not be easy, but I promise you that the strength that I will give you will make this journey less arduous.

Accept what you witness in the world as the purification continues with great intensity. For this is necessary.

Pray, pray, pray for patience and endurance because you must rise above the darkness and help Me to bring all of humanity into the Light.

Never lose hope. Just remember that all that matters is the unification of mankind. Your prayers, suffering and love for Me, will help unite My holy and precious family in My New Paradise on earth.

Look forward, children, for this is the life for which you are destined when you obey My Holy Will.

I love you and bless you, dear children for your love and compassion for Me, your beloved Saviour.

Your Jesus

Virgin Mary: The evil one will not rest until the Catholic Church is knocked to the ground
Wednesday, February 08, 2012 20:30 hours

I am the Immaculate Conception. I am the Virgin Mary, Mother of God.

My child, this poor world is in turmoil and as this continues, so too, will the time for The Warning draw closer by the day.

It is foretold that the hatred for my Son will extend to His Holy Church on earth. This has already happened. The evil one will not rest until the Catholic Church has been knocked to the ground.

When the Church breaks down, two sides will emerge. No matter how much the Church will suffer, it cannot, nor will it, die. This cannot be, children.

For while God the Father may allow the Church on earth to be dealt the same scourging as that suffered by His beloved Son, Jesus Christ, it will, as my precious Son, rise in glory once more.

Never forsake the Catholic Church.

Never deny my Son's other Christian Churches. For you are all followers of Christ. All of you with a devotion to my Son must put your differences aside and join together to fight the antichrist.

Crusade Prayer (28) Virgin Mary prayer for unification of all Christian Churches

O God of the Most High, we kneel before You to beg for the unification of all Your children in the fight to retain Your Christian Churches on earth.

Let not our differences divide us, at this time of great apostasy in the world.

In our love for You, dear Father, we beseech You to give us the graces to love one another, in the Name of Your Beloved Son, Our Saviour, Jesus Christ.

We adore You. We love You. We unite to fight for the strength to retain Your Christian Churches on earth in the trials we may face in the years ahead.

Amen.

Trust in me, children, to guide you towards the New Paradise and my Son's Reign on earth as it is meant to be.

Your loving Mother
Mother of Salvation

Very soon a man will come who will profess to be Me
Wednesday, February 08, 2012 20:45 hours

My dearly beloved daughter, it will not be long now before all prophesies foretold will be unveiled before a disbelieving world.

Even those unclean souls who shun Me, their Divine Saviour, and My Eternal Father, will not fail to notice. They will wonder why this is happening and for the first time will finally realise that they do not control their own destiny.

For all their misguided beliefs, and their perceived right to personal gain, they will soon realise the Truth.

My daughter, the way forward is to pray that these souls, however lost to Me, do not follow the allure of the antichrist and the false prophet.

Very soon a man will come who will profess to be Me. But, of course, this cannot be, for I will not come until the very end.

Yet he will display all the qualities that will deceive poor souls into believing that it is I.

He will perform wonders; great acts of peace, humanitarian deeds and acts of public affection.

He will be idolised and his powers will come from Satan, the king of darkness. So convincing will he be, that when he displays signs associated with the great saints, many of My sacred servants will drop in humility at his feet.

My Word, given to you the true end time prophet, will be rejected and dismissed as heresy.

I give you, My daughter, plenty of warning now so that as many of My children can be given the Truth before this happens.

Do not be fooled by those who exalt themselves in your eyes as being holy. Never confuse humanitarian deeds as always coming from Me.

The evil one is a liar. He is cunning and will present, at times, a loving charitable exterior.

Watch for those organizations, which are fronted by very wealthy individuals who boast about their efforts to save humanity. Many of them work in secret to denounce My Word.

This type of deception, will be used by the antichrist to recruit well meaning, but gullible, followers.

Once seduced you will become trapped. Then you will be fooled into accepting the mark of the beast, which you must avoid at all costs or you will become lost to Me, forever.

Be on your guard at all times.

Your task is simple. Remember there is only One God, Three Persons in the Blessed Trinity, God the Father, the Son and the Holy spirit.

Anything else that is presented to you otherwise, does not exist.

Your beloved Saviour
Jesus Christ

Fornication, pornography and prostitution all mortal sins
Thursday, February 09, 2012 15:00 hours

My dearly beloved daughter, man must turn away from sin and soon. So many sins today, are no longer seen as such.

So many grievances, against My Father, are committed without any guilt.

Children, you must stop. You are destroying your lives. Satan taunts Me, as he boasts of those souls he steals from Me, every single second. If you saw the souls, millions of them, tumbling into the fires of eternity, you would die of shock.

How it breaks My Heart to witness the terror that these souls, who lived in terrible sin when they were on earth, have to suffer. The sins they were guilty of are not always those you presume to be mortal sin.

I talk about fornication so easily accepted in the world today, participating in and viewing pornography, prostitution and sexual abuse.

I refer to hatred for others, as well as, those who cause pain and misery to those less fortunate than themselves.

So, too, is the sin of idolatry where you worship material goods, above everything else, yet they are nothing, but, ashes.

Do you not understand that once you sin in this way, you become further removed from Me, every day? Then it becomes very difficult to free yourself from the grip placed upon you by the king of darkness.

Wake up, children. Be aware of the existence of Hell and be very fearful of entering the gates of eternal damnation.

I tell you this not to frighten you, but, to ensure that you understand that mortal sin will lead you there unless you turn back to Me now.

Prayer, and much of it, will be needed to turn back to Me, but, hear this. To those of you who are desperate, sorrowful and feel helpless, because of the abyss of sin you are in, just ask and I will forgive you.

You must show true remorse and go to Confession, now. If you cannot go to Confession then say My **Crusade Prayer for a Plenary Indulgence** for Absolution for a period of seven consecutive days.

O My Jesus, You are the Light of the earth.
You are the Flame that touches all souls.
Your Mercy and Love knows no bounds.

We are not worthy of the Sacrifice You made by Your death on the Cross.

Yet we know that Your Love for us is greater than the love we hold for You.

Grant us, O Lord, the gift of humility so that we are deserving of Your New Kingdom.

Fill us with the Holy Spirit, so we can march forth and lead Your army to proclaim the Truth of Your Holy Word, and prepare our brothers and sisters for the Glory of Your Second Coming on earth.

We honour You. We Praise You. We offer ourselves, our sorrows, our sufferings as a gift to You to save souls.

We love You, Jesus. Have Mercy on all Your children wherever they may be.

Amen.

I never give up on sinners and feel a particular affection for them. I love them in a very special way, but detest their sins.

Help Me to save you, children. Do not leave it until it is too late.

Your Beloved Jesus

God the Father: Earthquakes will be felt as part of a small chastisement before The Warning
Friday, February 10, 2012 19:50 hours

I am God the Father, Creator of all things. I come in the Name of the Holy Trinity.

My beloved daughter, I announce today that all the preparations have now been completed for My Son's Great Mercy.

Please inform My children of their duty to pray for all souls who have removed themselves from Me, their Eternal Father. Only you can, children, help save these souls.

I also wish to inform you that a number of earthquakes will be felt, as I cast down a small chastisement, to punish those wicked souls who torment their fellow countrymen.

My daughter, once this chastisement is over it will be time for The Warning. Mankind will honour My Son, when they will seek forgiveness, for the way in which they have offended Me.

Many will convert. Many will die. Of those who will die their souls can be saved through your prayers. After that, the world will calm a little, and time will be given to repent.

Remember, I love all of My children, but, like any good father, I must punish My children, in order for them to understand the difference between right and wrong. This cleansing will waken up My children and many more will accept the graces, with gratitude, when they are poured over humanity during The Warning.

I love you, children, and it is My desire to save each of you, including those, hardened of soul, who will not accept the Existence the Holy Trinity.

Your beloved Father
God of the Most High

My poor Holy Vicar, Pope Benedict XVI will be ousted from the Holy See of Rome
Saturday, February 11, 2012 11:30 hours

My dearly beloved daughter, the wars are escalating everywhere, and very soon, the Hand of My Father will intervene, to bring this evil to a halt.

Fear not, for the plans to save humanity are completed, and it will not be long now for My Great Mercy, which will be given to each of you.

Never fear the works of the antichrist, when you, dear children, have the power within you, to weaken his grasp on the world, through your prayers.

Other world leaders will be killed soon and My poor Holy Vicar, Pope Benedict XVI, will be ousted from the Holy See in Rome.

Last year, my daughter, I told you of the plot within the corridors of the Vatican.

A plan to destroy My Holy Vicar was devised in secret, on the 17th March 2011, and this will come to fruition, for it has been foretold.

Spread My Holy Word to every corner of the world now, and arrange for the printed versions of My Messages to be spread to as many countries as possible.

You are being guided so you must do what is best. Ask Me, in prayer, to send you help and it will be done.

Your Jesus

Other countries will follow England to ban public prayer
Sunday, February 12, 2012 10:30 hours

My child, how I weep when I see how many are trying to stamp out homage to my beloved Son.

I told you before that the battle has begun. Plans have already commenced to ban public prayer to God, the Father, and His precious Son, Jesus Christ, in England.

This is only the beginning. Very soon it will apply to schools and other public places until it will become unlawful to pray in Churches, consecrated to my Son, Jesus Christ.

Hatred among men. and those in high places, towards my Son, means that they will do everything they can to ban the public practice of Christianity.

Those who hate my Son say they don't believe in my Son. But, how can they show so much hatred for someone they don't believe in?

Their contempt for my Son will become clearer as other countries will follow England to ban the public practice of Christianity.

It will become an offence to honour my Son.

Other religions, who believe in God, the Father, will suffer also.

However, they will not suffer as much as the Roman Catholic Church and other Christians. Their suffering will become intense.

Pray, children, to avert much of this evil as it becomes more apparent now.

For so long those who claim not to believe in my Son have stayed hidden.

Now they will surge forth in confidence and persecute my Son through the suffering they will inflict on His followers.

Pray hard, children, to protect your faith and your right to honour my Son in public without being made to feel ashamed.

Please pray this, the **Crusade Prayer (29) to protect the practice of Christianity**.

O my Lord Jesus Christ, I beseech You to pour down Your Holy Spirit over all of Your children.

I beg You to forgive those who have hatred in their souls for You.

I pray that atheists open up their hardened hearts during Your Great Mercy and that Your children who love You can honour You with dignity to rise above all persecution.

Please fill all Your children with the Gift of Your Spirit, so that they can rise with courage and lead Your army into the final battle against Satan, his demons and all those souls who are slaves to his false promises.

Amen.

Go in peace, my child, and tell the world to prepare for this great injustice.

Thank you for responding to my call today.

Mary Queen of all the Angels
Mother of Salvation

The Holy Bible is not being shoved aside in favour of these Messages
Sunday, February 12, 2012 15:00 hours

My dearly beloved daughter, I missed you yesterday. I woke you during the night do you remember? You were too tired, but how I wanted to speak to you then.

Today I must urge you to tell the world that war is to escalate and that, unless more of My followers pray, there will be a nuclear war inflicted.

This is close and prayer can avert this along with the Hand of My Eternal Father.

I need more of My followers to spread My Holy Word given to all of humanity for the good of your souls.

You, My daughter, are being attacked by those who say that the Holy Book of My Father is being shoved aside, in favour of these Messages. This is not so.

My Messages today are to reinforce the Teachings contained in the Holy Bible because so many in the world today do not know what is contained therein.

Nor will they know the warning signs of the end times unless I reveal them to you now. Why is this? I must prepare your souls for My New Paradise. Never feel I am trying to bring you on a different path.

For there is only one path to Paradise and I am the One who will guide you to its Gates.

Heed My Word. Listen to My call. Walk with Me with your heads high without fear in your hearts as I lead My army to help Me to reclaim My Kingdom on earth.

Your beloved Jesus

Satan's last days: Like a wasp when dying the sting will be the most painful
Monday, February 13, 2012 15:30

My daughter please remember that man only has to look around him to know that big changes have come into the world.

Normal every day events no longer seem the same. The joys you receive from material gain have lost their lustre. They no longer appeal. They are tinged with a mask of nothingness.

Why is this? Don't you know that it is the scourge of the antichrist and his presence on earth which casts these shadows?

He, the spawn of Satan infects every level of your society including politics, the military forces, financial institutions, humanitarian organisations and even your churches. Not one sector has been spared in order that he can inflict pain on humanity in these his last days on earth.

Remember that I, your Jesus, have given you, My followers, the power of the Holy Spirit to render these evil perpetrators impotent. The more you rise in battle, through the strength of your faith, then the weaker will be the grip of the antichrist.

Prayer, and especially the Crusade Prayers given to you, My messenger, will help drive out this evil. All evil can be destroyed through prayer. It is that simple.

The days are numbered for the survival of Satan and his army. However, like a wasp when dying, the sting will be the most painful. Show patience and perseverance during these trials and you, My army, in hope and confidence will march in unity towards the gates of My New Paradise on earth.

Your saviour Jesus Christ

God the Father: Europe will be first target of Red Dragon, followed by the USA
Tuesday, February 14, 2012 18:00 hours

My daughter, My timing, in relation to My Chastisement and The Warning, is not for your knowing.

There is no need for concern about My Divine timing, for this will be only according to My Holy Will.

Know this, though, the Red Dragon you were told about some time ago, has now risen his head coyly, but, with a deadly intent of devouring Christians all over the world.

Patient for so long in waiting, he will now swoop down and, with fire from his mouth, destroy everything that represents homage to Me, God of the Most High, and My beloved Son, Jesus Christ.

Europe will be his first target and then the United States of America.

Communism will be introduced and woe to those who oppose the reign of the Red Dragon.

My daughter, I realise that the recent Divine Messages given to you are distracting, but the Truth must be revealed.

It is only through the prophecies made known that faith will be restored. This is the reason why prophecies are being given to My children now, so that they will recognise the Truth of My Teachings.

All prophecies given to My prophets, Daniel and John will unfold layer by layer.

Details will be given to you, My daughter, to help build the remnant of My Church on earth.

They, My children, will need to be consoled through My Messages of Love and I will reassure them of this.

Lean on Me, children, your beloved Father, and I will give you the graces you need to defeat the enemy.

They cannot win and their power will not only be short-lived, but the Red Dragon and his blind allies will be thrown into the fires of eternal damnation.

Pray for their souls, because you can help them through your prayers, in order to save them.

The Warning will matter little to Satan's followers, the Red Dragon and his armies.

So hardened are their hearts, that they will deliberately side with the evil one. Their allegiance is to the false paradise he promises them.

Just as chosen souls are given the gift of apparitions or, as in your case, the gift of seeing Me and My Beloved Son, Jesus Christ, certain souls are shown visions of Satan and his fallen angels.

So close is their commitment to the evil one, that many of Satan's followers would rather die, than acknowledge Me, their Almighty Father.

My promise is this, children.

I will protect all of My children, who have the Seal of My Love, embedded in their souls.

You will be spared the persecution so that you remain strong to pray with all your might for these wicked people.

This will help dilute the terror and avert war, famine and religious persecution.

Prayer to Me, your Father, must now be included in your daily prayers with this special **Crusade Prayer (30) Prayer to avert war, famine and religious persecution**

O My Eternal Father, God the Creator of the Universe, in the Name of Your precious Son, I beg You to make us love You more.

Help us to be brave, fearless and strong in the face of adversity. Accept our sacrifices, sufferings and trials as a gift before Your Throne, to save Your children on earth.

Soften the hearts of unclean souls. Open their eyes to the Truth of Your Love, so that they can join with all of Your children, in the Paradise on earth, You have lovingly created for us according to Your Divine Will.

Amen.

Please do not ignore My Heavenly Intervention in your lives today, children.

For those of you with a deep love for Me, your Father, know that I must prepare you for this important journey.

I would not be doing My duty as your loving Creator and Father were I not to communicate with you during these, the end times, as you know them on earth, as it is now.

To those who may be frightened by My Most Holy Words, let Me console you, by telling you that this does not mean the end of the world, because it does not.

It is simply the end of Satan's reign on earth, which is to be welcomed children. The time is drawing closer for My Son to take up His rightful Throne when He will come, for the Second time, to reign over the New Perfect Paradise on earth.

My Heart bursts with joy when I tell you children of the new earth, which I have prepared for you.

My children will live for 1,000 years in the Paradise I created for Adam and Eve.

There will be peace, love, harmony and you will want for nothing.

People will marry, have children and the flowers, rivers, seas, mountains and lakes will take your breath away.

Animals will live with My children in harmony and you will be governed with Love, under the Reign of My Son, Jesus Christ.

Only then will My Holy Will be done on earth as it is in Heaven.

Your Loving Father
God the Creator of all mankind
God of the Most High

Wicked Group perpetrating biggest lie in order to seize control of countries
Thursday, February 16, 2012 20:00 hours

My dearly beloved daughter, you must tell My children, all those followers of Mine, to link and form a chain of protection in prayer.

By joining as brothers and sisters in prayer for those lost children, who wander seeking love for Me, but who cannot find peace in their souls, you can save them.

They need you to pray for them because The Warning won't convert these poor souls.

You, My loyal followers, bring Me the consolation I need when I see the terrible pain and hardships, which are now being endured by My children in almost every corner of the world.

This wicked group, made up of some of the worlds most powerful and elite are perpetrating the biggest lie through their deliberate plotting to seize control of countries in the Middle East, Europe and the US.

Their plan is unveiling before your eyes. Can't you see? This plan has taken decades to develop.

Every one of My children needs to stay awake at all times.

Do not allow them to take your countries. Stand up to them. Money is their weapon of deceit. The collapse of your banking systems was deliberate. Now they move to complete the next phase of their plan.

You, children, can stop this evolving through your prayers.

Already My Father is placing obstacles in their way.

My followers span many countries. Now you must join together in prayer to stop European leaders, some of whom, are intrinsic in bringing about terrible hardship on innocent people, in their wicked ways.

I urge you to say this Crusade Prayer to stop them.

Crusade Prayer (31) Chain of Protection

O My Jesus, let my prayer invoke Your Holy Spirit to descend on those leaders driven by lust, greed, avarice and pride to stop the persecution of Your innocent children.

I ask you to stop poverty, famine and wars from devouring Your children.

And I pray that European leaders will open their hearts to the Truth of Your Love.

Amen.

My daughter, the chain of prayer will spread out far and wide and the Power of the Holy Spirit will help stop those people, who have the power to stop suffering and halt them in their actions.

Spread My Word in order to spread conversion.

My time to come to Reign is close. So, there will not be time enough to save all souls.

Do all you can for Me, your Jesus, Who loves and cherishes you all.

We must work together, children, for the sake of all of mankind in our battle to prevent the antichrist and his atrocious plan of deception.

Hope, love and prayers, children, this is what I expect of you.

I thank you for all your loyalty and obedience.

You have not seen, yet you have believed. Once you heard My Voice, through these Messages, you recognised Me.

You were able to do this because of the Holy Spirit, which reigns in your souls.

You must share this great gift so that you can bring all of your loved ones with you into My New Paradise on Earth.

I love each and every one of you. You bring Me such consolation and joy.

Your beloved Jesus

Virgin Mary: Introduce abortion in Ireland and you sever the link to my Heart
Friday, February 17, 2012 15:30 hours

I am your beloved Mother, Queen of the Angels, the Virgin Mary, the Immaculate Conception.

O how I weep today as Ireland, the country most dedicated to me, their beloved Mother, falls prey to the evil one.

Great darkness has descended over this nation. So many have lost their faith, just as so many have turned their hearts away from my beloved Son, Jesus Christ.

My children in Ireland have allowed the evil one to turn their hearts to stone.

Those who love my Son are in pain as they witness the secularism, which has taken control over this, once holy, country.

Attempts are now being made to introduce abortion, and if this were to happen, it will deeply offend my Precious Son.

My children, should you introduce abortion in Ireland, you will sever the link that has brought you so close to my Heart.

So many people in Ireland now insult my Son; through the disrespect they show Him. I also am no longer tolerated and my Name is demeaned.

Children of Ireland, chosen as special souls to impart the Word of my Father, throughout the world, you must listen to me.

Pray, pray, pray that these plans to introduce abortion laws do not take place.

Should this happen, Ireland will lose much favour in my Father's Kingdom.

The sin of abortion is the most grievous in the Eyes of my Father. It is the worst kind of genocide.

You must fight this evil, children. You must do it now or the last Divine link, which needs to be strengthened, will, instead, be weakened.

You must rise, children, and reclaim your Catholic and Christian Faiths, for they are being stolen from you.

Do not allow those in power to sneer at you when you proclaim the Holy Word of God.

This spirit of darkness has now, not only covered your country, but, the Holy Shrines at which I am supposed to be revered.

I weep in sorrow as I see my beloved Ireland fall by the wayside.

Yet there is hope, children, but you must now join, in force, to protect your Faith.

Soon you will be forced to abandon, not only your Catholic Faith, but, your Christian Faith.

Reclaim your country from socialism and secular dictatorships.

They will plead for the right of citizens, but will deny the very rights they claim to protect, including the right to pray.

They will force you to accept, in law, the right to murder children, not yet born.

Remember, each soul was lovingly created by God, the Almighty Father.

Any man who chooses abortion or assists in the wicked act of abortion commits mortal sin.

Pray, pray, pray my Crusade Prayer for Ireland.

Crusade Prayer (32) Pray to stop Abortion in Ireland

O Mother of Salvation, pray for your children in Ireland to prevent the wicked act of abortion from being inflicted upon us.

Protect this holy nation from sinking deeper into despair, from the darkness, which covers our country.

Rid us of the evil one, who wants to destroy your children yet to be born. Pray that those leaders will have the courage to listen to those who love your Son, so that they will follow the Teachings of Our Lord Jesus Christ.

Amen.

Go now, my child, and tell my children in Ireland that they must be strong. They must stand up for what is right.

They must never be afraid to proclaim the Truth, the Holy Word of God, no matter how difficult this may be.

Your beloved Queen of Heaven
Mother of Salvation

European countries will succumb to dictatorship, no better than the days of Hitler
Saturday, February 18, 2012 16:00 hours

My dearly beloved daughter, it is My intention to protect as many of My followers as the Hand of My Father will descend shortly to punish mankind for their wickedness, and to prevent terrible atrocities from being committed by sinners who want to destroy many nations.

All of you will be protected, but your responsibility is to the others.

Watch now, as European countries succumb to dictatorship, no better than the days of Hitler.

The plans are in place by the world group to take over each country in Europe.

Babylon will topple as foretold.

The Bear and the Red Dragon will go to war just as prophesised.

Rome will become the seat of wicked rule and domination.

Italy will crumble.

Greece will be the catalyst, which will provide the excuse to bring down Babylon.

All will now be revealed to the world.

Prayer can ease the torment of My poor children who will be forced to beg for the food they put in their mouths.

They will be treated as children, but will be trodden upon, as they become enslaved by the global group, which works in tandem with European leaders.

They are traitors, all of them, not just to those they serve, but, to God, My Almighty Father.

His Name is hated by this group, who have banned homage to Him in their countries.

For this they will suffer. They will be punished and prevented from fulfilling their wicked mission. The Anger of My Beloved Father has now reached unprecedented heights, as the rise of the big Red Dragon is imminent.

So much destruction, children, so much lust for power and control, so much hatred for Me, their Divine Saviour.

Satan's four messengers have descended and work now within these groups.

Those wicked and powerful leaders are being controlled by the antichrist, who is now very active. The antichrist runs a very large organisation.

So cunning are they that few realise what they really do.

My children, they will try to take over and all their plans will seem to be unfolding.

But, that is when, My Father, will intervene.

Woe to those who will face the Anger of My Father.

They will not even be given the chance to tremble before Him if they do not repent immediately.

Very few of you, children, are being given the Truth because many of these people control the news you believe to be the truth.

You have no other means of knowing what is going on in the world.

For those you consider to be responsible organisations, who care about nations, are, in fact, the very groups run by the antichrist.

The nations you consider to be wicked are being victimised and used as pawns so that they, instead, seem wicked to the outside world.

You must not always believe what is presented to you in the name of justice.

Pray hard for all your brothers and sisters who will be trampled upon by these people.

Pray that The Warning will delay their action and pray to dilute the impact of the plan being orchestrated to abolish your rights to your money, your food and your right to practice Christianity and other religions, which honour My Father.

Your beloved Jesus Christ
Saviour of mankind

The Beast with the Ten Horns is the European Union
Sunday, February 19, 2012 03:00 hours

My dearly beloved daughter, you must not be frightened by these Messages for they are being given to the world because of the Love that I have for the whole of mankind.

Knowledge of events to come will help prepare My children so that they can defend the Truth.

My warnings can help spread conversion and will enable My children to, once again, acknowledge the Truth of My promise to come back again.

My Second Coming will take place in your lifetime children.

You, of this chosen generation, will reap the wonders of My Glorious Reign on earth.

I include among you, my chosen children, those who have turned their backs on Me and deny the existence of My Beloved Father, God the Most High.

My Love will envelop those who despise Me. In time they will convert.

Acknowledging My Messages given to you, My end time prophet, given the responsibility of the opening of the Seven Seals, will not be enough.

What really matters is the salvation of all your brothers and sisters in the world.

The two allies Russia and China will join forces. This will happen as the Beast with the Ten Horns rises to dominate their long-suffering innocent people.

The Beast with the Ten Horns is the European Union, My daughter, referred to as Babylon in the Book of Revelation.

Babylon will fall and be dominated by the big Red Dragon, China and its ally the Bear, Russia.

When this happens communism will rule and woe to anyone seen to practice their religion in their presence.

All religions will be banned, but Christians will suffer the biggest persecution.

Roman Catholics will not be tolerated at all and they will have to hold Masses in secret. The time has come, children, all My followers, to start planning your future.

I will guide you at all times.

Start preparing now, because you will be given the time to do this.

Again, I say to you, prayer and much of it will dilute the power of the Beast, the Bear and the Red Dragon.

They will rule for a very short time. For after that they will be destroyed.

Your Beloved Saviour
Redeemer of Mankind
Jesus Christ

God the Father: Rise now and accept My Seal, the Seal of the Living God
Monday, February 20, 2012 00:20 hours

My beloved daughter, My Heart heaves in sorrow for the sins of My children.

Like any loving Father their wicked hatred for each other tears My Heart in two.

It is like a sword piercing My Heart, which will not go away.

I am God of the Most High who, because of the free will I have given to all of My children, will have to suffer enduring pain until the New Paradise on earth evolves.

Then you will, My children, join in unison with My Holy Will. Until that happens there can be no peace on earth.

Only when the evil one, and those who slavishly follow the lies he promises, are destroyed, finally can the world become calm.

My daughter, tell My children that I do not relish the thoughts of punishing My children, for I love them.

They are mine, My cherished Creation. To see how the evil one has corrupted their souls is a constant torment to Me, their beloved Father.

I desire to take all of you loving children who know and understand My Love for you, into My beautiful New Paradise on earth.

I promise you that the persecution will be swift and that you will be protected.

For I now bequeath the Seal of My Love and Protection.

With this you will escape the notice of those who will cause hardship in your countries.

My Seal is My Promise of Salvation. My Power will surge through you with this Seal and no harm will come to you.

This is a miracle, children, and only those who bow before Me, their Lord and Creator of all things, as little children with love in their hearts for Me, can be blessed with this Divine Gift.

Rise now and accept My Seal, the Seal of the Living God.

Recite this Crusade Prayer to acknowledge My Seal and accept it with love, joy and gratitude.

Crusade Prayer (33) Rise now and accept the Seal of the Living God

O My God, My loving Father, I accept with love and gratitude Your Divine Seal of Protection.

Your Divinity encompasses my body and soul for eternity. I bow in humble thanksgiving and offer my deep love and loyalty to You, my Beloved Father.

I beg You to protect me, and my loved ones with this special Seal, and I pledge my life to Your service forever and ever.

I love You, dear Father. I console You in these times, dear Father.

I offer You the Body, Blood, Soul and Divinity of Your dearly beloved Son, in atonement for the sins of the world and for the salvation of all Your children.

Amen.

Go, My children, and do not fear. Trust in Me, your beloved Father, Who lovingly Created each of you.

I know every single soul; every part of you is known to Me. Not one of you is loved less than the other.

Because of this I do not want to lose one soul. Not one.

Please continue to pray My Divine Mercy Chaplet every day.

One day, you will understand why this purification is needed.

Your loving Father in Heaven
God of the Most High

God the Father: You are either for Me, or against Me. The choice is yours
Tuesday, February 21, 2012 00:30 hours

I am God the Father, Creator of all things. I am speaking with you tonight in the Name of the Holy Trinity.

My daughter, the time has come for the first of the Seals to be broken, and how this saddens Me.

I have promised that before this happens I will offer My Seal of Protection on the foreheads of all those who believe in Me.

Now I give you, children, a last chance to stand up and decide.

You are either for Me, or against Me. The choice is yours.

To those who reject My Holy Word given to this, the end time prophet, you must hear Me now as I speak.

I give you the prophets to guide you.

Why do you reject My Love?

Why do you allow doubts to blind you to the Truth?

Much as I Love you, there is little time and you will be given seconds to decide on your own fate. For in time, My Patience will run out.

Ignore My Calling and you will find it difficult to find Me in the wilderness ahead.

If you accept My Seal of Love, you will be within My Protection at all times.

This Protection will cover your families.

This is My final call to offer you My Seal of Love.

After that you will have to face the bleakness of the Great Tribulation exposed, alone and without a crutch to lean on.

I will never force you, children, to love Me. That is your own choice and, of course, love can only come from the heart.

I extend My Hand of Love now. If you know Me, you will recognise Me.

If you say you know Me, but reject My gesture of love and protection, then you do not really know Me at all.

My children, keep close to Me now for the first Seal has been finally opened.

The earth will shake all over in various parts of the world and then you will be without doubt. Because I love you I will await your response after that.

Never reject My prophets, for you reject Me.

Harm or slander My prophets, and you do the same to Me, for it is My Voice from Heaven that you insult.

Far better, if you do not speak at all, and remain silent, if in doubt.

It is now the time for the prophecies to be proven.

Many will fall on their knees in shame and regret when they will see how their rejection of My Messages, through My end time prophets, have torn Me in two.

How their condemnation and ridicule have made a mockery of My Holy Word.

How the Truth was too bitter for them to swallow and how the lies from the false prophets and fortunetellers gave them the shallow comfort they sought.

How far My children have fallen away from Me.

How ungrateful they are.

To those who know Me, and accept My Seal, know that you will have eternal life. You never doubted My Word, because your humility and childlike love for Me, meant that you did not allow intellectual reasoning to block your ears to the Truth.

So many of My true prophets sent to you over the last twenty years were mocked, abused, tormented and cast into the wilderness.

To those of you who slandered My Messages, you should be ashamed.

Yet you idolised the false prophets and bowed before them.

To you I ask, which God do you bow before?

You know who you are. The time has come for you to face the Truth for you are either for Me or against Me. If you cannot recognise Me then you are lost.

To those who do hear My Voice, follow Me, and help Me build My remnant Church on earth.

I will lead you through the havoc, which will be wielded by the antichrist.

You will not suffer the torment, which will befall those who refuse to reject false idols, greed, materialism and lust for power.

I call on all of My children, to listen.

I ask you to open your eyes, before it is too late.

Your beloved Father
God of the Most High

Why do you reject My Warnings to prepare for My Second Coming?
Tuesday, February 21, 2012 19:45 hours

My dearly beloved daughter, how you suffer in My Name, and that of My beloved Father.

You must be strong, as these Messages will provoke outrage in some quarters, although they will inspire and give strength to other souls.

My Holy Word was rejected by learned men, during My time on earth.

I was dismissed as a fraud, by the priests, and those who claimed to be holy men.

Those of you who say that the treatment meted out to Me was barbaric, would be right that people who lived in those days were uneducated, coarse and wicked, that they were cruel in their treatment of Me, their beloved Saviour.

Some may say that they were ignorant and knew nothing of Holy Scriptures. But, this is not true, because those living in the world today, although they are more educated and knowledgeable, are no different.

Those, whom you would expect, fully versed in the Holy Bible, to be alert to the Teachings therein, are blind to the Truth.

For all their understanding of My Father's Holy Book, they have failed to prepare for the time when I will come again.

When did they think they would be accorded this time?

The time is drawing very close to My Second Coming on earth.

Yet, mankind have not prepared themselves for My arrival.

Even My sacred servants do not preach of the importance of this most glorious event. Why is this?

Have you learned nothing? What is it that I have to do?

When did you think I might come, and why do you think that the time is not near?

What is it that blinds you, and blocks your ears to the sound of My Voice?

Drop your cloak of gold, silver and riches and accept that you are nothing, without Me.

Without My graces, you cannot prepare your souls for My glorious return.

My beloved Father always sends prophets to prepare His children. He has been doing this since time began.

Why then do you reject My warnings to prepare for My Second Coming?

I beg you to listen to Me.

I cannot command you to listen, for you have been given the gift of free will.

I can never force you or give you the command to take action. For this is impossible.

My Father will never interfere with your free will.

But, he will never hesitate to warn you, guide you and flood your souls with graces to make you strong.

For those with open hearts He will give them the Gift of the Holy Spirit.

Those guilty of pride, religious snobbery and arrogance, will find it impossible to open their hearts, because they lack the most important quality of all. Humility.

Without humility, and generosity of heart, you cannot come close to My Sacred Heart.

Come to Me, children. Let Me take you into My flock, so like a Good Shepherd I can lead you to safety.

Your Jesus
Redeemer of Mankind

Fasting is important for your souls
Wednesday, February 22, 2012 19:00 hours

Message received by Maria Divine Mercy during Adoration of the Holy Eucharist.

My dearly beloved daughter, tell My children that this time of Lent is a time of quiet reflection, of personal sacrifice, and an opportunity to pray for the mitigation of war in the world.

Emulate My fasting in the desert by making small sacrifices.

Fasting is important for your souls. It cleanses the spirit and gives Me great comfort.

You can save many souls by fasting just once a week. This can be according to your desire. All that matters is that you offer up this day for souls.

Use this time to help Me in My battle for souls.

Reflect on My life on earth, and the Gift I bestowed, by My death on the Cross, to provide all of My children with Eternal Life.

These few weeks of Lent must be used to prepare your souls and those of your brothers and sisters.

Please prepare for Holy Week and Easter by reciting this **Crusade Prayer (34) My Gift of Fasting to Jesus**

O My Jesus, help me in my own small way, to imitate Your life of Sacrifice, in order to save mankind.

Allow me to offer You the gift of fasting one day a week, throughout Lent, to save all of humanity so that they can enter the gates of the New Paradise on Earth.

I offer You, dear Jesus, my sacrifice with love and joy in my heart.

To show You the extent of my love through this sacrifice, I beg You for the salvation of every soul who may have fallen from grace.

Amen.

Do not allow fear to cloud your hope of eternal salvation, children. The purification will be swift.

You, My followers, who accept the Seal of the Living God, are blessed.

You must not worry.

You must be strong.

You must be hopeful and focus on Me at all times.

Only then will you rise and walk the thorny road, without hesitation.

I will guide and lead you on your journey every step of the way.

Your beloved Jesus

Virgin Mary: Pray that Nuclear War can be averted in Iran
Thursday, February 23, 2012 16:00 hours

My child, it is time for my children to join as one, in deference to My precious son, so that nuclear war can be averted in Iran.

This war is very close and you must pray hard to stop it, because it will kill millions of God's children.

Satan and his demons are working to cause terrible destruction.

If they kill souls, before they are given a chance to redeem themselves in my Son's eyes, then they are lost.

This is the evil one's plan.

He seeks so many souls to prevent them from entering my Father' Kingdom.

My Holy Rosary can, when recited by saying all the mysteries in one prayer, prevent war, children.

Unite now for one day and recite my Holy Rosary to stop this nuclear war, which is now being planned.

Pray for those poor souls, not just in Iran but, in countries who become embroiled unwittingly.

Pray also for those poor countries, who are being used as pawns in the wicked game of lies, being planned by groups, not of God, my Eternal Father.

Go now, my children, and bring all of my children together to pray in order to mitigate this great atrocity against humanity.

Your beloved Mother
Mother of Salvation

There will be no death, no illness no sin in the New Paradise
Friday, February 24, 2012 15:30 hours

My dearly beloved daughter, you must never forget that, despite My stern warnings to humanity, I hold a very special love in My Heart for all of My children.

It is necessary to purify the earth now for were I to return now it would not be fit for Me to walk upon it.

When mankind has been purified only those with love for Me and My Eternal Father will remain.

My chosen generation will be with Me for eternity. This Paradise will offer 1,000 years of peace, love and harmony.

After this period the second resurrection of the dead will take place.

Only then can eternal life be offered to all souls, with the Light of God shining through them.

Why do you hesitate, My daughter, don't you know that these prophesies have been foretold?

Let no man misunderstand. You, children of this generation, will be given the gift of living in the Paradise, even more beautiful than that prepared for Adam and Eve.

Age will be non-existent, as man will live in peace with families of generations.

So much love and enjoyment will be an everyday occurrence. Finally you will be accorded true lasting peace in your souls.

Why would this not be possible? This is the earth that was planned by My Father whose Divine Will, will at last finally be realised on earth as it is in Heaven.

Rejoice all of you. The New Paradise is to be welcomed with excitement and anticipation.

There will be no death, no illness, no sin. You will be given the gift of eternal happiness.

Pray for those who, through sin and disobedience, will forfeit any claim to their rightful inheritance, which was planned by My Eternal Father since the beginning of time.

Your Beloved Jesus

Never reject the prophets of the Lord
Friday, February 24, 2012 21:45 hours

My daughter, it is imperative that you remain silent as the persecution begins.

The Holy Word of My Eternal Father, will be rejected by those very sacred servants who claim to proclaim the Truth of His Most Holy Word.

The Catholic Church is the one True Church.

All Churches will unite to become one Holy and Apostolic Church at My Second Coming.

Until that happens every Word from My Father, given to a spiritually dry world, will be either, ignored, challenged or fiercely opposed.

Those who will fiercely oppose My Messages, given to you, the 7th messenger for the end times, will be divided into two camps.

Those who follow Satan through new age fortune telling and witchcraft.

The others will be those who are spiritually blind, but, who believe they are divinely inspired with the Gift of the Holy Spirit.

Both will reject the Word of God, given to you through the Holy Trinity and My beloved Mother.

Even good priests, forbidden to publicly endorse these Messages, will feel it is justified to vilify My Holy Word for all the world to hear.

With little true humility in their hearts, they will set out to undermine this call from Heaven, which is being given to help humanity.

These priests, clergy and other self-appointed apostles who claim to know Me will try to encourage souls to reject My Word.

They have no shame, for they will arrogantly pull My Book of Truth apart, as it is being revealed to all of mankind.

Then, they will shred the contents with venom in their hearts.

They do not want to hear the Truth, for it will upset and rattle the cocoon of false security within which they wrap themselves.

Oh how they offend Me.

How much damage they will cause and, yet, they do not realise this.

Pray that these souls, blind to the Truth, through the influence of the deceiver, will open their hearts and accept the Word of God as it is presented to them today.

They have no right to publicly dismiss these Messages without discerning them, with a clean soul, which must be humble in all things.

While God allows the sufferings experienced by His visionaries on earth to ensure that souls are saved He will not tolerate the abuse of His anointed prophets.

You, My daughter, are a prophet.

You accept suffering as a gift to me.

But, this is not about you for you are nothing without Me, and you know and accept this.

God, My Father, speaks to the world through His prophets.

It is His Word you reject, when you publicly slander His prophets.

For this is a sin in His Eyes.

Never reject the prophets of the Lord.

Never hurt or harm His prophets in any way.

Remain silent at all times if in doubt and pray for them.

Attack the true prophet and fire will pour forth upon you from the Heavens in punishment by the Hand of My Father.

No man will stop the Word of the Lord from being given to His children.

This is the promise made by My Father since the beginning.

Hear His Voice.

Accept that you are in the end times.

Pray that these Messages will be heard, so that all of God's children will have eternal life.

Your Teacher
Redeemer of all Mankind
Jesus Christ

God the Father: The balm you so desperately need to calm your souls
Sunday, February 26, 2012 21:45 hours

My daughter, to those of My children, called to proclaim My Holy Word, to prepare the earth for the coming of My beloved Son, Jesus Christ, I have this to say.

You, My children, who know Me, your beloved Father, must fight against the temptations placed before you every minute of the day.

You have been filled with the Holy Spirit, through a special blessing given to the world by My Son on 10th May 2011.

You must understand the responsibilities you now face.

Because you are joining as one army, which will form the beginning of My remnant army on earth, you will be attacked on all sides.

Your faith and allegiance to Me, your beloved Father and My precious Son, Jesus Christ, will be tested beyond your endurance.

You will, by following My Son, have to bear the weight of His Cross, and this won't be easy.

You will be filled with doubts, interior sufferings and trials, and at times, you will want to turn your back.

Many people in whom you trust may try to discourage you.

You will be told that you are imagining things, that you suffer from delusions and then you will be mocked, sneered at and rejected.

You may even find that you will succumb to lies and deceit, which will be designed to persuade you to reject these Messages.

It will require tremendous faith and courage to take up your cross and follow My Son to help prepare humanity for His Glorious return to earth.

You will be tripped and traps will be set.

Never fall into the trap of being asked to judge people, if they don't accept these Messages.

Never fight another, when defending My Holy Will.

Love each other.

Show patience to those who not only sneer and find fault with these Messages, but who pour scorn on you as a person.

Remain silent. Show patience. Show love to those who profess to speak in My Name.

Never judge another in My Name, for you do not have the authority.

Never slander another in My Name. When you do this you break My Commandments.

Pray for those who hurt you, even when it is in My Name.

Children I need you to unite as one.

Throw all your differences aside.

The poor souls who need your attention are not those who are already converted, but, those who do not know Me at all.

Pray now for all of My children who know nothing about Me.

Pray, too, for those who do know about Me, but who refuse to acknowledge Me, their Creator, their beloved Father, who loves them tenderly.

I wish to unite all of My children.

I urge you to drop all your weapons of fear, anger and impatience, and allow Me to take you on the journey to Paradise.

This journey will be torturous, but the love and peace you will find at the end will be the balm you so desperately need to calm your souls.

Calmness, children, is important.

Patience is needed.

Love for one another, including those who hurt or offend you, is essential in order to enter the Reign of My Beloved Son, in the New Heaven and Earth, in the Paradise, I promised you so long ago.

Your Beloved Father
God the Most High

The world is about to undergo the next stage of cleansing.
Monday, February 27, 2012 15:30 hours

My dearly beloved daughter, as the events of disruption in the world continue to increase the time is the drawing close for My Divine Mercy.

As the wars and unrest spread in every direction, the faith of My Church will continue to weaken.

The schism in My Holy Church is about to develop quickly.

Priest against priest.

Bishop against bishop.

The world is about to undergo the next stage of cleansing.

Anger against My Father will emerge in every country in the world.

My followers will now experience suffering for their faith in a way they have not experienced before.

The pain felt by those poor souls is a reflection of the pain that I am enduring right now.

All those in union with Me, their beloved Jesus, will know, without doubt in their souls, that My Holy Spirit now rests within them.

They will instantly know when they witness sin around them and how it pains Me.

When they see wars inflicted on the innocent they will feel My torment in every bone of their bodies.

When they see the sin of abortion paraded in front of them, as if it were of no consequence, they will be riddled with My pain.

Sin is escalating. The faith of My Church is dissipating.

The loyalty of My sacred servants is weakening.

Belief in My Teachings is being dismissed by My sacred servants, where My flock are told lies about the seriousness of sin.

Then there are My beloved priests, nuns and clergy, of all religious denominations, who believed in Me and My Eternal Father, who are enduring the pain of having to witness the spread of sin like wildfire, which is engulfing nations everywhere at a ferocious speed.

No matter how difficult this is, you must stay strong and keep united in My Name.

Prayer is now needed and you must spend at least one hour a day doing this in order to mitigate events, which will now unfold in the world.

Christian churches are being targeted and tormented by secular groups.

They will seek to abolish all things, which honour Me, their Divine Saviour, Jesus Christ.

The hatred being instilled in their souls is by the hand of Satan.

Pray, pray now that those souls who inflict pain and suffering on God's children can be saved.

Your Jesus

Don't you know that the Holy Spirit cannot and will not enter the souls of those with hardened hearts?
Wednesday, February 29, 2012 17:30 hours

My dearly beloved daughter, the timing of My Father's Will is not for your knowing.

My followers must be patient, as everything in the world will evolve as prophesised in My Father's Book.

All of this will be according to My Father's timing, and the effect that your prayers will have, in helping to avert global wars.

It is not long for all My promises to be fulfilled.

You, My followers, must trust in Me, your beloved Jesus.

Pray for souls and leave everything in My Hands.

Never forget to pray to My Father, as often as you can, for the Seal of the Living God, in order to protect you and your families.

Crusade Prayer (33) to ask for the Seal of the Living God and accept it with love, joy and gratitude.

O My God, My loving Father, I accept with love and gratitude, Your Divine Seal of Protection.

Your Divinity encompasses my body and soul for eternity. I bow in humble thanksgiving and offer my deep love and loyalty to You, my Beloved Father.

I beg You to protect me, and my loved ones with this special Seal and I pledge my life to Your service forever and ever. I love You, dear Father. I console You in these times, dear Father.

I offer you the Body, Blood, Soul and Divinity of Your dearly beloved Son, in atonement for the sins of the world, and for the salvation of all Your children.

Amen.

Ensure also that you encourage others to pray the seven-day **Crusade Prayer (24)** to seek redemption for your sins.

O my Jesus, You are the Light of the earth. You are the Flame that touches all souls.

Your Mercy and Love knows no bounds. We are not worthy of the Sacrifice You made by Your death on the Cross. Yet we know that Your Love for us is greater than the love we hold for You.

Grant us, O Lord, the gift of humility so that we are deserving of Your New Kingdom. Fill us with the Holy Spirit, so we can march forth and lead Your army to proclaim the Truth of Your Holy Word, and prepare our brothers and sisters for the glory of Your Second Coming on earth.

We honour You. We praise You. We offer ourselves, our sorrows, our sufferings as a gift to You to save souls. We love You, Jesus. Have Mercy on all Your children wherever they may be.

Amen.

To those who challenge this special gift of prayer, in which I offer Total Absolution, you must know this.

I am Jesus Christ, the Son of Man, and have been given the authority to forgive all sins.

My sacred priests have also been given the power to forgive sin, through the holy Sacrament of Confession.

I request that you accept My Gift of Absolution, for the benefit of those who cannot receive the Sacrament of Confession, or for those who are not members of the Roman Catholic Church.

Would you deny these precious souls the right to My Gift?

Why would you try to discourage those souls, who accept My Divine Word, from receiving Absolution? Would you rather they did not redeem themselves in My Eyes?

You must show love to your brothers and sisters and be happy that they are being given this special Gift by Me, their beloved Jesus.

Even if they never read My Messages given to you, My daughter, every sinner has the right to ask Me to forgive them once they show true remorse in their souls.

Open your hearts and pray for the gift of humility.

Don't you know that the Holy Spirit cannot and will not enter the souls of those with hardened hearts?

Your Divine Saviour
Jesus Christ

Join together as we enter the Gates of the New Paradise
Thursday, March 01, 2012 19:55 hours

My dearly beloved daughter, many of My children will now be saved, because of the prayers and suffering of My cherished followers, whose love for Me exceeds that known to much of mankind.

In this period of intensity, I hold out and rely on My followers to help Me to save souls.

Many of these souls will not survive the act of My Divine Mercy, and will die in mortal sin.

So many of you have responded to My call with such obedience and generosity of heart.

You bring Me great comfort.

I bless you, My dear followers, and ask you to continue to pray for the souls of others.

All of humanity will be given the Gift of My Mercy shortly.

Not one will fail to understand the Truth of My Existence. But, not all will want to embrace Me even when the Truth is revealed to them.

They are the souls I pine for.

These are the lost souls for whom My beloved Mother spills tears.

These are the sinners you must help Me save, because I want to save all of God's children.

Pray and join together to help Me draw every single soul together, as we enter the gates of the New Paradise.

Crusade Prayer (35) Prayer for souls to enter Paradise

O My Jesus, help me to help you salvage the remnants of Your children on earth.

I pray that You will, through Your Mercy, salvage souls from the spirit of darkness.

Accept my trials, sufferings and sorrows in this life to save souls from the fires of Hell.

Fill me with the graces to offer You these sufferings with love and joy in my heart so that we will all unite, as one, in love for the Blessed Trinity, and live with You, as one holy family, in paradise.

Amen.

Children, you know how much I Love you.

You who know Me will understand the depths of My pain and suffering, because of the number of people who reject My Hand of Mercy.

Only you, through your prayers, can help these souls and so bring Me the comfort I desire.

Keep close to Me now.

It won't be long.

Be patient and pray.

Relax, feel My Love.

All will be well.

Your beloved Jesus Christ

God the Father: Warning about satanic cults and new age doctrines
Friday, March 02, 2012 00:20 hours

My daughter, the trials of mankind will intensify during the final cleansing required before the Second Coming of My beloved Son, Jesus Christ.

The earth is being prepared for this Glorious Event, promised as the greatest Gift by Me, since the Creation of Paradise. Await this event with great anticipation for this New Paradise is what every man, woman and child will strive for.

Prepare yourselves so that you, your families and friends are fit to walk the ground in My New Kingdom, which will be under the Reign of My dearly beloved Son, Jesus Christ.

Ignore this request, children, and you will forfeit your rightful inheritance.

Were sinners to glimpse just one minute of this glorious Creation, they would fall to the ground and beg for Mercy to enter the gates.

Only those who hold a simple and pure love for Me, their Heavenly Father, and My beloved Son Jesus Christ, will be able to enjoy this new peaceful and glorious existence.

Sadly, Satan has blackened the souls of many of My children, so they will be unable to discern Truth from fiction.

My daughter, terrible lies are being perpetrated by satanic cults and new age doctrines.

My poor children, seduced by lies, which are couched in a colourful mirage, believe in a new planet.

They are being promised a different kind of paradise. But, it does not exist.

When Satan seduces and wins the hearts of those who believe in him, he torments them for eternity.

If you saw the terror in their faces when they, after death, find themselves in the clutches of Satan, it would tear your heart in two.

So wretched are they that it is important that you warn these souls of the torment that lies ahead.

Pray for them. Never stop. In many cases only the suffering of victim souls can save them from Hell.

To those who believe in Me, God the Father, I call on you now to denounce false gods, false idols, false doctrines, fortune tellers and new age doctrine all of which amount to nothing.

All have been created by the king of deceit, Satan, a cunning liar.

He will stop at nothing to draw away from Me, My precious children.

I beg you, children, to pray for these souls as a consolation for Me, your beloved Father.

Comfort Me. In time you will understand the mystery of My Heavenly Kingdom.

In time the mystery of My Divine Will, will be revealed. In time you, through your loyalty and love for Me, will help Me unite My family, at last, in the kingdom created for all of My children in the beginning.

Thank you, My daughter, for your suffering. Thank you My children, for responding to My call from the Heavens.

I give all My Blessing now, but you must ask Me.

"Heavenly Father, help me to become little, as a child, in Your Eyes. I ask for Your Graces to fall upon me so I can respond to Your Call to save all of Your children.

Amen."

Your beloved Heavenly Father
God the Most High

Virgin Mary: Wake up children. You must embrace the Truth.
Saturday, March 03, 2012 14:33 hours

My child, the suffering of my Son today, is equal to that of His suffering when He was on earth.

The pain He endured then, which caused Him the greatest torment, was not His Crucifixion, but the way in which He was rejected.

His Word today is rejected, just as it was then.

He is mocked today, in a way, which brings tears and suffering, not only to me, His beloved Mother, but, to His devoted followers on earth.

How hurtful it is to see how many children of God have turned away from the Holy Sacraments and the Teachings of the Church.

So many souls are lost. I beseech you, children, to pick up the Cross of my Son and lead by example.

Embrace my Son with simplicity of heart.

To love my Son, and honour my Eternal Father, is very simple children.

Never analyse the Word of my Son.

Simply follow His Teachings, which have never changed.

Listen to the Words of my Son as He speaks to you now, from the Heavens.

He calls you to prepare your souls for His Second Coming.

When He speaks with you now, He does this out of His Love for mankind.

His Holy Word will nourish your souls and make them strong again.

Do not reject His call to you now.

He wants to save each and every soul. But, in order to do that, he must remind you of the difference between right and wrong.

So many of you are not being guided or informed of the grievousness of sin.

Tolerance in your society, and within the churches, means that what many of you think is of no consequence, may well be a serious sin, in the Eyes of God.

The Church is in great darkness at this time and has been a target of the deceiver for many years.

My Son must intervene and guide you now, as the schism within the Church will erupt soon.

Wake up, children. You must embrace the Truth.

The world will now change beyond recognition.

You have been sent many messengers in the past to prepare you for this event.

These are the last warnings being given to humanity, to enable them to prepare for my Son's great Mercy.

After His Divine Mercy, when He will open the eyes of all of mankind to witness their sins, he will give a little more time for them to seek redemption.

Then you will be given direction to prepare your souls for the Second Coming of Christ, my beloved Son, who will come again in glory as foretold.

Mother of Salvation

Catholic Church and House of Israel will be persecuted
Sunday, March 04, 2012 15:30 hours

My dearly beloved daughter, the time for the opening of the Seals, which will result in you opening the Seventh Seal, is almost upon you.

Because of your prayers, much upheaval is being averted.

You, My followers, are accepting My Cross, and you will unite with the Immaculate Heart of My Mother, as you march towards My glorious Kingdom.

As the falsities and depravities of the world escalate, so too will the faith of those who lead My army.

The churches will be persecuted, namely, the Catholic Church and the House of Israel.

Many will be pleased. These two religions will be tormented and every effort, both externally and within, will be made to eradicate any trace of either.

There will be great rejoicing around the world when they have fallen.

Many will consider them to be destroyed. People will then ignore their corpses.

But, this would be foolish. For they will rise again to form the New Heaven and the New Earth as the Gates of My Paradise are opened. No one can nor will destroy My chosen people on earth.

They may inflict pain, torture, death, and demolish the very buildings and temples set up by them to honour My Father.

But, then they will rise and reclaim their rightful thrones, when they will reign with Me in Paradise.

Never reject God.

Never reject His Churches, for if you do you will be following the path of deceit to eternal damnation.

Your Saviour Jesus Christ

The Book of Truth is being revealed to you, the seventh messenger for the end times.
Monday, March 05, 2012 15:30 hours

My dearly beloved daughter, I come today to comfort you in this time of torment, which assails you on every side.

Know that John the Evangelist was given the unsealed Book – the Book of Truth – for the world to hear now in these times.

This Book was given to him no longer sealed for the Seals were already opened. They were then closed and not to be revealed until the end.

This time has come for you to open the Book of Truth and reveal the contents therein for all of God's children to prepare their souls for eternal life.

The Book of Truth is being revealed to you, the seventh messenger for the end times.

By the sound of your voice, the Truth will finally be revealed, and the mysteries contained in the Book of Revelation will be presented to a disbelieving world.

But, not for long, despite the apostasy, which will not only affect believers, but those sacred servants within the church, the time for the Great Confession is close.

Once this takes place, great conversion will occur throughout the world.

Then they will be hungry for the Truth contained in the unsealed Book promised to the world for these, the end times.

You are the messenger who has been given the task not only to prepare the world for the salvation of souls, but who will also announce My Reign.

Your beloved Jesus

Watch now, as the man of peace will present himself to the world
Tuesday, March 06, 2012 15:20 hours

My dearly beloved daughter, you must continue to carry out My Holy Instructions and let no man stop you in this Mission, although you will continue to be attacked on all sides.

Never doubt My Word, even when you do not understand what My Messages mean.

Everything you are being given for the world to hear has been foretold, My daughter.

It is just that mankind needs to understand what is contained in the Book of John.

All things foretold must come to pass.

Watch now, as the man of peace will present himself to the world.

He will be seen to create peace in the Middle East.

This will be a false peace, and is a guise for the lie he presents, in order to hide the real reason for this untruth, which is being perpetrated.

Pray for My Holy Vicar, Pope Benedict XVI, for he will face a terrible persecution. This time is close now.

Pray all of you because your prayers will ease the severity of these times, which can be diluted.

Much is not known, My daughter, about the end times.

Many are fearful and so they should be, but, only if their souls are unclean.

For those of you in the Light of God, you have much to look forward to, because it will mean the banishment of sin from the earth.

At last the world will emerge in a new beginning filled with My Divine Light.

There is not much time before these things take place.

All that matters is that all of God's children will see the Truth, in time and convert.

Otherwise they will not be part of the New Heaven and the New Earth, which will merge to become one.

For then I will come to Judge.

So only those who acknowledge Me, their Saviour, Jesus Christ, and My Eternal Father, will have life.

Pray for all your souls. This is all you need to focus on right now and trust in Me completely.

Your Jesus

The First Seal is the Apostasy
Wednesday, March 07, 2012 15:40 hours

My dearest beloved daughter, tell My children that no man has the knowledge or the authority to reveal the Truth contained in the Book of Revelation.

No matter how knowledgeable they may consider themselves to be, it is only I, Jesus Christ, Saviour and Redeemer of mankind, who has the authority to reveal to the world what is contained in the Book of Truth.

Only, I, the Lamb of God, has the right to deliver the Truth, given to My disciple, John the Evangelist, the instrument of the Truth, to the world today.

The First Seal is the apostasy, seen not only among unbelievers, but, among those who profess to know Me, and those who publicly proclaim their love for Me. This is the time when the True Faith will be twisted, when you, My children, are presented with a watered down doctrine, which is an insult to My Teachings. I tell you, children, that when you see new false faiths and religious doctrines spring up, you will know that this is now the time for the First Seal to be revealed.

Look around and what do you see, religions that pay homage to new gods, which you have never heard of. Science fiction based religions, which amount to nonsense and which are empty of substance. Spiritual entities that are not of this world, but which many believe represent the Heavenly realm of My Father.

Heed now, for you are living in fantasy.

None of these metaphysical beliefs represent the Truth.

Any doctrine, which teaches you the importance of putting yourself before everything else, is a doctrine, which springs from Satan.

Do not listen. Turn your backs on this cruel deceit.

Those who seek out false gods and devote their lives by idolising false gods, are lost to Me.

Unless you stop, and pray to Me for guidance, I cannot save you.

You, and all those who knowingly withdraw now from the king of darkness, will be given the gift of discernment if you ask Me in this **Crusade Prayer (36) Help me to honour the True God**

Jesus, help me for I am lost and confused. I do not know the Truth of life after death.

Forgive me if I offend You, by honouring false gods, which are not the True God. Save me and help me to see the Truth with clarity and save me from the darkness of my soul. Help me to come into the Light of Your Mercy.

Amen.

There is only one God, the Father, the Son and the Holy Spirit, in One the Holy Trinity.

Any other god comes from Satan, no matter how attractive the guise.

Please do not waste your eternal life by pledging your allegiance to those faiths which honour new age practices including reiki, yoga, new age meditation, tarot cards, clairvoyance, psychic readings and angel worship, connected with ascended masters.

Slowly, but, surely these practices of the occult are being accepted not only by your society, but, by Catholic and Christian Churches.

These false religious doctrines are spreading so fast, they have consumed billions of God's children, who have now found so much false solace within them, that they no longer acknowledge the Existence of the One True God.

Your Jesus

My Second Coming, cannot be prevented, nor can it be stopped
Wednesday, March 07, 2012 20:30 hours

My dearly beloved daughter, I will protect you with the special graces needed, to give you the strength to deal with the forces of evil, which are underway to stop this holy Mission.

It is important to understand that human opinion is not important.

All that matters, is My most Holy Word.

My Word is the Truth. I am the Truth. Anyone who tells you these Messages are not in accordance with My Teachings is a liar.

They do not know Me. They may think they do, but, they can only know Me, if they remain humble of heart.

Those whose opinion contradicts My Word, are guilty of the sin of pride.

Pride blinds even My sacred servants to the Truth of My Holy Word.

My promises to mankind, to come again in Glory to Judge the living and the dead, must come to pass.

This, My Second Coming, cannot be prevented nor can it be stopped.

My warnings to humanity, given to them because I love every soul, are important.

I must prepare all of God's children, adequately, for this most glorious event.

Many will attempt to block you. Many will try to undermine My Holy Word and many will try to harm you in order to prevent My Holy Word from being heard.

All of these attempts will be useless.

Only I, Jesus Christ, have the Power to provide eternal salvation to the whole of humanity.

Only I have the Power to prepare the souls of all mankind for their inheritance in Paradise.

No one, not even Satan, the king of darkness, or his minions, can stop this from happening.

Always remember this. I will protect all of those who abide by My Holy Word.

You may be frightened by global events as the forces of darkness envelop your countries.

Events will distress you, but you must never fear, for I will bring you with Me into My New Kingdom on earth.

All I ask is that you trust in Me.

Let Me guide you.

Allow Me to show you the way to purify your souls, through the Crusade of Prayers I give you.

Then leave all to Me.

Remember, My Love for all of you is so strong, that no man can ever dilute this Pure Love and Compassion I hold for each of God's children in My Sacred Heart.

Your beloved Jesus
Redeemer of Mankind

My Seal of Protection is foretold, as the Second Seal is broken
Thursday, March 08, 2012 19:52 hours

My dearest daughter, the world has awaited this moment for two thousand years.

Some with fear in their hearts, others with anticipation and wonder, as to when this moment would come, and now it has.

This is the time I send My end time prophet, you, Maria, to finally present the Book of Truth, which reveals the contents of the Book of Revelation.

I am the God for whom all of My children are crying out, in these terrible times.

It is I to whom they, My distressed children, must call out for now.

I gather My family together, at this time, so that we can unite in the final battle to slay the dragon, who has tormented the earth for so long.

Children do not be afraid. No harm will come to those who wear My Seal, the Seal of the Living God.

Satan and his fallen angels, who infest the world at this time, do not have the authority over those who have the Mark of the Living God.

You must listen to Me, children, and accept My Seal for it will save not only your lives, but your souls.

Recite the prayer to receive My Seal every day*. (See end of this Message.)

Ensure that each member of your family and loved ones understand the significance of My Seal.

Your love for Me, your Heavenly Father, will be your saving grace, and it will give you the strength that you need. My Seal of Protection is foretold, as the Second Seal is broken.

The rider of the red horse is the avenging dark angel, who will slay My children in the many wars to come. But, he will pass over those of My children with the Seal on their foreheads.

Prepare now for these wars are already happening, and more are being planned in every corner of the earth and, especially, in the Middle East and in those lands upon which My precious Son, Jesus Christ, walked during His time on earth.

Your beloved Father
God the Most High

* Seal of Protection Prayer to God the Father (originally received by Maria Divine Mercy on February 20th 2012)

Recite this Crusade Prayer (33) to acknowledge My Seal and accept it with love, joy and gratitude.

O my God, my loving Father, I accept with love and gratitude Your Divine Seal of Protection.

Your Divinity encompasses my body and soul for eternity. I bow in humble thanksgiving and offer my deep love and loyalty to You, my Beloved Father.

I beg You to protect me and my loved ones with this special Seal and I pledge my life to Your service forever and ever. I love You, dear Father. I console You in these times, dear Father.

I offer You the Body, Blood, Soul and Divinity of Your dearly beloved Son, in atonement for the sins of the world and for the salvation of all Your children.

Amen.

Virgin Mary: Recite Rosary across all nations between now and Easter Sunday
Friday, March 09, 2012 19:15 hours

My sweet child, how I weep, as I see the hatred mounted, not only against you, but, against the Holy Word of my beloved Son, Jesus Christ.

Now you know how He suffered in the Garden of Gethsemane, and how He still suffers today as every attempt by Him to intervene to save souls is thwarted by the evil one.

As the wars are now being plotted it is important that my Holy Rosary be recited every day before Easter.

Children if you could devote each day of the week to my Holy Rosary with every Friday to saying the four mysteries, between now and Easter, much destruction in the world can and will be mitigated.

My Son is so happy with those who accept His Holy Word, with love and purity of heart.

Great graces are being bestowed on those clean souls who trust in Him completely, without any doubts in their hearts.

You, my children, are the remnant, the little acorn of believers, who will help swell the army now required to deplete sin in the world.

Your prayers, and especially my Most Holy Rosary, are the weapons needed to destroy the evil one and those he infests in every corner of the earth.

Go now, my children, and organise global prayers so that my Rosary is recited across all nations, between now and Easter Sunday.

Go in peace, my child. The graces you are now being given will help you to deal with the daily attacks from Satan, as his anger with this work increases.

Your heavenly Mother
Mother of Salvation

Time for the Second Seal to open, as wars will increase
Saturday, March 10, 2012 15:30 hours

My dearly beloved daughter, it is time for the Second Seal to open, as wars will increase and spread.

The avenging dark angel comes from one source, My daughter, and these wars are all connected.

They did not happen because of regional unrest, they were planned by the West.

These wars have been ignited, deliberately, in order to control, and many of these nations are painted as demonic, with lies spread about their political leaders.

Children, these wars have been cunningly set up, all at once, the objective being to remove leader after leader.

Peaceful solutions will be presented and applauded, but they are false.

You, My children, are being deceived.

Rumour of war is just that – rumour. How do rumours start? Who starts them and why?

Why do you think so many countries became embroiled in these wars at the same time?

This was not a coincidence.

There is a plan being organised by the antichrist to control and conquer these nations who have rich resources.

Once they control these countries they will become very powerful.

As these wars increase and become wearisome, then the antichrist will make himself known, as the peaceful negotiator.

Few of you are being told the truth, because of the control that the antichrist and his organisations hold, in the world of communications.

Pray now, as the wars will increase, so as to render their plans impotent.

Know that Israel, so influenced by the West, will be rejected and betrayed by the US, when they least expect it.

It will be then that the holocaust I speak of will take place.

Pray, pray, pray for the people of Israel, who will continue to suffer for their sins, until My Second Coming.

Your Beloved Jesus

Virgin Mary: Never before has there been so much opposition to Divine Revelations
Monday, March 12, 2012 19:00 hours

My child, it is at this time that all of God's visionaries, seers and chosen souls, will suffer the greatest persecution.

Satan's days are almost at an end, and he will use every weapon, especially some sacred priests, to try and discredit the Word of me, your beloved Mother, and my precious Son, Jesus Christ.

Never before has there been so much opposition to Divine Revelations, as there are today.

The darkness continues to invade the Church, and many within the Church are doing all they can to quieten the word of visionaries.

They do not want the Truth to emerge and will block the prayers, given to visionaries to save souls, from being proclaimed.

Pray, children that their efforts will not block the Work of my Son, or blind believers to the gift of the Holy Spirit, as it continues to be poured over souls who see these Messages.

Your prayers and loyalty to my precious Son have never been so important, as this cloud of darkness continues to fall upon my Son's Church.

Pray, pray, pray for the Light of my Son to shine through so that lost souls can be enlightened through His Most Holy Word.

Thank you for responding to my call, my child, especially at this time of great sadness in your soul, caused by the torment you have had to endure at the hands of those who profess to speak in the Name of the Lord.

Your heavenly Mother
Mother of Salvation

Now, a concerted effort being made to silence you, by a certain fragment within My Church
Tuesday, March 13, 2012 18:30 hours

My dearly beloved daughter, today you finally realised how much My most Holy Word is not only opposed, but, rejected, by certain members of My Church.

Those who are not fit to fall at My Feet and beg for Mercy, proclaim themselves fit to judge My Sacred Words, given to mankind to save their souls.

I am a God full of Mercy, full of desire to save all of My children, and am slow to anger.

Today, My patience was tested as another assault, this time from a man who professes to speak in My Name, was made to undermine these Messages.

You, My daughter, may not, from this day forth, engage with any such representative without first asking for My permission.

There is now a concerted effort being made to silence you, by a certain fragment within My Church.

My children, these are the times when the faith of My most ardent followers, including members of My Church, will be put to the test in ways not witnessed since My Crucifixion.

Just as I was viciously treated and condemned to death for daring to speak the Truth, when I came the first time so, too, will the same treatment be meted out to My prophets in the lead up to My Second Coming.

They will be sneered at, ridiculed and made to look foolish, when they spread My Word.

They will be accused of heresy, by those who proclaim My Teachings, but who fail to recognise My Word given to the world today.

Be fearful, those of you who attempt to block the pathway I now lay down before you, in order to save humanity.

You will be punished.

You will have to answer to Me for the injustice you inflict on those sent to proclaim the Word of God in these, the end times.

Reject the prophets of the Lord, and you reject the Word of the Lord.

Your arrogance blinds you to the Truth and you do not have the right to represent Me.

You offend Me greatly and your rejection of My Holy Word wounds Me deeply.

I weep at your cruel rejection of Me, while at the same time, you preach a watered down version of the Truth of My Teachings.

You must spend time now in Eucharistic Adoration before you can communicate with Me, to enable Me to guide you on the path of discernment.

Examine your reasons for rejecting My Words.

Is it because you do not want to hear the Truth of the schism, which is to grip the Catholic Church?

Is it because you do not accept that the Church has been infested by the deceiver?

Don't you understand that this has all been foretold?

You must pray so that you will see the Truth and come to Me for guidance, before it is too late.

Your Jesus
Redeemer of all Mankind

Love is more powerful than hatred
Wednesday, March 14, 2012 15:30 hours

My dearly beloved daughter, I embrace you tightly, within My bosom, as you endure this pain in union with Me.

My children, and especially My followers, feel a tenderness towards each other, which they cannot explain.

They may be strangers, living on opposite sides of the world, yet the love they feel is My Love.

They love each other as natural brothers and sisters do in any loving family.

I am the Light that Creates this spontaneous love, which brings souls together.

It is My Holy Spirit, which unites all of God's children together as one family.

You, My children, are My family.

The Holy Trinity heads up the family, and when your love is pure and humble, you are automatically part of this holy family.

Love of the Father is through Me.

When you love Me I will take you into the Arms of My Father who will place the Seal of Protection around you and your family.

My Heart is tender, as I witness with joy, the love that you have for each other.

You bring Me such comfort from the torment that I have to endure, as My poor children in war torn countries are being persecuted.

Unite with Me now, so that My family of devoted followers will join as one, no matter what their background is, or what country they come from, in order to conquer the hatred in the world.

Love is more powerful than hatred.

Hatred is diluted, if it is responded to with love.

If someone treats you unjustly, you must respond with love, and Satan will cower in pain.

If you feel tempted to seek revenge on those who hurt you, then you must pray for them, forgive them and show them love instead.

Love, which permeates through My family on earth, is a very powerful force.

You must never believe, for one instant, that hatred can defeat love.

The power that hatred wields, although ugly and painful to witness, can be defeated through the power of love.

How can love weaken hatred in the world today?

Prayer is the answer.

Love Me.

Listen to Me.

Respond to the requests of My beloved Mother and Me, her Son, through the various prayers given to you.

Here is a special Crusade Prayer for the unification of God's children.

It will spread love in the every corner of the earth, and dispel the hatred that grows every day.

This hatred, caused by Satan through the weakness of humanity, and which creates atrocities such as torture, murder, abortion and suicide can be averted through this prayer.

Crusade Prayer (37) for the unification of all God's children

O dear Jesus, unite all Your beloved followers in love, so that we can spread the Truth of Your promise for eternal salvation, throughout the whole world.

We pray that those lukewarm souls, afraid of offering themselves to You in mind, body and soul, will drop their armour of pride and open their hearts to Your Love, and become part of Your holy family on earth.

Embrace all those lost souls, dear Jesus, and allow our love, as their brothers and sisters to lift them from the wilderness and take them with us into the bosom, Love and Light of the Holy Trinity.

We place all our hope, trust and love in Your Holy Hands.

We beg You to expand our devotion so that we can help save more souls

Amen.

I love you, children.

You must never feel disheartened when you see the wickedness around you.

Your prayers can dilute this wickedness.

Your love will defeat it.

Your loving Saviour
Jesus Christ

Same sex marriage a grave sin
Friday, March 16, 2012 22:20 hours

My dearly beloved daughter, the pain and suffering of My poor followers, who have to watch, helplessly, as new laws, contrary to My Teachings, are reaching unprecedented levels in the world.

Not only do you have to witness sin, children, you then have to watch as sin is presented to you, where you are forced to accept it as being humane.

I refer to one sin in particular, same sex marriage, which is presented as a natural right.

You are then expected to accept this abomination, as it is set before My Father's Throne in a Church.

It is not enough for these people to condone same sex marriage in the eyes of the law, they then want to force God the Father to give them His Blessing. He could never do this, because it is a grave sin in His Eyes.

How dare these people think it is acceptable to parade this abominable act in My Father's Churches?

Children, I love every soul.

I love sinners.

I detest their sin, but love the sinner.

Same sex sexual acts are not acceptable in My Father's Eyes.

Pray for these souls because I Love them, but cannot give them the graces they desire.

They must know, that no matter how much they try to condone same sex marriages, they are not entitled to participate in the Holy Sacrament of Marriage.

A Sacrament must come from God. The Rules for receiving Sacraments must stem from My Father's Teachings.

You cannot force My Father, God the Most High, to give His Blessing, or access to, His Holy Sacraments, unless they are respected in the way they are meant to be.

Sin is now presented in the world as a good thing.

As I have said before the world is back to front.

Good is presented as evil, and those people who try to live by the Laws of God the Father, are sneered at.

Evil, no matter how you dress it up, cannot be turned into an act of goodness, in the Eyes of My Father.

My Father will punish those who continue to flaunt their sins before Him.

Heed this warning, for your sins, which are carried out when you refuse to obey God, will not and cannot be forgiven.

This is because you refuse to accept sin for what it is.

Your Saviour
Jesus Christ

I will come in the clouds surrounded by all the angels and the saints in Heaven
Sunday, March 18, 2012 16:00 hours

My dearly beloved daughter, My children must know that the reason the world is spiritually empty is because they no longer know the difference between right and wrong.

If it were not for My Light, which fills each soul, including sinners, the world would cease to exist.

It is My Light, which keeps the world alive.

Many of My followers who consecrate themselves to suffer in union with me, also help keep this Light alive.

Just before I return, My Light will disappear in the world, for a period of three days.

This will happen at the very end and must not be confused with The Warning.

It will be during these three days, that there will weeping and gnashing of teeth and people will scramble looking for My Light, even though they rejected Me.

This will be the time for the Truth.

My followers must not fear these three day,s for while you may not be aware of My Presence, I will be with you.

Then after the three days, I will return to earth, exactly the way in which I ascended into Heaven.

I will come in the clouds, surrounded by all the angels and saints in Heaven in great glory.

How beautiful and joyful will that day be when I come to Reign over the earth according to My Father's Will.

No man will be in any doubt that it is I.

Nor will they have any doubts about their future.

This will be the day I come to judge.

I will divide My people into those who love Me and those who hate Me.

Those, who rejected Me and paid homage to all things evil, will be banished in the eternal fires of Hell.

The rest will come and live with Me, in Paradise, along with the resurrected righteous.

This is the goal, which every soul must look forward to, when I come again as I promised you.

To Christians, I say this:

Know that this great and glorious event will take place soon.

Your generation will witness My glorious return.

I will never reveal the day for only My Father knows this, but I can assure you that the time for My Second Coming is close.

To My sacred servants I tell you that it is your duty to prepare My people, those souls for whom you are responsible, so that they are included in the Book of the Living.

I plead with you to work hard, through the power of communications and prayer, to prepare the world for My Second Coming.

Your Loving Saviour
Jesus Christ
Redeemer of all Mankind

Virgin Mary: Pray for Pope Benedict XVI who is in danger of being exiled from Rome
Tuesday, March 20, 2012 20:30 hours

My child, there is stillness, like the calm before the storm, as the Catholic Church will soon be plunged into crisis.

I call on all of my children, everywhere, to pray for Pope Benedict XVI, who is in danger of being exiled from Rome.

He, the most Holy Vicar of the Catholic Church, is hated in many quarters within the Vatican.

An evil plot, planned for over one year, will be seen all over the world shortly.

Pray, pray, pray for all of God's holy servants in the Catholic Church, who will be persecuted, because of the great divide within the Church, which will come about soon.

The great schism will be witnessed by the whole world, but it will not be seen to be the case immediately.

The false pope is waiting to reveal himself to the world.

Children, do not be deceived, because he will not be from God.

The Keys of Rome have been returned to my Father, God the Most High, who will rule from the Heavens.

Great responsibility will be placed on all those holy priests, bishops and cardinals, who love my Son dearly.

They will need much courage and Divine fortitude to lead souls towards the New Paradise.

Every effort by these holy disciples, to prepare souls for the Second Coming of my dearly beloved Son, will be opposed by the other dark side.

I urge all of my children to pray for the strength needed, as the antichrist and his partner the false prophet will rise to prominence.

You must ask me, the Mother of Salvation, for prayers to ensure that the Catholic Church will be saved and that the True Word of my Son is salvaged.

The Truth of my Son's Promise to return in great glory will be tampered with.

You, my dear children, will be given a series of untruths, which you will be expected to honour and accept in the Holy Name of my Son.

My Crusade Prayer must be said for the next month, every single day, to ensure that God's holy priests do not fall for the wicked deceit, which is being planned by the false prophet and his followers.

Crusade Prayer (38) Salvation Prayer for the Catholic Church

O Blessed Mother of Salvation, please pray for the Catholic Church in these difficult times and for our beloved Pope Benedict XVI, to ease his suffering.

We ask you, Mother of Salvation, to cover God's sacred servants with your Holy Mantle, so that they are given the graces to be strong, loyal and brave, during the trials they face.

Pray too that they will look after their flock in accordance with the True Teachings of the Catholic Church.

O Holy Mother of God, give us, your remnant Church on earth, the gift of leadership, so that we can help lead souls towards the Kingdom of your Son.

We ask you Mother of Salvation to keep the deceiver away from the followers of your Son, in their quest to safeguard their souls, so that they are fit to enter the gates of the New Paradise on Earth. Amen.

Go, children, and pray for the renewal of the Church and for the safety of those sacred servants, who will suffer for their faith under the rule of the false prophet.

Mary
Mother of Salvation

The time for the schism in the Church is almost here and you must get prepared now
Tuesday, March 20, 2012 21:20 hours

My dearly beloved daughter, I wish to embrace all of My disciples and followers everywhere in My Arms at this moment.

I need your comfort, children.

I need your consolation in My suffering, as I cry tears for My Church on earth.

So far removed have some of My sacred servants become, that many do not believe in My Second Coming.

Those priests, bishops and cardinals who do believe are being pushed aside and forced to keep silent.

How I weep for these poor precious disciples of Mine who have pledged their lives to Me and to the spreading of My Teachings to humanity.

Soon they will have to watch what they say about My Holy Word, for they will be forced to proclaim the teachings of a liar, whose soul does not come from the Light.

Unite, My children, My beloved priests and all those who love Me, now and help Me to save souls.

To do this you must not waste one moment. You must tell others of the Great Glory that lies ahead for each and every one of you at My Second Coming.

This great and glorious event will be the moment when you will finally unite with Me, your precious Jesus, who loves you all so much.

You, My beloved followers, must remain on your guard at all times.

You will be tempted to forsake Me, to denounce My True Teachings, and be forced to honour and obey the wolf in sheep's clothing.

So many poor souls will not only fall under the spell of the false pope – the false prophet foretold so long ago – but, he will have you believe that he has divine powers.

Children the time for the schism in the Church is almost here and you must get prepared now.

Join together as one.

Hold onto each other.

Protect each other and pray for those who will follow the wrong path and pay homage to the false prophet.

Much prayer is needed, but if you do as I tell you, you can save souls.

You, My precious followers, will form the remnant Church on earth and will be led by those brave sacred servants, who will recognise the false prophet for what he is.

Do not fear, as I am bestowing graces of wisdom, calm and discernment on each of you who ask Me to do so with this prayer:

O Jesus, help me to see the Truth of Your Holy Word, at all times, and remain loyal to Your Teachings, no matter how much I am forced to reject You.

Stand up now and be brave, all of you, for I will never forsake you.

I will walk with you the thorny road and lead you safely to the Gates of the New Paradise.

All you have to do is trust in Me completely.

Your Beloved Saviour
Jesus Christ

Tell humanity that all is now in My Most Holy Hands
Wednesday, March 21, 2012 20:30 hours

I come to you this evening, My dearly beloved daughter, to tell humanity that all is now in My Most Holy Hands.

I refer to the plans underway by the global group, who want to control your currency, your healthcare systems and your sovereignty.

They will not be allowed to control you, and My Father's Hand will fall swiftly, should they try to hurt you, children.

All believers who have My Eternal Father's Seal of Protection, the Seal of the Living God, will come to no harm.

This is why you, My daughter, must ensure that as many of God's children are given immediate access to this, instantly, in every corner of the earth.

Your prayers, children, have been very powerful and especially those of you who recite My Crusade Prayers, My Divine Mercy and the Holy Rosary daily.

Already they have delayed and prevented a nuclear war, saved millions of souls from the fires of Hell, as well as prevented many earthquakes.

Never forget that it is your prayers, which are your greatest weapon against evil.

Your love for Me, Jesus Christ has spread because of your allegiance to Me.

You, children, are My modern day disciples, and you have now been given the authority and the Gift of the Holy Spirit to spread My Most Holy Word.

In order to receive the Power of the Holy Spirit, you must invoke My help, so that you will speak the Truth at all times when proclaiming My Holy Word.

Crusade Prayer (39) is now being gifted to you so that you can walk amongst all of God's children and help them to prepare their souls for the New Paradise and My Second Coming.

Crusade Prayer (39) Help Prepare Souls for the New Paradise

O Jesus, my beloved Saviour, I ask You to cover me with Your Holy Spirit, so that I can speak with authority Your most Holy Word, to prepare all God's children for Your Second Coming.

I beseech You, Lord Jesus, for all the graces that I need, so I can reach out to all faiths, creeds and nationalities, wherever I go.

Help me to speak with Your Tongue, soothe poor souls with Your Lips and love all souls with the special Divine Love, which pours out From Your Sacred Heart.

Help me to save souls so close to Your Heart and allow me to console You, dear Jesus, when lost souls continue to reject Your Mercy.

Jesus, I am nothing without You, but with Your generous aid, I will fight in Your Name to help save the whole of humanity.

Amen.

My army, which has emerged from these My Holy Messages, has reached seven hundred thousand souls already.

Help Me to convert more of God's children, so that not one soul is lost to Satan at the time of Judgment.

I will keep you strong in all your work for Me, children.

I love you, My precious remnant Church.

Your beloved Jesus

The opposition to My Second Coming will be fierce.
Thursday, March 22, 2012 23:00 hours

My dearly beloved daughter, My pain has now become yours, in full union with Me. While this will be very difficult for you, it will bring you much joy and many new graces.

I now bestow upon you the Gift of being able to read souls. I bequeath this special Gift for two reasons. The first is to offer you the protection you require when you will begin to mingle with some of My followers.

The second is to convert those hardened of hearts who will confront you as they challenge My Most Holy Word.

You must accept this new suffering, which you are experiencing, and know that it is intensifying because of the increased wickedness in the world.

You, My daughter, and many of My other chosen souls, are all now experiencing both physical and interior suffering, at the same time.

This is due to the suffering My Most Holy Vicar is also experiencing in these days, when he will face his biggest trial.

Accept My Cup, My daughter, and for those who accept My Holy Word, through these Messages, know that your generosity of spirit is saving millions of souls every day.

Not one minute of your suffering goes to waste.

I realise, My children, that when you take up My Cross and follow Me, that you will suffer as a result.

But, know that by doing this you are helping Me to save most of humanity. You will also help Me in My Reign on earth, when the deceiver is banished and as My New Paradise on earth emerges.

Know also that you, who suffer with Me, by following My path to Paradise, will take the very same road to Calvary, when I came the first time.

Christians today may believe, that were I to come again a second time, that I would never be treated with such cruelty again. Well they are wrong.

The opposition to My Second Coming will be fierce.

My Holy Word will, and already is, being ridiculed and questioned.

My children, especially those with rigid and firm beliefs, fail to understand that My prophets will be outwardly rejected by the majority, just as they were in the past.

My Word, given to you this time, is already being ignored in many quarters of the Church and dismissed just as it was by the Pharisees during My time on earth.

The Truth of My Teachings, which have never changed, will be deemed to be lies.

Why is this? I tell you, it is because so many have twisted the Truth of My Teachings to such an extent that they no longer believe in mortal sin.

So many chose to ignore the Truth contained in the Holy Bible.

Why do you deny, for example, the existence of the 1,000 years of the New Heaven and Earth?

This revelation is very specific and the Truth is there for all to see.

Yet My Holy Word is challenged.

The Book of Revelation, just as the prophecies contained in the Book of Daniel, have been given to you only in parts. Many of you are confused.

But, this is because the contents revealed to both these prophets were closed and hidden until the end of times.

Only I, Jesus Christ, the Lamb of God has the Authority to reveal the contents to mankind.

How can you claim to know everything about My Second Coming when you know only parts? When they have not been revealed yet?

You must listen to My Holy Word for it is being given to you to save your souls.

Should you continue to deny My Word, after The Warning takes place, as these My Messages to the world will continue to unfold, you will be guilty of rejecting My Hand of Mercy.

No matter how much you believe in Me, or claim to know Me, you will commit the sin of denying Me. As such you will be lost to Me, and will not be fit to enter the Gates of Paradise.

It is My duty, given to you out of pure love and compassion, that I now try to prepare you for the end times.

Please do not reject Me, this second time, as I come to save mankind from eternal damnation and offer you the keys to eternal salvation.

It is because I love you that I must be firm and lead you to the Truth.

Do not wait until My Day of Judgment to discover the Truth.

Come with Me now and help Me salvage the souls of the whole of humanity.

Your Teacher and Redeemer
Jesus Christ

You do not have much time before I come to Judge
Saturday, March 24, 2012 11:45 hours

I come to you today, My dearly beloved daughter, to inform the world of My Great Mercy.

I also wish to inform the world of My Justice.

Children, you do not have much time before I come to Judge.

It is the period between now and My Day of Judgment, which will take place at My Second Coming, that you must use wisely to prepare your souls.

As your Divine Saviour, it is My duty to guide you, instruct you and reveal ways, in which you can ensure that you are fit to enter My Paradise.

Do not reject My prophets. I refer, in particular to My sacred servants.

You must ask Me to cover you with My Holy Spirit for discernment with humility and purity of soul.

When you do, I will reveal to you the Truth of My Most Holy Word, given to you now through this prophet.

After that, it will be your duty to ensure that all those souls who look to you for guidance, are helped to prepare their souls for My Second Coming.

Never be afraid to utter the phrase The Second Coming of Christ, for many of My flock do not know what it means.

So few of them have been taught about this great and Glorious Event, or the importance of preparing their souls so that they are in a state of grace.

Never be afraid to preach about the existence of Purgatory or Hell. It is your responsibility to tell My people the Truth.

Look to Me for guidance through this prayer.

Crusade Prayer (40) Prayer for the Clergy to prepare souls for the Second Coming

O my Jesus, I am but a humble servant and need You to guide me, so I can prepare souls for Your Glorious Second Coming.

Help me to convert souls and prepare them according to Your Holy Will so that they are fit to enter the New Heaven and Earth, which You promised all of mankind, through Your death on the Cross.

Give me the graces I need so that I can impart Your Word to thirsty souls and that I never waiver in my duty to You, dear Jesus, to Whom I pledged my allegiance through My Sacred Vows.

Amen.

Go now My sacred servant and accept the role for which you were chosen.

The challenge of preparing souls for My Second Coming is the biggest ever in your ministry, and you must accept this with love and joy in your hearts.

Accept also the Gift of being chosen as a sacred servant in these, the end of times, when the New Heaven and Earth emerges as My New Paradise.

You are blessed to be living in these times.

But, you will be tormented and obstructed on every part of your journey, when you help to save My souls on earth, by the deceiver and all those he tempts to turn your hearts away from Me, your Divine Saviour.

Never give up in your Holy Mission and know that I, your Jesus, will walk with you every step of the way.

Your Beloved Jesus

Even The Warning will not convert all non-believers
Sunday, March 25, 2012 15:30 hours

My dearly beloved daughter, today I urge all of My followers to devote their time to pray for those who do not believe in Me, Jesus Christ, or eternal salvation.

These souls are close to My Heart and are the ones who need to be converted, so that they can be saved first.

Those who are blind cannot see that their life does not end on earth.

Many do not accept that they will exist for eternity.

These souls wound Me deeply and I feel terror as I watch them destroy the life in their souls in this life on earth.

Even The Warning will not convert many of them who proclaim to be atheists.

Their only salvation is through the prayers and suffering of victim souls.

I urge you to pray for these souls through this **Crusade Prayer (41) For the Souls of Non-Believers**

O my Jesus, help Your poor children, who are blind to Your promise of salvation.

I beseech You, with the help of my prayers and suffering, to open the eyes of non-believers, so that they can see Your Tender Love and run into

Your Sacred Arms for protection.

Help them to see the Truth and seek forgiveness for all their sins, so that they can be saved and be the first to enter the gates of the New Paradise,

I pray for these poor souls, including men, women and children, and urge You to absolve them for their sins.

Amen.

Go now, My precious army, and focus on My poor lost children. Help Me, your Jesus, to save their souls.

Your beloved Saviour
Jesus Christ

Virgin Mary: Ask my children to do one day of fasting on Good Friday to prevent one world currency
Tuesday, March 27, 2012 18:00 hours

My child, your suffering, along with other chosen souls, will intensify during Holy Week.

This is the week where the deceiver will hurt as many of God's children as he can, through wars, persecution and violence.

It is at this time that he inflicts great suffering just as my precious Son endured during His Passion on the Cross.

My child, you must tell all those who have encouraged souls everywhere to recite my Holy Rosary every Friday up to Easter, that I am most pleased.

The souls they are saving, along with the suffering of their own nations, are all being helped through these devotions.

The Love of my Son is being felt now by more people all over the world, at a time of great suffering.

He eases their pain with His special graces, and soothes their souls, by the Power of the Holy Spirit.

Children, your prayers, which are so lovingly presented by you in the Heavens, are being heard.

You must seek the help of my Son, and my Eternal Father, at all times. Every single prayer, no matter how small, is heard and answered, according to the Will of God Most High.

My child, ask my children to do one day of fasting, on Good Friday, to prevent the one world currency from being introduced.

Your prayers and fasting can do this.

As soon as this prayer is said during your fast, my Eternal Father will stop these people from inflicting the austerity they are planning so that they can control you.

These same people want to abolish Christianity, so it is important that you stop this from happening through special sacrifices.

Crusade Prayer (42) Prayer of fasting to stop One World Currency

O God Most High, I offer you my gift of fasting, so that You will stop the grip of evil in the world, being planned to starve my country of food, including the Bread of Life.

Accept my offering and listen to my pleas for other nations to prevent them from the suffering being planned by the antichrist.

Save us, dear Lord, from this wickedness and protect our Faith so that we can honour You with the freedom we need to love and adore You forever and ever.

Amen.

My child, one day of fasting, on Good Friday, will bring much freedom to nations, from the evil one and those who follow his wicked desires to control the finances of all nations.

Your beloved Mother
Mother of Salvation
Mother of God

Jesus reveals details of His Crucifixion
Thursday, March 29, 2012 13:15 hours

My dearly beloved daughter, My time for more suffering will come about, as My Passion on the Cross, will be commemorated.

No man understands the extent of My suffering, during My Crucifixion, or the way in which I was scourged.

My scourging was the worst. I was beaten savagely; by ten men and every inch of My Body was slashed.

The flesh on My Back was torn and My Shoulder Blades were visible.

I could barely stand and one Eye was bruised and crushed. I could only see through My left Eye.

By the time they took Me before Pontius Pilate and placed the Crown of Thorns on My Head I could barely stand up.

They then stripped Me bare before placing a short red garment over My Head and then placed a palm branch in My right Hand.

Each thorn was like a needle, so sharp was it. One of these thorns also pierced My right Eye, which left Me barely able to see.

I lost so much blood that I vomited and was so dizzy that when I began My ascent to Calvary I could not hold the Cross.

I fell so many times, that it took hours before I reached the top of the hill.

I was scourged and whipped each step of the way.

My Body was bloody all over and covered with a thick sweat produced by a scorching sun.

I fainted a few times.

Much as this was painful and agonizing, the most frightening of all was the hatred shown to Me, not just by the adults along the way, but, by young children who kicked Me because they were following their parents' example.

The screams that poured out from their mouths and the hatred was nothing compared to the fear they had of Me.

Because, behind it all, they were still not sure whether or not I was, in fact, the Messiah, they were awaiting for so long.

It was easier, therefore, to hate Me, denounce Me, rather than accept Me, for that would have meant that they would have had to change their ways.

My most agonising moment was when I lay on the ground on My side, having being kicked in the back again, and saw My beloved Mother looking at Me.

She was heart broken and had to be held up by two of My disciples.

I could only see her through the one remaining Eye and I could not bear to watch her torment.

The jeers, screams and roars from the crowds of hundreds could be felt from the ground I lay on, and it took six hundred soldiers to organise and supervise the Crucifixion of Myself and six others.

I was the main focus of their attention and the others did not suffer like I did.

When My Wrists, at the base of My Thumbs, were nailed to the Cross I could no longer feel.

My Body was so battered and bruised that I had gone into shock.

My Shoulders were dislocated and My Arms were torn out of their sockets.

The worst physical damage was inflicted on My Body, before I was nailed to the Cross.

I let out no scream.

No protest.

Only a whisper.

This infuriated My executioners who wanted a reaction to satisfy their lusts.

I never engaged with them, for to do so would have meant that I would have had to engage with Satan and his demons, who infested their souls.

This is why their viciousness towards Me was so intense.

I was hanging on the Cross for five hours.

The sun was scorching and without clouds to help reduce the burning of My Skin.

As soon as I took My last breath, My Father sent forth black clouds, as well as, thunder and lightning.

The storm that took place was of such a frightening magnitude, and so sudden, that My spectators were left in no doubt, at that stage, that I was, indeed, the Saviour ,that had been sent by God the Father.

I reveal this to you, My daughter, as a Gift to you in return for the huge act of suffering you have offered Me.

Tell My children that I do not regret My Passion on the Cross.

What I do regret is that My Sacrifice has been forgotten, and that so many deny that My Crucifixion took place.

Many have no idea as to what I had to suffer, as many of My apostles did not witness My climb to Calvary.

What hurts Me today is that so many deny Me still.

My appeal to you, My followers, is do not allow My Crucifixion to go to waste.

I died for ALL sins, including those committed today.

I want and I need to save, even those who deny Me, even today.

Your Beloved Saviour
Jesus Christ

I beg you. Do not Crucify Me again
Friday, March 30, 2012 15:00 hours

My dearly beloved daughter, it is important that all of God's children understand why I died to save the world from eternal damnation. Satan has reigned in the hearts of mankind since the fall of Adam and Eve, and this has meant that he has successfully stolen souls. Most of humanity would not accept the Word of God especially the Commandments given to them by Moses.

I was then sent to ensure that humanity was given the Truth, in the hope that the world would accept this and turn back to the Father.

While many did accept My Most Holy Word, the majority refused to accept Me, as being the Messiah.

The Truth is that they would not have accepted anyone, including the prophets because they were content to live in sin, which entrapped their souls.

If they had accepted Me, I would have Reigned on earth and the whole of humanity could have enjoyed eternal salvation.

Instead I was rejected.

The Jews, My own people, despised Me.

The Pharisees looked down on Me, yet when they heard My Holy Word, they could not simply ignore Me.

This is because My Words sparked a Light in their souls, which they found hard to dismiss.

So they kept coming back to Me, again and again, to question Me.

Today the same is true. Those of you, who claim to deny My Word, spoken through My prophet, cannot simply walk away.

Despite your claims of rejection, you keep coming back, again and again.

In time, you will accept My Word, spoken to you today.

You must not make the same mistake, made by those who not only rejected Me, but who crucified Me.

I beg you. Do not crucify Me again.

Allow Me to lead you to salvation by listening to Me now, as I call on you from the heavens, to prepare you for salvation and My New Paradise.

Your beloved Jesus

Virgin Mary: I am the intercessor. Through me, I will bring your prayers before my Precious Son
Friday, March 30, 2012 23:45 hours

My child, you must know that as my Son's Messages to you change, and reveal events, both past and future, that you will be attacked more.

My Son's Holy Word will always be rejected, by those who refuse to listen to Him.

Human opinion is not important.

My Son' communication to the world, at this time, is too important to allow those who oppose these Messages to delay and divert you from this Work.

Now is the time for humble reflection on my Son's Passion on the Cross.

My children must honour the Sacrifice He made, for the whole of humanity, by making their own private sacrifice for Him during Holy Week.

Pray, pray, pray, children, for peace in the world.

Pray, too, for the protection of the Pope, during these times of fierce opposition to the Catholic Church.

Prayer, humility and simple allegiance towards My Son, is necessary, for you to become close to My Son's Heart.

I am the Intercessor. Through me, I will bring your prayers before my precious Son.

Through me, I will help you to love Him more and give Him the comfort He needs at this time, when the world commemorates His Death on the Cross.

Your beloved Mother
Mother of Salvation

My new miracles will be presented to the world
Saturday, March 31, 2012 11:00 hours

My dearest beloved daughter, you must remain brave throughout your suffering and not allow fear to enter your heart.

In union, truly with Me, your suffering coincides with the week, which commemorates My death on the Cross.

This is not a coincidence. For the suffering that you and other such chosen souls endure, during this week, will save millions of souls from the fires of Hell.

Just as I endured pain, torture and death, to save mankind from eternal damnation, so too, do victim souls save other souls, so that they can be given the Gift of eternal life.

No matter how difficult and frightening this suffering is, always remember the Gift to humanity that it represents.

Children, as Holy Week commences, please meditate on My Passion on the Cross.

Not just on the suffering, but, on the Gift of freedom that it offers the whole of humanity.

Not one soul, including the cruel and hardened sinner, influenced by Satan, will be excluded from My Mercy.

The Mercy, which has been made possible, because of the Gift My beloved Father gave the world.

When He sent Me, His one and only Son, He made the biggest Sacrifice of all.

This Sacrifice, proof of His ardent Love for all of His children, has meant that it is possible to destroy Satan once and for all.

Because of the free will, given to humanity by My Father, each man will be given the choice.

You will either be for My Father or against Him.

You will choose either the Paradise of Eternal Life or the horror of Hell.

Satan, as his days are almost at an end will not sit back, while My new miracles will be presented to the world at this time.

Not only will he attack those dark souls, in order to tempt them into further darkness and closer to his domain, he will target devout Christians.

The miracles I speak of are firstly, My communications through you, My daughter. My Voice is being heard and conversion is multiplying.

Millions of souls are now being claimed by Me, through these Messages.

The other miracles include the great Gift of My Mercy I bring into the world shortly when The Warning takes place.

For the first time every single man, woman and child will be given the proof that, not only does God, the Father, exist, but that I, Jesus Christ, His only Son, also exists.

This means that all those religions, including the Jewish people, My chosen people from whom I came, will realise the Truth.

The miracle of global conversion will infuriate Satan, who will not give up even at that stage. Those poor souls, already in terrible sin, will find it very difficult to pull away from him.

Other miracles will include global events, which will involve ecological wonders, which will be given by My Father, out of His Love for His two witnesses the Christians and the Jews.

Power will be given to these two Faiths when they are being persecuted.

Their enemies will suffer as they inflict terrible punishment on them.

And then there will be My Second Coming, the greatest miracle since My Resurrection.

This will be the day I come to Judge the living and the dead.

This is the day I come to gather My family so that we become one.

This will be the beginning of My Reign, as Heaven and earth merge, to become one for 1,000 years.

At this time, all will live by the Divine Will of My Father.

Your beloved Jesus

Let them pray to Me, for discernment
Monday, April 02, 2012 15:30 hours

My dearest beloved daughter, you must rest now, for the attacks by those who cannot accept My True Word, continue.

You are not permitted to defend My Word, but now I am instructing you not to engage with those who doubt My Word, for that is not your responsibility.

My daughter, no matter how tempting it is to prove the authenticity of My Most Holy Word for humanity in these the times, you must not do this.

I never responded to My executioners, during My Crucifixion. You must not try to respond to those who wish to persecute Me, through My Messages.

It is not you, my daughter, they are angry with; it is I.

I can only tell the world how to prepare for My Second Coming. I cannot force them.

Ignore such taunts. Many are from genuine souls, who feel the need to ask questions. But, you are not permitted to do so. Let them pray to Me for discernment. Only I have responsibility for their souls. Even when you offer suffering to save souls, it is still not your responsibility.

So go, and tell those who are in doubt, like My apostle Thomas, it was I who faced him, after My Resurrection, when I stood before him. It was only when he touched My Wounds that he fully believed.

Sadly, many souls in the world are not afforded this luxury.

They must know time is short, in order to prepare their souls. It is their own free choice whether or not they respond to My Call.

Your Jesus

Only through the prayers of intercession can those souls in the dark be saved
Tuesday, April 03, 2012 20:00 hours

My dearly beloved daughter, there is a period between now and The Warning, which I want My followers to understand.

Your intense prayers are needed to save souls, who are beyond helping themselves. Many of these souls will not survive The Warning, so it is important that they, and all others, who are all in a state of mortal sin, are saved by Divine Intervention.

Your prayer, begging for the salvation of their souls, is needed now. This must be your priority, now, during Holy Week for when you ask My beloved Father, in My Holy Name, to save such sinners; your prayers will be answered.

Crusade Prayer (43) Save Souls during The Warning"

O God, the Almighty Father, on behalf of Your beloved Son, Jesus Christ, and in commemoration of His death on the Cross to save us from our sins, I beg You to save souls who cannot save themselves, and who may die in mortal sin during The Warning.

In atonement for the sufferings of Your beloved Son, I urge You to forgive those who are unable to seek redemption, because they will not live long enough to ask Jesus, Your Son, for Mercy to free them from sin.

Amen.

Pray for all sinners. My greatest wish is to save all of humanity. Only through the prayers of intercession can those souls in the dark be saved.

Your beloved Jesus Christ

Please say My Divine Mercy and start My Novena on Good Friday
Wednesday, April 04, 2012 01:00 hours

My dearly beloved daughter, the time is almost here for the world to reflect on My death on the Cross.

This is the time, during 2012, that I urgently need your prayers for those who will not recognise Me and for those who do not know about Me.

It will be up to you, My beloved followers, to help Me save those poor souls, whom I need to bring close to My bosom, so that I can prepare them for My New Paradise.

Children I need you to say My Divine Mercy Chaplet and commence the 9-day Novena of the Divine Mercy from Good Friday.

It is important that as many of you complete this Novena for other souls. You will receive great graces and for this I will never forsake you. I will salvage your soul when you come before Me on the Day of Judgment.

You must never become tired of praying to save other souls. You are My army and through the graces I give you, you will work with Me to clean the earth of Sin, before My Second Coming.

Praying does not come easy to all of you. The best way is to unite yourself in My Sorrowful Passion, and meditate on My suffering, and, in particular, My Agony in the Garden. My Great Mercy is at its most potent then. It was precisely because of sinners, including those pagans who were never given a chance to know Me, whom I agonised over the most.

For those of you who love Me know this.

The more you trust in Me completely, the stronger is My Mercy. The more I can forgive. My Mercy is so powerful that it can wipe out the sins of all mankind.

Those who believe in Me, trust Me, can achieve great sanctity by helping to save the souls of their brothers and sisters, as a priority. They do this out of their love for Me for they know that this brings Me much consolation.

You, My pure and just followers, who love Me so much, know that it is through your generosity of heart, that I can save sinners.

Sinners, you must understand, are who I died for, and are the ones I thirst for most of all. I show great compassion for sinners.

But, you, My followers, who are also sinners, must trust in Me completely. By doing this, I grant a number of special graces.

The more you ask for My help, the more you receive. It is because of this bond that you and I hold between us, that you can help Me to save other souls from drowning in despair and hopelessness.

Remember the Power of My Divine Mercy Novena and the number of souls you will save for Me, this year.

Your beloved Jesus

Good Friday is the day I desire, and this year, especially, to be remembered for what it really means
Thursday, April 05, 2012 08:00 hours

Good Friday is the day I desire, and this year especially, to be remembered for what it really means.

My Father sent Me into the world, and offered Me, as a ransom, to save the world from the fires of Hell.

I came to serve you, children, not to condemn you. My death was a special grace, free of any obligation on your part, other than to accept the Hand of Mercy, given to you by My Eternal Father.

This Gift was offered to allow mankind to receive the Gift of Reconciliation, so that they can be made fit to enter My Father's Kingdom.

Before I was crucified I attended a very important Passover Supper with My Apostles the night before My Death on the Cross.

This Last Supper provides another special Gift. The Gift of celebrating the Holy Eucharist, is a Sacrament of Love, to provide you with a unique Gift where you can truly receive Me in Holy Communion.

My True Presence, contained in the Holy Eucharist in the world today, when celebrated during Holy Mass, provides very special graces to those in a state of grace who love Me, who receive Me.

My Presence can be felt in a way, which will strengthen your faith, when you accept My True Presence, in the Holy Eucharist.

If you reject My Presence, in the Holy Eucharist, you reject one of the most significant Gifts I left behind when I came to earth to atone for your sins.

I died to save you and this is, in itself, a great Gift.

But, I left you a very special Gift where you can receive Me, in mind, body and spirit.

Accept My Presence and your soul will become closer in true union with Me.

Accept Me. Do not forsake Me. Do not deny Me.

Believe, without any doubts in your hearts, that it was because of the Love of God, the Father, that these Gifts were bestowed upon you.

Reflect now on the real Truth of My Teachings

Do not accept My Crucifixion, without accepting the Gifts also offered to you at My Last Supper. If you do, you will be starving your soul of the Food of the Life.

Your beloved Jesus
Redeemer of Mankind

Easter is the time when My death on the Cross is contemplated properly
Friday, April 06, 2012 22:20 hours

My dearly beloved daughter, how you console Me, in My time of sorrow. How you give Me the love and comfort I so desire from souls.

Oh were all souls to unite and intertwine their hearts with Mine, God's Holy Family would be fully complete. Only when all souls are salvaged will My Father's Divine Will be done.

Easter is a time when My death on the Cross is contemplated properly and My Resurrection from the dead is fully acknowledged, for the freedom it brings humanity.

My Resurrection means that all of you who love Me and proclaim My Holy Word, can also be raised from the dead.

All those who have died in a state of grace, and favoured by My Father, will also be raised in glory from the dead on the day I come to Judge.

They will join those, who are alive not just in body, but in the Spirit of the Lord, and be awarded eternal life.

Many people do not understand My Promise.

All those whose names are contained in the Book of Life will be raised body, mind and soul, free of bodily corruption and in full union with Me.

All those chosen, will live according to the Divine Will of My Father.

You will live in love, peace and harmony during my Glorious Reign on earth for 1000 years.

You will join in glory, with the first resurrection of the dead. Those souls, including your beloved family and friends, who are deemed fit to enter My New Paradise on Earth.

This is the life you must all seek out. Let there be no doubt.

For those poor souls who cannot accept the Truth of My Existence or My Promise to Judge the living and the dead, they will tear their hair out when faced with the terrible fate, which will lie ahead of them when the Truth is revealed.

For those believers, you must also be careful.

Many of you who do not love Me enough, or take Me for granted, making the mistake of believing that My Mercy ignores sins, where no remorse exists.

My Mercy is abundant, I want to lavish My graces upon every sinner. But there are those, who are smug in the false assumption, that their knowledge of My Teachings is enough to save them.

They are indifferent to My Love. They lack a tender heart, have little humility in their souls and believe that certain sins are not worth repenting.

This thinking is dangerous, and serves only to remove such souls from Me further.

There is not one sin so small that can be ignored. Absolution can only be given when you repent. You can only repent if you are free from pride and humble of heart.

Rejoice, My children, this Easter. Just as My Death on the Cross gave you the gift of salvation, it was My Resurrection from the dead that will also give you the Eternal Life, which has been planned by My Eternal Father for so long.

You have much to look forward to. For the eternal life promised to you, means just that. Eternal life, in body, mind and soul.

It is important that you strive for this new life and that you prepare your souls.

Every effort will be made by Satan and his demons to convince you that eternal life in My New Paradise does not exist. That My Second Coming is a lie.

Priests, members of the clergy and devout Christians, will be the first target.

Pray, pray, pray to My Eternal Father to protect you with My Precious Blood so that not one of you strays from the Truth.

Your beloved Jesus Christ
Redeemer of Mankind

I Am the Church. The Church was founded by Me and it can never die
Saturday, April 07, 2012 10:00 hours

My dearly beloved daughter, the schism I spoke of has begun in the Catholic Church.

My Teachings, which have never changed since My Holy Scriptures ended with the Book of Revelation, are now being challenged.

There have been a number of challenges, opinions and theological assessments of My Holy Word throughout the centuries.

Many fine men questioned the instructions and the Teachings, which I imparted to mankind.

Some of My Teachings were taken apart, analysed, new interpretations sought and then accepted.

Yet this has been unnecessary, for the Truth was given to man by the prophets who came before Me and then by Me during My time on earth.

The Truth has never changed. The Truth is simple.

Other information, not contained in Holy Scripture was given, as a Gift to the world, through chosen souls, for one reason only. To help you contemplate on My Sacrifice for mankind, and to show and remind you of the Love I hold in My Heart for all of God's children.

Any Divine Revelations given to the world today are to help you prepare for Eternal Life.

My Teachings, honoured by the Holy Catholic and Apostolic Church, are now being attacked in the first of many challenges, which will result in the division of the Church.

New laws will be introduced to suit modern opinion and so that they sit comfortably with those who, with pride in their souls, feel a need to pacify mankind, rather than show obedience to the Teachings of the Church.

I Am the Church. The Church was founded by Me and it can never die.

Many, including those from within, as well as from outside the Church, will attempt to break down its structure.

Pray that My Holy Vicar, Pope Benedict XVI, will remain strong amidst the opposition he now faces.

This is a deliberate attempt, by those connected with the false prophet, to create a new church.

These cunning people will have you believe it will be the same Church, but it cannot be.

How can My Church, with new laws, twisted versions of the Truth I gave to the world, represent Me?

It can't. This is why My Father will direct His Church, the true loyal believers, from the Heavens.

He will hold the Keys, until the Second Coming, when the New Jerusalem will rise, the One True Catholic Church, out of the ashes to be reclaimed by all of God's children, all religions, all creeds as one.

This is the way it was meant to be in full and final union in the New Era of Peace on earth.

Your beloved Jesus Christ

Heaven and earth will become one. One won't exist without the other
Sunday, April 08, 2012 15:30 hours

My dearly beloved daughter, the time for My Reign on earth is drawing closer, and there is only so much time for humanity to grasp My Mercy, and repent.

It is also important that My Church prepare its flock for eternal life and use every opportunity to encourage reconciliation.

This is an important time of the year and you must turn to Me, your Jesus, and pray for the graces to ensure that you, My followers, have the strength of conviction to spread the Truth of My Second Coming.

The suffering of humanity and that of My Eternal Father and Me, His beloved Son, is coming finally to an end.

Satan's reign on earth will cease and I will take over My Rightful Throne.

While My Reign, within My Church, has meant that My Spirit has been present with great graces, offered to deserving souls, it will not be until Satan is bound that My Father's Will can finally be fulfilled.

No man truly understands what Eternal Life is.

No man understands fully what will happen at My Second Coming.

No man, because of the limitations of human understanding, can know of My plans for the gathering of My twelve nations on earth.

So many believe that My Second Coming is the end of the world.

It may be the end of times as you know it, but it is only the beginning of the glorious future planned by My Eternal Father for all His children.

Heaven and earth will become one.

One won't exist without the other. The righteous will live in My New Paradise and there will be great abundance in all things.

So much wonder can never be described in human terms. Great peace and joy will be felt by every soul who inherits the right to be part of My Kingdom.

My Heart breaks when I see fear in your eyes, children, when I refer to the end times.

Instead, I ask you to trust in My great Love for you all, and know that My Promise is that you will be truly at home with Me and your sorrows will be banished for eternity.

The New Paradise I promise is to be revealed to humanity very soon.

Do not waste one single moment in fear. Rejoice. Look forward to your future.

Trust in Me completely for I love you too much to ever let you down.

Pray that all of My children will be humble in heart to accept the keys to Paradise.

Your Jesus

Virgin Mary: The Era of Peace I spoke about in Fatima has been forgotten
Monday, April 09, 2012 10:00 hours

My child, the world is about to undergo the final changes, as the battle for souls intensifies.

Satan will hurt the Catholic Church and I, the Mother of God, will be implicated in the division of the Church.

My role as Co-Redemptrix, Mediatrix, Advocate, is not being accepted by divisions in the Catholic Church.

I am not accepted in many quarters as to the role I must play in the salvation of souls.

My poor Son is so hurt by the way in which I, the Mother of God, have been dismissed.

My role, as the destroyer of the serpent, is not understood.

I have been blessed with the graces, and the power, to defeat and destroy the Evil One.

He, the Evil One, has many followers from inside the Catholic Church who want to oppose the power I have been given by God the Most High.

The Era of Peace, I spoke about in Fatima ,has been forgotten.

This Era of Peace will take place after the Second Coming of My Son and will last 1,000 years.

This will come about when Heaven and Earth will merge as one glorious New Paradise.

Because of the faith of my children and their devotion to me, their beloved Mother, many souls will enter the New Paradise.

Satan is now working hard to persuade members of the Catholic Church that this is not to be.

My role as the Mother of Salvation, and Co-Redemptrix, working alongside My Beloved Son to herald the Second Coming, is being denied.

Children, pray that those souls, victims of the deceiver within the Catholic Church, do not drive my children away from their moment of salvation.

Pray that Pope Benedict can stop this evil from permeating throughout the Catholic Church.

Never give up children in your fight to stand up to the Truth.

My Son's Promise to return to bring humanity to eternal life in Paradise is about to be fulfilled. But, He will be opposed every step of the way by those souls who have allowed the deceit of the Evil One to turn their heads.

Loyalty, within the Church, towards My Son will weaken.

My role as Co Redemptrix, Mediatrix, Advocate, will not be accepted.

Pray that My Son's priests will stay strong and that they will defend the Truth.

Your beloved Mother
Mother of God
Mother of Salvation

Virgin Mary: The time for me to crush the serpent is drawing nearer
Tuesday, April 10, 2012 20:45 hours

I am your beloved Mother, Queen of the Earth. I am the Immaculate Conception, the Virgin Mary, Mother of Jesus, Who came in the flesh.

My child, the time for the Triumph of My Immaculate Heart is close.

The time for me to crush the serpent is drawing nearer, until the day when Satan and his demons are cast into the wilderness, much confusion will erupt on earth.

For believers in my Son, it will be a time of torment. They will be pulled into two different directions, by the Catholic Church.

One half will believe, out of duty, the need to follow the false prophet, the Pope who will follow Pope Benedict XVI.

He, the beast, is dressed like a lamb, but, is not from my Father, God the Most High, and will fool poor souls, including priests, bishops and cardinals.

Many will follow him and believe him to be sent by God to rule over His Church on earth.

Sadly, many souls will follow his Teachings, which will be insulting to My Father.

Others, filled with the Holy Spirit and given the graces of discernment because of their humble souls, will know instantly, that an imposter sits in the Church in Rome.

The new false Pope is already scheming, even before he ascends to the Throne of the Seat of Peter, to denounce the Teachings of my Son. Then he will denounce me, the Blessed Mother of God, and ridicule my role as Co-Redemptrix.

My child, your role is going to become even harder than before. For many of my children are very confused. The insults you face every day, the torments you endure on behalf of my Son, will increase.

Never be afraid to tell the world the Truth, my child.

You are being made stronger, as a result of the physical and mental suffering you accept on behalf of my Son, in order to save souls.

Every effort, especially by one division in the Catholic Church, will be made to dismiss my Messages given to you.

Your obedience and loyalty to me, and my beloved Son, will be tested as never before. This may lead you to pull away, but should this happen it will not last long.

Pray, my child, for all of God's children who, through no fault of their own, are being pulled into the final battle for souls.

All of this must come to pass for it is contained in my Father's Book.

All the angels in Heaven protect you, my child, in this somewhat lonely mission.

Always remember how important prayer is.

Pray, pray, pray for without prayer, especially the recital of my Holy Rosary, Satan can pull you away from the Holy Word of my precious Son.

Remember also the importance of fasting, for it keeps the deceiver at bay.

Without regular prayer, my children, will find it hard to remain close to my Son.

Never fear the future, children, for once you remain close to my Son you will be protected and given the necessary graces to prepare your souls, and those of your families, for the New Era of Peace foretold so long ago.

Your beloved Mother
Queen of the Earth
Mother of Salvation

The hatred will mount against you. You will be told that this Work is from Satan
Wednesday, April 11, 2012 21:20 hours

My dearly beloved daughter, why is it that you, sometimes, question the graces I have given you?

The Gift of reading souls was given to you so that you can discern the intentions of those poor souls who will try to undermine My Holy Word.

This Gift will enable you to feel compassion for such souls and help them to find the true path to eternal life and to free their souls from the torment that they endure.

This Gift will also enable you to identify false prophets.

You will know instantly, who comes in My Name, and who does not.

At first you will feel a terrible sinking feeling of fear because you will recognise Satan's work. You will know immediately when he is present in others.

When he attacks you, through others, you will feel like you have been kicked in the stomach.

You will feel nauseous when you come face to face with someone whose soul has been stolen by Satan and you will tremble and feel dizzy.

You will speak, however, to such souls with My Words and with a strength you will not recognise as your own.

Many who come to you with pure souls, will feel the Light and My presence surge through their bodies.

Few, of humble heart, and a deep love for Me, will fail to respond to My Holy Spirit, which has flooded your soul.

My daughter, this is now a difficult stage of your Mission.

The hatred will mount against you.

You will be told that this Work is from Satan.

Don't you know how Satan, the deceiver, works? He convinces good souls that when My Word is spoken, that it is not from Me?

He tries to convince others, through their fear of him, that the traits associated with him are present in others.

He causes doubts and distress in souls by deceiving them. By blinding them to the Truth and by preventing them from receiving graces, designed by Me, to sanctify their souls.

Those he attacks the most, are those who are closest to Me.

This includes not only visionaries and prophets, but, the very souls I need to help form My army.

This army will defeat Satan. He knows this and will never give up in his quest for souls.

Remember this though. Satan does not have the power that I have. He cannot defeat the Holy Trinity. He is powerless against My Mother who has been given authority to destroy him. He fears her.

To all those who doubt My Word, given through these Messages, please ask My beloved Mother to bring you closer to My Sacred Heart.

Ask her to cover you with her Holy Mantle and give you the protection you need from the evil one.

Remember the evil one is full of hatred.

When you find hatred of any kind in your heart, especially towards My holy messengers, know that Satan has tempted you to sin.

That is when you must ask Me for the graces to make you strong.

Remember, I will never turn My back on any of you including those of you who hate My messengers and those souls who reject Me.

Your loving Saviour
Jesus Christ

The next Pope, may be elected by members within the Catholic Church, but, he will be the false prophet
Thursday, April 12, 2012 11:27 hours

My dearest daughter, many people still reject Me in the world and it has to do with public opinion. So much darkness has descended over all of God's children that very few have the courage to publicly proclaim My Word.

Believers are frightened of the verbal abuse and vicious mockery they would have to endure were they to speak openly of My Holy Word.

Even devout followers lack the nerve to stand up and fight evil laws introduced in their countries, which defy the Word of My Father.

Priests are embarrassed to be seen to stand up for the Truth of My Teachings, for fear of being ostracised.

Now, more than ever, because of the shame they have to endure, because of the wicked sins of some of their own orders, they find it impossible for their voices to be heard.

When a brave sacred servant decides to stand up and defend the Truth of My Teachings, they suffer terribly. They are accused of lack of tolerance, lack of compassion, lack of love and lack of respect for human rights.

You see, children, the Truth of My Teachings, spoken through My sacred servants is treated as a lie.

Lies, those twisted versions of the Truth contained in Holy Scripture, are presented as the truth instead.

Satan has won over so many souls, including leaders within My Own Church, which has meant that many innocent people find it hard to pledge allegiance to My Holy Will.

How I have been deserted and pushed to one side, to allow the lies, planted in the minds of My sacred servants, to be accepted by the majority.

These wicked lies extend way beyond this.

The Truth of My Scripture contained in the Book of Revelation has been interpreted by My many churches, so many variations, all of which are based on human interpretation.

My beloved Pope Benedict XVI is the last true Pope on this earth.

Peter the Roman, is My Peter, the original apostle, who will rule My Church from the Heavens under the command of My Eternal Father. Then, when I come to Reign, at the Second Coming, he will rule over all of God's children when all religions will become one Holy Catholic and Apostolic Church.

I only speak the Truth, My daughter.

I must warn you that many new self-proclaimed prophets will now emerge, who will contradict My Holy Word given to you, the end time true prophet.

First they will convince believers that their words come from Me.

Their words will be carefully chosen and their meaning will be vague and a little confusing. But, many will dismiss this weakness and embrace their Messages, because they seem to be in line with Holy Scripture.

When many souls have been seduced, the attack will begin.

They, My daughter, are being sent to prepare God's children to accept the next pope, who comes after My beloved Vicar Pope Benedict. This pope may be elected by members within the Catholic Church, but he will be the false prophet.

His electors are wolves in sheep's clothing and are members of the secret Masonic and evil group led by Satan.

This is how Satan will try to destroy My Church.

Sadly, he will, this false prophet, attract a large following. Those who oppose him will be persecuted.

Run children, while you can. Denounce the lies, which will be presented by those who attempt to convince you of the authenticity of the false prophet.

Be strong. Stay faithful to Me, your Jesus. Never doubt My Holy Word.

The Book of Revelation is the True Word of God. It does not lie.

Not all of the secrets contained within are known to you; yet. I will reveal all through Maria Divine Mercy, although the Truth will be vehemently attacked and treated as heresy.

Remember one important lesson. My Word, when I was on earth, was treated as heresy when I came the first time.

My Word, given to you now, at My Second Coming, will also be treated as such, by believers, including My sacred servants, who represent My Church on earth.

Satan will sacrifice many souls to satisfy his final cravings to cause the greatest heartache.

Be assured that it will be the Catholic Church, founded by Me, and placed under the command of My beloved apostle, Peter, which will suffer the greatest in the end times.

Be on your guard at all times. Please recite this Crusade Prayer.

Crusade Prayer (44) Strength to defend my Faith against the false prophet

Dear Jesus, give me the strength to focus on Your Teachings and to proclaim Your Holy Word at all times.

Never allow me to be tempted to idolise the false prophet, who will try to present himself as You. Keep my love for You strong. Give me the graces of discernment, so that I will never deny the Truth contained in the Holy Bible no matter how many lies are presented to me to encourage me to turn my back on Your True Word.

Amen.

The Truth is written in Holy Scripture.

The Book of Revelation does not reveal all because I come only now, the Lamb of God, to open the Book for the world to see.

Any human interpretation regarding the 1,000 years is not to be trusted.

You must only trust in the Word of God.

Your beloved Jesus

So many lies, where the existence of Hell is denied, will be the downfall of Christians.
Saturday, April 14, 2012 15:27 hours

My dearest beloved daughter, no matter how difficult your physical suffering is, you must recognise that as it continues to intensify, that it is as I feel. Your suffering reflects just a fraction of My own suffering. In union with Me, you will know that for every pain and interior darkness of the soul you experience, you will know the torment I endure because of the sins of mankind.

Many people mistakenly believe that My suffering, began and ended, on the Cross.

My suffering will not end until all of God's children are united in love and harmony, where no sin will exist in My Father's New Paradise.

No matter how much humanity has been told about My Existence, I am still hated.

Amongst believers, although I am accepted, My Teachings are only tolerated by them, based on their own terms.

Many will treat others with love and kindness, but, only if those, to whom they offer this gift, come up to their own ideologies.

For example many will condemn sinners when they should show kindness and pray for them. They must, instead, lead by example.

Some will pour scorn on others instead of showing the love that is expected of them as Christians.

Never condemn others even if you do not agree with them for that is not your right. No one, only God, has the authority to Judge another.

While many believers continue to pay homage to Me, it will be on their own terms.

Some will feel the need to set themselves apart from their brothers and sisters to show the world how learned they are in spiritual matters. They then use their own interpretations of what My Mercy really means.

How many times have you heard that God is every Merciful, He is so Merciful that because He loves everyone He would never condemn them?

That He would never send a soul to Hell?

Well this is a lie. So many lies, where the existence of Hell is denied, will be the downfall of Christians.

People condemn themselves to Hell. I do not put them there. They choose it by refusing to turn their backs on mortal sin.

Nor will they seek forgiveness, or show remorse. This is dangerous thinking and it is the duty of all Christians to warn others of the dangers of Hell.

So many, including those who refuse their children the Sacrament of Baptism, speak as if sin no longer matters.

They believe that all sin 'will' be forgiven. This is not correct.

All sin 'can' be forgiven, no matter how black the sin, but, only if the sinner seeks forgiveness.

Now I speak to you from the Heavens, to prepare all of God's children, for My Second Coming and what do I find?

I speak to you from behind prison walls and in a cell into which you have cast Me because you refuse to believe that I could speak to you in this way.

Oh how you offend Me!

To those who have spent your lives devoted to Me, and who are knowledgeable about My Holy Scripture, but, who now reject Me I say this.

Your rejections of Me now, will leave you tormented and in great sorrow when the Truth is revealed to you.

Because, then you will realise the souls which you cast aside, when I needed your help to salvage them.

How you make me weep with frustration at your blindness caused because of your lack of humility.

You doubt My Holy Word, when you should embrace it, grasp it, because you are a drowning soul and lack generosity of heart.

I beg you to respond to My Call.

Your beloved Jesus
Redeemer of Mankind

My remnant Church, the Two Witnesses, referred to in the Book of Revelation
Sunday, April 15, 2012 19:16 hours

My dearly beloved daughter, I realise that some of these Messages do not make sense to you, but you must trust in Me and know that I must reveal the contents of the Book of Revelation, so that souls know what to expect in these times.

To those of little faith but who accept My Word, given to you through this prophet, know that your humility and desire, born of a pure love for Me, has brought you closer to My Sacred Heart.

You are My Remnant Church. You are the Church, referred to in the Book of Revelation.

You are the product of the woman who gave birth to a male and who was cast out into the desert, where you will be isolated, yet united as one, to proclaim My Holy Word and preach the True Gospels.

The woman gives birth to My True Church, My loyal flock, who will not be misled by the false prophet.

You, My Church, will be cast aside into the desert for 1,260 days, where you will take refuge. But with the Gift of the Holy Spirit, you will be fed with the Fruits of My Love.

It will be the loyal members of My Christian Churches, including My sacred servants, and those of My followers who reject the false prophet, who will have to keep My Church together.

You will have to honour Me in secret, because the Mass will change beyond recognition, under the rule of the false prophet.

You are My true followers and all the graces of Heaven are being poured over your precious souls.

How I love you children and how you ease My suffering. But how much pain is in My Heart because of those of My followers who will refuse to listen to Me. They will be drawn in a web by the false prophet; into the darkness and I cannot save them.

By their own will they will slap Me on the Face.

My Remnant Church will need to spread the Word to My other children, including those who do not know Me at all.

You, My Remnant Church, will need to proclaim My Prophecies and My Holy Word to those, who are not Christian or who do not know the Ten Commandments.

Your job will be to ensure that the Holy Bible is read and understood.

It will be up to you, to inform the world of the full meaning of the Seals contained in the Book of Revelation, which I will reveal to Maria Divine Mercy.

The Two Witnesses in the Book of Revelation:

You, My followers, are one of the two witnesses referred to in the Book of Revelation and who will be protected from the Heavens.

My Word, given to you My Remnant Church, may be cast aside as a corpse, but My Word will never die.

The Jews will be the second of the two witnesses.

The two lamps are My Christian Churches, the traditional True Church, and those followers of Mine who will be cast aside by the false prophet.

The two olive trees are the Old Jerusalem Israel and the New Israel.

They, the Jews, will know that I Am the Messiah at last and their preaching of the Truth will also be cast aside and thrown out by the False Prophet and the antichrist to rot like a corpse. Again, this chosen race will not die.

Both will feel defeated, but this will not be the case, for you will form, along with all other religions, the One True Church – the New Jerusalem which will rise from the ashes.

You will survive the terrible evil monarchy, which will arise under the dual leadership of the false prophet and the antichrist, both of whom will be cast into the lake of fire that is Hell.

This persecution will not last long and you will be given great strength and protection.

Help will be given to you and many leaders will arise amongst you to guide you through this period.

Many of you will become saints in My New Paradise and, having helped build My Remnant Church on earth, will reign with Me in the New Heaven and Earth, which will emerge at My Second Coming.

Those of you who are not with Me, will be given a very short time to choose.

You will either be for the false prophet and against Me or you will be for Me.

Choose the first and your soul will be stolen by the deceiver. Harsh as this sounds it is the Truth.

Proof of My Presence will be given to all of God's children during The Warning.

Pray that you will accept the Truth then, that it is I, your beloved Jesus, who calls to you from Heaven to open your eyes so that you can see and so that you will listen so that you can hear before it is too late.

Your beloved Jesus

I, your beloved Jesus, could never undermine My Own Church.
Monday, April 16, 2012 18:00 hours

My dearly beloved daughter, I call out to all of God's children and assure you that I, your beloved Jesus, could never undermine My Own Church.

However, I will not stand back and watch My Church, by the hand of one particular sect, who has no right to play a role in the Holy See, to disintegrate.

For that is precisely what the false prophet, and the imposters who idolise Satan, are trying to do. They want to topple the Catholic Church and break it into little pieces.

This, My children, is how Satan will stand in final rebellion against God, the Creator of all things.

This wicked plan to destroy My Church has been underway for 100 years, but, since 1967, it has intensified.

Many imposters, who are members of this evil sect, who worship Satan, entered the seminaries to gain a foothold in the Vatican.

Their powers, while allowed by God the Father, were restricted up to now. As the end times draw nearer that will change.

This evil sect will now unleash every power to ensure that they will elect a new replacement for My Holy Vicar, Pope Benedict XVI.

All those who know My Teachings will see changes in the recital of the Holy Mass.

New secular laws will be introduced which will be an affront to My Death on the Cross.

Many devout followers of Mine will see this and will feel hurt. Their views will be dismissed and many Sacraments will cease to be offered.

This is why much preparation is needed.

For those Catholic, who will be hurt and dismayed, please, remember that I am here.

Call out to Me, your beloved Jesus, and know that you must not be afraid to proclaim the Truth of My Teachings.

You must not be afraid to turn your back on heresy.

I will guide and protect you on your journey and you will be guided by the Power of the Holy Spirit.

Your beloved Saviour
Jesus Christ

My Messages are for all religions and creeds including those who do not believe.
Tuesday, April 17, 2012 18:30 hours

My dearest beloved daughter, know that My Messages given to you, are for the whole world.

They are being given to all religions and creeds, including those who do not believe in the Existence of God, the Eternal Father, Creator of the whole world.

Children, you must know that because you have been given the Truth of The Triune God, the Holy Trinity that is made of the Father, the Son, and of the Holy Spirit, that you have a responsibility to proclaim My Holy Word to the whole world.

Whether you believe that I speak to you through these Messages or not, you must help those poor souls who need My protection, so that they can be saved.

Many question why these Messages refer to Satan so many times. My answer is this.

Satan and his fallen angels roam the earth looking to infest human beings.

They attack them through the senses mainly to encourage them to commit sins of the flesh.

They put thoughts into their minds so that they commit atrocities, which offend My Father.

In the case of souls, already in sin, they can possess the body. When this happens these poor possessed souls create havoc around them.

If they are in positions of power they can inflict terrible injustice among those over whom they rule.

They will introduce laws, which defy the Ten Commandments, laid down by God, the Father.

In other cases they will cause great anguish in people's lives.

Negativity is caused by Satan and his demon angels. This does not come from God.

Only peace and love can come from God.

For all those who want to rid their lives of negative thoughts and feelings, all that is required, is devotion to Me, their beloved, Jesus Christ.

Prayer, simple conversation, is enough. In your own words ask Me to help you.

Said from the heart I will respond immediately and help you to come closer to My Sacred Heart.

Please, children, let Me hold you close and give you the comfort you crave in a world full of unhappiness, injustice, cruelty and hatred.

I am your lifeline. Only I can help you. Please call out to Me in this Crusade Prayer.

Crusade Prayer (45) Prayer to conquer negative thoughts

O Jesus, I know very little about You.

But, please help me to open my heart to allow You to come into my soul, so that You can heal me, comfort me and fill me with Your Peace.

Help me to feel joy, conquer all negative thoughts and learn the way to make me understand how to please You, so that I can enter Your New Paradise, where I can live a life of love, joy and wonder with You, forever and ever.

Amen.

I love all of you, dear children, no matter what creed you are, no matter how much you have sinned, caused hurt or harm to others.

Only I can change the way you live.

The only way to free yourself from the difficult life you lead, is to call Me, so I can help you.

Your beloved Jesus

Never take unfair advantage of others, even in business, politics or any walk of life.
Thursday, April 19, 2012 20:00 hours

My dearest daughter, I want you to tell all of My followers that their prayers are being heard and that many evil events are being mitigated as a result.

I also wish it to be known, that as a result of your suffering, My daughter, that I have been able to save four million souls. My Mercy has been poured over these children of God, who are still alive in the world today.

Other sacrifices, offered by those followers of mine who through prayer and fasting, are helping Me to save people from a terrible destiny.

Your strength, love, loyalty and perseverance means, that Satan's power is being diluted.

It also means that the power of the global, One World Group, is weakening.

You must know that prayer weakens evil in the world, the more prayer the less power that Satan holds.

Never underestimate, even one person's prayer and suffering, for it wields great reprieve, for those who would otherwise, face the fires of Hell.

The love you feel children, given to you as a natural gift at birth, is a pure thing.

Rarely does hatred enter your life, until you reach the age of reason.

Children under this age are innocent, pure and humble in My Eyes, and see things in a simple uncomplicated way. This is the true love you must try to recapture in your lives.

When you look at life in a simple way, honour God the Father, Creator of all things, and obey His Commandments, then you become like a child again.

You become pure, loving, simple of heart and empty of malice. Then you will be given the strength of the Holy Spirit so that your faith will be unshakeable.

You will become like a child, but will be given the armour of a warrior, a true and honourable member of God's army.

In time, you will reign with Me, side by side, in the New Paradise.

Keep your love for others simple. Never offer love on condition it offers you something in return.

Instead offer love with no strings attached. Offer love to others as a gift to God.

See everyone you meet in your life, through the Eyes of God.

Each person was created by God. Each brought into the world through the Love of God.

Even though certain souls are born with a severe cross to bear, they are presented into the world by God with Love.

Love each other, despite the faults of each other, in honour of My Father.

Search out each face and look upon it as if you are seeing this person in the Eyes of God.

Only then will you find it easier to refrain from judging others.

Try to find the best and the good in everyone. Show love and kindness to each other.

Never take unfair advantage of others even in business, politics or any walk of life.

When you come across evil present in others, pray hard for their soul and offer a small token sacrifice to Me, your Jesus, in atonement for their sins.

Suffering a little, making small sacrifices for the souls of others and prayer, can mitigate the intensity of future prophesised persecution.

When you do this, the Mercy of My Father can be poured out over the world in a deluge of graces.

Pray, pray, pray that your prayers will help prepare mankind, adequately, before The Warning takes place so that few are lost before they are given the chance to see Me present to them My Great Gift of Love, Mercy and Reconciliation.

Your loving Jesus
Saviour of Mankind

Even those, who commit terrible sin, are loved by God, the Father
Friday, April 20, 2012 15:45 hours

My dearest beloved daughter, My children must be told of the intense Love that I hold in My Sacred Heart for every child born on this earth.

Even those, who commit terrible sin, are loved by God the Father.

Each one of you is a child of God.

Because of this you are abused, tormented and hurt by Satan and his demons.

To those hardened sinners, members of Satan's army, who know that God exists, but who chose to idolise the beast, know this.

No matter how much homage you pay Satan, remember, he does not love you.

He hates you and will destroy you.

His promises to offer you a paradise, both on earth and beyond, are empty lies.

Very soon you will be given proof of My Love for you. There will be no doubt in your heart that I, your beloved Jesus, want to embrace you, forgive you and bring you eternal peace, love, joy and happiness in My New Kingdom, the New Paradise.

Never be afraid to turn your back on the life you lead where you idolise all the perceived gifts of wealth, sex and other material comforts offered to you by Satan, whose reign on this earth comes to an end shortly.

Only I, your beloved Jesus, can save you.

My Mercy is so great that I will forgive you anything when you feel remorse. Hurry. Come to Me now.

Do not waste one second for your future happiness is at stake.

I promise you eternal life, peace, love, joy and a beautiful Paradise where you will be loved, cherished and where you will want for nothing.

If you cannot accept My Hand of Mercy now, then when the time comes on the last day, you will be given one more chance to ask Me for Mercy.

When this day comes you will, many of you, realise the mistake you have made.

Yet I will still embrace you, like a long lost and much loved child of God, no matter how much you have suffered by the hand of evil.

All you have to do will be to call out to Me and ask for My Mercy.

If you are involved, at this time, in a web of deceit and evil, from which you cannot escape, then I ask you to call on Me by reciting this;

Crusade Prayer (46) Free me from the chains of Satan

O Jesus, I am lost. I am confused and feel like a prisoner caught in a web I cannot escape from. I trust You, Jesus, to come to my aid and free me from the chains of Satan and his demons.

Help me, for I am lost. I need Your Love to give me the strength to believe in You and trust in You, so that I can be saved from this evil, and be shown the Light so I can find peace, love and happiness at last.

Amen.

Billions of souls, not millions, will convert.
Saturday, April 21, 2012 16:00 hours

My dearly beloved daughter, I must bring comfort to all those who may fear these Messages.

Let Me calm you all, My dearly beloved followers, by assuring you of My Great Mercy for the whole of mankind.

Because of the prayers of My cherished followers, all of which are heard and answered according to the Divine Timing of My Eternal Father, much conversion is beginning to flourish.

Never give up hope. You are the backbone of My Mission on earth to help Me save the whole of humanity. As such, you will suffer the pain of the sins of others.

Never assume that the sins of others can blacken the Light of God, the Most High, to such an extent that all is lost.

Very soon all will witness the Glory of God, through My Divine Mercy, which will be revealed during The Warning.

Billions of souls, not millions, will convert. This will mean that Satan's power will dwindle when God's army will rise in strength to defeat the beast.

All of humanity will know the Truth of their existence soon. This will

208

be the turning point for God's children, who will unite in preparation for the New Era of Peace, where no sin will exist.

Prayer is important because God the Father gave each person on this earth, at the time of their birth, the Gift of free will. Because of this, although He has the Power to do anything He wishes, He wants His children to come to Him, of their own free will.

God the Father does not want to force His children to love Him.

This must come naturally. But, how can you love someone you don't know?

This is the problem in the world today. Very few know God the Father. Very few know Me, His beloved Son Jesus Christ.

You, My followers, must use prayer so that My Father can bestow special Gifts on those souls who are in darkness.

Then they will be shown His Glorious Light and they will be saved.

Through your gift of prayer, God the Father will use Divine Intervention to bring those who do not know Him or who do not know He exists, closer to His Heart.

Many souls, however, who do know My Father, and who deliberately turn their back, will face terrible chastisements.

They will be given every opportunity, but will reject God.

For these souls who conduct despicable acts, common in certain parts of the world, the chastisements will come in the form of earthquakes.

For those global groups who will continue to destroy the countries over which they control, they will be stopped and punished harshly, by the Hand of My Father.

Again, your prayers are needed to mitigate such sin and subsequent chastisements.

A little more time is needed in preparation for My Divine Mercy to allow for more souls to be prepared for this great event.

It is important that most of humanity can be saved and that all souls, including hardened sinners, are given a chance to re-unite as one with God.

It is My greatest wish that I will Reign over most of humanity in the New Paradise.

Your prayers will help Me fulfil My great desire so that we can all become one family in love and unity forever and ever.

Your beloved Jesus

Virgin Mary: When times seem difficult or painful, children, always call on me
Sunday, April 22, 2012 10:00 hours

My child, my Son is so happy at the way in which His beloved army obey His Holy Wishes to recite His Crusade Prayers.

These prayers are for modern times to help all of God's children to seek the protection they need to deal with the difficult times, which so many souls are facing.

When times seem difficult or painful children, always call on me, your Beloved Mother, to intercede with my Precious Son on your behalf.

Always remember that your personal sacrifices, offered up to God, help to save so many souls on earth.

Your prayers are always heard.

They are never ignored, but are dealt with according to the Will of my Father.

So you must be patient, children. Always place your full trust in my Son.

Hand Him over all your fears and suffering. Then, you must trust that all will be dealt with, by Him.

For those of you, believers, who find it hard to pray or to keep your love for my Son alive, here is a special Crusade Prayer (47) to help re-kindle your love for Jesus.

Crusade Prayer (47) Re-kindle your love for Jesus

O blessed Mother, Mother of Salvation, for the whole world, pray that my love for Jesus can be re-kindled. Help me to feel the Flame of His Love so that it fills my soul.

Help me to love Jesus more. Pray that my faith, love and devotion for Him, becomes stronger.

Allay any doubts, which torment me, and help me to see clearly the Divine Light of the Truth, which radiates from your beloved Son, the Saviour of all humanity.

Amen.

Go in peace children. Remember when you ask me to pray for you, from the heart, I, the Mother of Salvation, will present your request to my beloved Son.

I will never ignore one request once it is in line with the wishes of my Son and according to the Holy Will of the Father.

Learn to trust more, children. When you trust my Precious Son you demonstrate your love for Him.

If your love is weak then your trust in Him will also be weak.

Only those of you, who humble themselves before my Son, will be blessed with the graces given to strengthen your faith.

Never give up when you feel despair.

Despair is created by the evil one.

Just turn to me and I will pray for peace to return to your soul.

When you do this you will be able to reject temptation placed by the Evil One and you will become free.

Your Blessed Mother
Queen of the Angels
Mother of Salvation

Help Me prepare the world for My Second Coming
Sunday, April 22, 2012 15:30 hours

My dearly beloved daughter, humanity must know that the time for Me to present Myself to a disbelieving world is not far away.

All of God's children who are devout believers must now, out of their loyalty to Me, their beloved Jesus, help Me prepare the world for My Second Coming.

So much time has already been accorded to entice souls back into My Sacred Heart.

This was important for, without this time, very few souls would be able to enter My New Paradise.

I urge all those, in My Holy Name, to allow Me to guide you, to help you proclaim the Truth of My Teachings in every corner of the world.

Preach My simple Teachings first.

Love of one's neighbour is expected of all those who say they are followers of Mine.

Speak only of My Second Coming.

Anyone who denounces you, remind them that, My promise to come again in glory to Judge the living and the dead, is to be fulfilled during the lifetime of this generation.

My Holy Spirit will flood the souls of those to whom you impart My Holy Word.

But, first, you must ask Me for this special Grace. Before I sanction you to do this most Sacred Work, I call on you to ask Me for this Grace through the recital of this Crusade Prayer.

Crusade Prayer (48) Prayer for the Grace to Proclaim the Second Coming of Christ

O My Jesus, grant me the grace to proclaim Your Holy Word to all of humanity so that souls can be saved. Pour Your Holy Spirit over me, your humble servant, so that Your Holy Word can be heard and accepted, especially by those souls who need Your Mercy the most. Help me to honour Your Holy Will at all times and never to insult or condemn those who refuse the Hand of Your Mercy. Amen.

Go now, My army, for you have been given the armour you need to convert mankind.

You will be ridiculed in your Mission, insulted and challenged.

Know that, when this happens, that you will truly be a child of God.

Fear not for I will give you the strength to overcome such obstacles.

I will lead you the whole way. Go in peace and love.

Your beloved Jesus

To My sacred servants I say this. Do not make the mistake of your forebears who rejected Me when I came the first time.
Tuesday, April 24, 2012 19:45 hours

My dearly beloved daughter, know that when a Mission like the one I now bequeath to the world, is as important as this, that many people, will try to stop it.

They will try to attack you and belittle those who recognise My Voice as I try to impart My Messages to the whole world.

The scale of the hatred shown towards these Messages, delivered through you the end time prophet, will continue to escalate.

Hear Me now, all those who say they know Me. I am preparing mankind for My Second Coming.

If you believe in Me, My Teachings and say that you know Me, then know that I am sending My end time prophet, along with other prophets, to make you worthy to enter My Kingdom.

To My sacred servants, I say this. Do not make the mistake of your forebears who rejected Me when I came the first time.

Take heed and listen to My calling, for I need you to help Me prepare the souls of My flock, before the Great Miracle takes place.

Did you think that I would not send My prophets to warn you?

Did you think I would just herald My return without preparing you and allow souls to perish?

For those of you who denounce My Second Coming, and yet claim to understand My Promise to humanity, shame on you.

Your lack of humility means you cannot be cleansed with the Holy Spirit.

You must call on Me for this gift of discernment or walk away from Me.

You have let Me down. You make Me weep with frustration, for you are My servants, given the responsibility for the salvation of souls, which is your ministry.

Now that I call to you from the Heavens. I beg you to respond to My Call.

I have many chosen souls who work with Me, to bring Me the souls, for whom I thirst.

It is your duty to rise from your slumber and be alert to My Call.

Only those of you who truly love Me will recognise My Voice.

Like a mother, an infant will recognise his own and so you, My beloved servants, must call out to Me as an infant, to seek reassurance that it is I, your beloved Jesus, who beckons you to take My Hand.

I will lead you through a jungle of thorns over which you will have to step in order to reach the Gates of My New Paradise.

Did I not tell you that I would come again to Judge the living and the dead?

Well I will come soon and I need you to help Me bring all of God's children together as one.

Very few now recognise Me because of the veil of deceit, which has fallen over the whole world. Many do not believe in God the Father.

Few accept that I, Jesus Christ, His only Son died to save them. Yet they are willing to believe in, and idolise, false gods, which do not exist.

How I weep with a terrible sadness when I witness young people laugh when My Name is mentioned, and when they sneer at others who publicly admit that I exist.

How I suffer the pain of My Crucifixion when I see those who claim to be Christians refuse to proclaim My Teachings publicly for fear of ridicule.

The world has been deceived, by the king of lies. Only I can now bring hope and save God's children from the terrible destiny, which is being planned to inflict terror across every nation, by those armies of global powerful groups, including those under the control of the false prophet and the antichrist.

All My warnings, given to My end time prophet Maria Divine Mercy, will come to pass.

Until this happens, never forget that your allegiance is to Me, your Saviour, Jesus Christ.

Without My Love and direction, you will find it impossible to steer the ship, that is My Holy Church on earth.

Wake up. Do not reject God's prophets. Many now claim to come in

My Name, as the Scriptures foretold, but, do not offer the spiritual food, which can only come from Me.

Many are coming forth now so that My main public Voice to the world contained in these Messages, in these the end times, will be dismissed.

Prayer is your route back into My Arms.

Pray, pray, pray for the graces to open your eyes, so that you can recognise Me before it is too late.

I need your help, your love and your loyalty.

Remember it was because of Me that you took your Sacred Vows. Now that I call out to you, do not reject Me.

Embrace Me, and allow Me to guide you, so that you can lead My remnant Church and salvage souls.

I give you My special blessing, and await you to respond to My Call as follows in this **Crusade Prayer (49) Pledge of loyalty for Christian Clergy**

O Jesus, I am Your humble servant. I pledge my love and loyalty to You. I beg You to give me a sign of Your calling. Help me to open my eyes and witness Your promise.

Bless me with the Grace of the Holy Spirit, so that, I will not be deceived by those who claim to come in Your Name, but who do not speak the Truth. Show me the Truth.

Allow me to feel Your Love so that I can fulfil Your Most Holy Will. I ask You, with a humble heart, to show me the way, in which I can help you to save the souls of humanity. Amen.

Do not ignore My call. Do not reject Me when I come once more.

This time I come not only to save mankind once more, but, to fulfil the Divine Will of My beloved Father, God the Most High.

Go in peace.

Your beloved Jesus

All mankind will have free will until their will unites with the Divine Will of the Father.
Wednesday, April 25, 2012 15:50 hours

My dearly beloved daughter, many souls do not acknowledge Me, simply because they don't want to.

They know Who I am.

They know that they have been Created out of nothing, by God, the Father, yet they choose to ignore God.

They use My Name in the most casual way many, many, times and My Name is included in the curses spewed by those possessed by demons.

It is only when people are afflicted by tragedy that they stop and think of death and any future life they believe may be ahead.

This is why I sometimes punish those souls, out of My Mercy, to bring them to their senses, so I can save them.

Through suffering, all those material attractions, sought out by the senses, will become meaningless and be seen for what they are. Fleeting novelties, which will vanish within a short period of time.

Many souls are born into this world sent from Heaven. They choose suffering, including those aborted children, as a means of seeking salvation for sinners.

It is difficult for the human mind to understand the Divine Kingdom, for no man has been blessed with this gift.

When the fallen angels rebelled against My Father, He – My Father – never forfeited the right of His children to their free will, for He will never take away the Gift he gave to humanity.

All mankind will have free will, until their will unites with the Divine Will of the Father.

Satan takes advantage of free will. What he cannot fight is when those chosen souls forfeit their own free will and offer it to God to save sinners.

By making this sacrifice, through the acceptance of suffering, Satan's influence is weakened.

Then sinners can be saved even when they have not repented. This is the miracle that is suffering.

Your beloved Jesus

Those who are loyal to Me will be taken, in the blink of an eye, without suffering into the New Heaven and Earth.
Thursday, April 26, 2012 20:30 hours

My dearly beloved daughter, again, I must tell all of God's children not to feel worried or frightened of events to come.

All of humanity will witness My Mercy soon, and many, while remorseful for their sins, will not fear Me.

Instead their souls will be flooded with My Divine Love. My Light will radiate through their bodies and they will rejoice.

The time for the New Era of Peace brings tremendous joy and excitement for those who acknowledge My Hand of Mercy.

Every single sinner is invited to live eternal life and must not walk away because they are confused. My Era of Peace will be a new earth, where twelve nations will rule, under My Guidance.

You will live in peace, love and harmony. The natural surroundings you see on the earth today will pale into insignificance when compared with the world, which lies ahead.

For those worried or frightened for your family or loved ones – bring them with you to My wonderful New Paradise.

Pray for them and I will give them special graces so that they will be given the Gift of recognising My Love.

This is My Father's greatest wish, to see the wonder, joy and love, shine through each of His precious children when He unveils the New Paradise.

You will be reunited with your loved ones who died in a state of grace and who will be resurrected from the dead.

Why would you not believe in such a Gift? When you trust in My Promise to come again, then you will feel peace.

All I ask is that you prepare through prayer. When you pray for grace and for others, all will be well.

My Mercy is so great that few will fail to recognise My Divine Promise to gather all of God's children and take them home and away from the vice-grip of Satan and his demon angels.

The Truth of My Kingdom will be seen even by atheists who will be shocked, yet, their disbelief will in most cases turn into humble love and acceptance. While many difficult times lie ahead none will be so hard that you cannot overcome them, through your love and devotion to Me, your Jesus. Please do not allow fear to get in the way of accepting, with joy, the Gift of My New Paradise.

Those who are loyal to Me will be taken, in the blink of an eye, without suffering into the New Heaven and Earth.

What should concern you, are those hardened sinners who will not ask Me to forgive them, who will refuse My Hand and who will, instead, hold onto their wicked ways.

They need your prayers.

Pray hard for the salvation of their souls.

Your beloved Jesus

God the Father: As the Father of all humanity I am ready to send My Son to reclaim His Rightful Throne
Saturday, April 28, 2012 15:40 hours

My daughter, these months have been a difficult time, not only for you, but, for all of My beloved children.

I am the Father of Creation and Love, with a deep passion for each child of mine, no matter how they offend Me.

There is so much preparation required to help prepare souls for the Coming of My beloved Son Jesus Christ.

Much of humanity is suffering at this time because of persecution. This persecution not only consists of poverty and lack of money, but hunger of spirit.

As the Father of all humanity, I am ready to send My Son back to reclaim His Rightful Throne.

Only I know of this time. Not even My Son is aware of the date.

I can tell you it will be soon and that most of this generation, alive in the world today, will live for the day of My Son's Return in Great Glory.

I now prepare to gather all of My children as I take them away from the terrible abyss of suffering they have had to endure in the wilderness.

This wilderness was created by the hand of Lucifer and all his fallen angels who have roamed the earth since the fall of Adam and Eve.

Today many of My children find it impossible to believe in Me, God their Creator and Father.

I have blessed My children with intelligence and an independent free will where they can choose whatever way they decide to live their lives.

To guide them towards My Kingdom I gave them the Ten Commandments, which are cast in stone.

They have never changed, yet My children feel they were smarter than they are, and created new meanings, which are unacceptable to Me.

This time for the end of the reign of all of the demons cast out, and who flood the earth, is almost at an end.

I call out to all My children to listen. Your time on earth, as you know it, is drawing to an end.

Yet there is a new earth, a New Paradise waiting for you.

It will surpass anything you could ever imagine, and it has been prepared for some time, with love for every single man, woman and child.

At last I will unite all of My precious family and we will all live in harmony, peace, love and joy for eternity.

For those who refuse to enter the New Paradise I will do everything in My Power to stop you from turning your back on the inheritance, which is rightfully yours.

Because of the Gift of your free will, which I will never take away from you, the choice is yours.

All it takes is a turn of your head and the opening of your heart.

Then you must run into My Arms, so I can take you home.

This is My dearest and most treasured wish, to take all of My cherished children home to the rightful place to which they belong.

Your Loving Father
God the Most High

Virgin Mary: My child there will be no death for those who love My Son.
Sunday, April 29, 2012 10:00 hours

My child, you must never think that because of the loneliness of this special calling that conversion is not taking place.

Your Mission, sanctioned by my Eternal Father, is to spread the Truth of my Son's Second Coming, to all of God's children.

It is important that those children, who do not spend time in honour of and devotion to my Son, are told what is to come.

All of God's children are to be included in all of your prayers, for He, my Father, loves everyone.

Even those who have hardened their hearts towards my Father, and do not want to acknowledge My Son, must be given eternal life.

When the Gift of The Warning takes place, many sinners will be enlightened and will turn to My Son, begging for His Mercy.

Only then will humanity want to listen to the important Messages, given by my Son, through you.

When they realise the Truth that the time for His New Reign is to commence they will devour His Holy Word.

Many of God's children are confused about the existence of heaven and earth. Many are too frightened to think of life after death.

My child, there will be no death for those who love my Son.

Instead they will be taken into the New Era of Peace and the Paradise promised by my Father for all of His children.

You must pray that all of those wandering and lost souls find their way back into the Loving Arms of my precious Son, or they will not be fit to enter the Gates of the New Paradise

Your beloved Mother
Mother of Salvation

First Secret in Book of Truth reveals plot, against the Church, by Masonic Groups
Sunday, April 29, 2012 15:33 hours

My dearly beloved daughter, you have been given a gift, which many would reject out of fear.

Because of the graces afforded you, the strength given and the Fire of the Holy Spirit, you are fully armed to proclaim the prophecies promised to the world so long ago

The prophecy given to Daniel when he was told to seal up the Book of Truth until the end times, when the contents would be revealed, has now come to be.

Revelations given also to John the Evangelist, were given only in part, but some secrets were shown to him in The Scroll of the Seven Seals.

He was not granted the authority to disclose the contents. Instead he was instructed to put the scroll down and eat it so that the Seals could not be broken nor the contents revealed until this era. By swallowing the Scrolls a clue was given to humanity.

Bitter to eat, the Truth causes fear.

It can also offend those, who profess to know all of God's plan for humanity. Yet the Truth, the powerful Love that God has for every single person on this earth, is sweet for those who acknowledge the Truth.

The Truth is that only I, Jesus Christ, can reveal the secrets given to John the Evangelist. The sweet Truth, will be welcomed with love, by those who follow God's Teachings.

It may cause fear, but God's Power will overcome all evil and all persecution for He can do anything.

The first secret lies in the fact that God and all His Works have been plotted against, by Masonic groups, established in the Middle Ages.

Their allegiance is to the evil one. He, Satan, is their God and they are proud to pay homage to him, through black masses.

Then there is the Holy See, which has been under fierce attack, by this group since 1967.

Slowly they have infiltrated My Church, not just within the Vatican but, within the ranks beyond in every country.

Their deliberate contamination of My Church, has resulted in evil atrocities, inflicted on innocent victims.

Their love of money and power is nothing compared with the sickening devotion they show to the king of lies, Satan himself. He is openly worshipped, in groups and in secret. Priests and other holy servants, including bishops, cardinals, have aligned themselves in certain quarters with this group.

The evil acts they participate in are too serious to reveal to you, but, know that they offer human sacrifices to the evil one in churches set up to offer the Holy Eucharist of the Holy Mass.

This group, so careful to hide their true activities, from those genuine and holy priests, holy bishops, holy cardinals and other sacred servants commit vile acts.

They hate God with a ferocity that would shock you. The powers, given to them by Satan, has meant that their wickedness, greed, lust and sexual deviations are welcomed by their followers in all countries.

They greet each other with private signals designed to show allegiance to each other.

One thing is certain. Their wicked acts will come to an end and, unless they turn to Me during The Warning, they will have little time left before they are cast into the lakes of fire, where they will suffer a terrible persecution for eternity.

They have created and stirred up the apostasy that exists all over the world.

They achieved this by infiltrating My Church.

Your beloved Jesus
Lamb of God

I call on all of you, who don't know Me
Monday, April 30, 2012 17:45 hours

My dearest beloved daughter, I must explain to those people, who believe in God, but who do not go to Church or pray. Many do not know how to pray. A little like the way in which you, My daughter, find it difficult.

Prayer means to ask.

Prayer means to communicate.

Prayer means to show love and give thanks.

Many people today, well meaning and of generous heart do not know how to pray. Some will find it distasteful and will feel awkward.

Others will feel that their prayers won't count.

Oh how I love these special souls. So far removed and yet how I yearn to show them My deep Love.

I call on all of you who don't know Me. There is no need to fear Me. All you have to do is to ask Me to take you and give you comfort.

Let Me prove My Love. Speak to Me in your own simple words. Nothing will shock Me.

Confide in Me your worries, as I will soothe your heart. Let Me help you to feel true peace.

Ask Me to sort out your concerns. I will show you the Truth so that your worries will no longer seem as bad.

How will you know I hear you? How will you be sure that I will respond to you?

Just sit down quietly and ask Me to help you with this prayer, to help you open your heart to Me and to ask for My help.

Crusade Prayer (50) Jesus help me to know Who You are.

O dear Jesus, help me to know who You are. Forgive me for not speaking with You before now. Help me to find peace in this life and be shown the Truth of eternal life.

Soothe my heart. Ease my worries. Give me peace. Open my heart now, so that You can fill my soul with Your Love.

Amen.

Many of you will not come to Me at this time. But, that is okay.

In times of hardship, confusion and fear, you will.

I stand with you every day, although you do not realise this yet, but very soon you will see Me and know the Truth of My Promise to grant you eternal life in body, mind and spirit.

I await your call. Then I can take you, when the time is right, to the Gates of the New Era of Peace and My New Paradise on earth.

Your friend
Your beloved Jesus

Hear My Call and prepare for the pouring out of My Holy Spirit.
Tuesday, May 01, 2012 20:00 hours

My dearly beloved daughter, My Love for all of you means that I now pour the Holy Spirit, once again, over humanity, to entice them to open their hearts.

Many souls will feel the Power of the Holy Spirit pour over them in mind, body and soul, very soon.

This is essential in order to wake up all of God's children to the Truth.

Some people will now see the world in a different way.

Then they will begin to question everything. No longer will they be willing to remain slaves to masters, whose only goal is to control them, for personal gain.

No one will be able to ignore this pull of the Holy Spirit.

All of Heaven awaits, so that the moment of enlightenment will create a new dawn, a new beginning.

The lies you are being confronted with hide a master plan, born out of a world alliance, designed to control all of your countries.

By making your country rely on giants to feed their families you will become slaves. Already they are taking away everything you own, but you are blind to this.

Now with the Gift of the Holy Spirit, millions will see through this mask of deceit and oppose these wicked, Masonic controlled groups.

This Gift will give you the armour you need to throw this army off the trail of your destruction.

Hear My Call and prepare for the pouring out of My Holy Spirit.

Your beloved Jesus

Holy Spirit will descend this Sunday. The second outpouring by the Power of the Holy Spirit
Friday, May 04, 2012 21:05 hours

My dearly beloved daughter, when you feel that this Mission is difficult, to convince all of God's children to acknowledge the Second Coming, and that it will be accepted as good news for all of God's children, just remember this.

Just as every single person is made in the Image of God, My Eternal Father, so too does the Light of My Father shine in some way through every soul.

Look into the face of every one you meet and you will see a glimpse of God the Father.

It may be just a look, a smile, a gesture or tenderness, but it is there.

There is good in everyone, even hardened sinners. In some this goodness is wholly enveloping and draws people towards the person blessed with this gift like a magnet. In others it is but a glimmer, but, present all the same.

When you look into the eyes of someone whose behaviour towards others is cruel you can still see a ray of hope, because of the presence of the Light of God. It is the Light in the souls of God's children that needs to be re-kindled through My Messages of love and hope. The stronger the Light, the more purified the person. The more people who are purified by the Light of God, the more purified will be the earth.

As God's Light becomes stronger in the souls of believers, then the work of evil will dwindle, because darkness cannot abide the Light.

This is why, yet another outpouring of the Holy Spirit, is being bestowed all over the world now.

This is the second outpouring by the Power of the Holy Spirit, since 10 May 2011.

It precedes My Great Divine Mercy, and will ensure that the Light creates a new understanding in the souls of believers

This Holy Spirit will descend upon the whole world this Sunday 06, May 2012.

Many will feel peace and love. I urge all to pray for this Gift to drench their souls, so that they will feel God's Love and respond to His call.

Crusade Prayer (51) For the Gift of the Holy Spirit

O come Holy Spirit. Pour Your Gift of Love, Wisdom and Knowledge over my humble soul.

Fill me with the Light of Truth, so that I can discern the Truth of God, from the lies spread by Satan and his angels.

Help me to grasp the torch and spread the flame of understanding to all those I meet through Christ, Our Lord. Amen.

Go in Love, Light and Peace.

Rest and allow My Holy Spirit to descend upon you.

I love you,

Your Precious Jesus

God the Father: Accept My Holy Spirit with wonder and with thanks.

Saturday, May 05, 2012 12:00 noon

My daughter, how great is the day that the Holy Spirit, the Light of My Love, will spill over the earth.

This is a very special Gift. It will open the hearts of many and prepare many souls for The Warning.

My Love has no boundaries.

There is not one man, woman or child, whom I exclude in My longing to hold each tightly in My Arms. Not one sinner is excluded.

My Gifts to mankind are generous, and I will continue to pour out My Gifts, in response to those who recite the Crusade Prayers given to you, My daughter.

These prayers are from Heaven and have not come from the pen of man.

They are for these times and are a powerful weapon against persecution.

These prayers are heard every time they come from your lips, My children.

They will bring you great rewards.

Accept My Holy Spirit with wonder and with thanks.

It is a miracle and it is being sent to each of you with My Love for all.

Go now in peace and love.

Your Father
God the Most High

My modern day disciples are being given an enormous Mission
Sunday, May 06, 2012 10:00 hours

My dearest daughter, many of God's children believe that those who lead holy lives are those favoured by My Father.

The Truth is that these souls, holy and devout as they are, must work towards the salvation of other souls.

The other souls are those ordinary men, women and children who lead busy lives with little time spent in prayer.

Many do not pray or communicate with Me. Some do not believe in God. Some do. Many of these souls lead good lives.

They treat other people with love and kindness of heart. They put others' needs before their own. They give to charity. They love one another. But, they do not go to Church, receive the Sacraments or accept that I, Jesus Christ, exist.

You would think, therefore, that they are lost souls. In Truth they are not.

They are God's children and His Light shines through them. They are not doomed. They are loved.

In time, when they are shown the proof of My Existence, they will immediately embrace Me.

It is only those souls who are aware of their grievances, against My Father, and who savour the delights of wicked and evil sins, who are lost.

Those who cannot live without committing mortal sin and whose souls are so blackened because they are possessed by Satan, who need to escape from this terrible darkness, they will not be strong enough to do this.

They will find it almost impossible to seek My help. They can only be saved through the prayers of holy and devout followers of Mine.

My modern day disciples are being given an enormous Mission equal to that, but, more urgent, than that given to My apostles, when I ascended into Heaven.

Your role, My followers, is to prepare these souls for My New Paradise, through your prayers. Prayers can convert them.

My Mercy is so great that I will forgive such sinners, through the generousity of My other loyal servants, through their suffering and prayers.

Never forget the power of your prayers. This power is a gift to you so that you can save the souls of your brothers and sisters.

Remember My Eternal Father loves all sinners. But, great rejoicing takes place, and tears of joy wept, for every blackened and lost sinner, who is saved from the fires of Hell.

Your beloved Jesus

Pain and persecution inflicted upon Me by those sects who work in secret to topple the Holy See is severe
Sunday, May 06, 2012 19:30 hours

My dearly beloved daughter, I come to beg My followers to ease My suffering.

The pain and persecution inflicted upon Me, by those sects, who work in secret to topple the Holy See, is severe.

How they hurt Me so.

The deceit and cruelty, of their plot against Me, is hard to bear.

I tremble when I see the absolute hatred that they hold in their hearts for Me.

Satan has stolen their souls, their minds, their spirits and their bodies. They are still God's children, but they do not want anything to do with My Father.

Their plans are now taking place before your eyes, including the eyes of My sacred servants, yet they cannot see this. The wicked ways, in which they hide, and yet manage to control My Church, breaks My Heart.

I will do anything to get them to stop, but their souls are so black.

Your suffering, My daughter, will be used to help salvage the souls of those who may still have a spark of love within, and who will respond to My call.

I urge you to pray for those souls, working as a dedicated army, with little love in their hearts for God.

There is still a light, the Divine Light of My Father, present in their souls. Only prayer and suffering can help them.

They will not and cannot, defeat My Church, for I Am the Church.

You, My followers, are the Church. They cannot fight those in the Light, for it would blind them.

In time they will realise they have but seconds to make the final choice.

Pray that they will accept the Hand of My Mercy, instead of allowing themselves to be sucked into the lake of fire for eternity.

It is because of these souls who defile My Church, that I relive the scourging at the Pillar, every second of the day.

I will never rest unless I can save them.

Help Me. I urge all of My followers to pray for such sinners.

Your beloved Jesus

Many Popes have been prisoners in the Holy See, surrounded by Masonic Groups
Monday, May 07, 2012 18:19 hours

My dearly beloved daughter, to My Churches through the world I say this:

Know that I will always be with you at your side, as long as you proclaim My Most Holy Word.

To My Catholic Church, even though you caused torment as a result of evil sin, know that I will never forsake you, although you have sinned. But, know this.

Your faith in Me, is not as strong as it should be. You do not love Me, as you once did.

All the wealth you accumulated, put a distance between Me, your Christ and Saviour, and God's ordinary children.

You scaled such lofty heights, that I could not reach up to you and offer you My Hand to salvage you from the rot within your core.

You were taught the Truth by My Peter, upon whose Rock you were built. And what did you do?

You built thick stonewalls around you.

This caused a lack of communication with those whom you needed to feed with My Body and Blood, so that their souls could be nourished.

The respect required of you in administering My Most Holy Eucharist, was lost, when you demeaned My Presence.

When Vatican II declared new rules, they were introduced, by those evil Masonic forces, from within your corridors.

They cunningly presented new ways to administer My Holy Eucharist, which are insulting to Me.

Your so-called tolerant Teachings proclaimed a series of lies, including the refusal to acknowledge the power of St Michael the Archangel.

He is the protector of the Church against Satan. Those forces among you knew this. This is why you stopped all prayers, requesting his help, before Me at Mass.

Then you perpetrated the biggest untruth, that Hell was not to be feared. That it was just a metaphor. For this lie, accepted as the Truth by many of God's children, has meant the loss of billions of souls.

How you offend Me. For those humble and sacred servants among you, I ask that you go back to My Teachings.

Never allow riches to accumulate amongst you, and think that they are acceptable in My Eyes.

Riches, gold and power accumulated in My Name, will be your downfall. You cannot profit from My Holy Word.

You have suffered because of the way you have offended Me.

Never think that I am blaming the many Holy Popes who have sat in the Seat of Peter. Their Mission has always been protected.

Many Popes have been prisoners in the Holy See, surrounded by Masonic groups, who do not represent God.

They hate God, and have spent fifty years spreading untruths, about the Mercy of God.

Their works have led to the collapse of the Catholic Church.

This was not an accident. It was deliberately and cunningly plotted in order to destroy the faith of the Church, to destroy the homage of ordinary Catholics, to the One True God.

For this, you will now be cast aside into the wilderness. After Pope Benedict, you will be led by Me, from the Heavens.

Oh how you have made Me weep.

I call on all of My sacred servants,who know the Truth, to stand up and follow Me, your Jesus, to spread the Truth of My Teachings in humble servitude. You must find the courage and the strength to rise from the ashes.

Above all, reject the lies, which will shortly be presented to you by the false prophet.

He will merge the Catholic Church with other churches, including pagan churches, to become one abomination, a one-world church without a soul.

Your Jesus

Virgin Mary: God the Most High can change the destiny of the world
Tuesday, May 08, 2012 12:30 hours

My child, this Mission is converting millions of souls, who would otherwise be lost.

You must never feel that the obstacles placed before you can stop the spread of the Holy Spirit.

My Son is so pleased with all those who follow the Word He imparts to the world at this time.

The devotion through your prayers, children, is saving so many lost souls. Never forget the power of prayer. So much evil has been thwarted because of your prayers.

The work of the one world group is now being disrupted and their plans in disarray.

God's Mercy is so great that prayer can mitigate any evil in the world.

The Light of the Holy Spirit now increases in Power, so that more and more souls will see the Truth of the Lord, as it is being re-kindled everywhere.

Children, you must continue to speak to my Father, and increase your devotion to Him.

By calling on the Father, God the Most High, in the Name of His precious Son, He will hear your prayers and respond.

You should call out to the Father more, for it will be He, God the Most High, who can change the destiny of the world.

It will only be through my Son, Jesus Christ, that you can approach the Father. So this is what you must say:

Crusade Prayer (52) Prayer to the Father

My dearest Father, in the Name of Your precious Son, and in remembrance of His Passion on the Cross, I call out to You.

You, God the Most High, Creator of the world and all that is, hold our salvation in Your Holy Hands. Embrace all of Your children, including those who don't know You, and those who do, but look the other way.

Forgive us our sin and save us from the persecution of Satan and his army. Take us into Your Arms and fill us with the hope we need to see the Way of the Truth. Amen.

Go in peace.
Your beloved Mother
Mother of Salvation

My Remnant Church, inspired by the Prophet Enoch, will create hatred everywhere My Holy Work is heard
Tuesday, May 08, 2012 19:00 hours

My dearly beloved daughter, I come this evening to tell you that a great token of My Love and Mercy will now manifest within the hearts of believers everywhere.

They will feel My Presence within their hearts in a way they will not be able to explain and they will unite their hearts with Mine.

This Gift will make them strong in My Faith and they will hunger for My Presence daily.

I urge all of God's children, who feel the Flames of My Love engulf their souls, to receive My Body and My Blood, in the Holy Eucharist, as often as they can.

You, My beloved disciples, will need the Gift of My Body, through the Holy Eucharist to give you strength, for you will need every ounce of strength, as you witness the falling apart of My Holy and Apostolic, Catholic Church.

My Holy Eucharist will be desecrated as I foretold some time ago.

Excuses will be made to render this Most Holy Gift as simply a gesture in remembrance of My Crucifixion.

Very soon My Real Presence will be denounced as part of a new modern catholic church, which will include other religious churches.

Once this happens, the love and devotion to the Holy Trinity will dwindle and fall away.

Instead false gods will take its place. While this will be difficult, you must remember, I will never forfeit My Church on earth.

My allegiance is to the Church founded by Me before I ascended into Heaven.

The Church upon the Rock founded by My beloved Peter, cannot and will never die.

For I will lead My Church now in the end times, and will renew the prophecies, foretold long ago.

My Gospels will be preached by My Remnant Church, in every corner of the Earth.

My Remnant Church, will be inspired by the Prophet Enoch, and this will create hatred everywhere My Holy Word is heard.

The Holy Spirit will ignite the faith of My Remnant Church who will never give up proclaiming the Truth of the Gospels, till its dying breath.

Go now and prepare My Remnant Church, by following My Instructions.

Trust in Me always, for all will be well.

Your beloved Jesus

Already, the work of the Masonic groups in your world, is weakening
Wednesday, May 09, 2012 21:00 hours

My dearly beloved daughter, more and more of those who know My Teachings are finally accepting that I am now communicating with the world through these Messages, given to you.

The Power of the Holy Spirit will awaken those dead in the love for My Father, to savour the Word of His beloved Son.

I, Jesus Christ, wish to give you encouragement in the suffering and trials, which you may be experiencing.

This suffering will not last long.

My Love for you is so strong and My Mercy so great, that I will not allow you to suffer the torments inflicted on you, by those who wish to control your nations.

Already, the work of the Masonic groups in your world, is weakening.

Your prayers have mitigated their evil deeds and rendered them to be ineffective.

They will try to destroy your faith, but, you, My Remnant Church, will keep the Flame of Truth alight.

You must not fear, if you trust in Me.

Only by trusting in Me, your Jesus, can you feel at peace.

Please keep close to My Sacred Heart and do not allow fear to destroy your lives.

Once you love Me, and live life, as you know I expect you to, then, you must live your lives in love, prayer and contentment.

When you suffer, offer this up to Me and move on.

Do not allow anything to turn your heart away from Me.

Keep close to Me, and I will protect you, guide you, and lead you to safety.

Your beloved Jesus
Saviour of Mankind

Virgin Mary: I weep tears of sadness for priests, within the Catholic Church, who suffer terribly at this time
Thursday, May 10, 2012 15:45 hours

My child, My Son Jesus Christ prepares now to save as many of God's children as possible before The Warning. For, after The Warning, not much time will remain before the Glorious Return of my Son.

I weep tears of sadness for priests, within the Catholic Church, who suffer terribly at this time.

These pure, lost and wandering servants, are caught in the middle of disruption, from which they cannot untangle.

Because of the sins of others, they suffer the torment of seeing allegiance to my beloved Son being thrown to one side.

Those wicked divisions, caused by Masonic groups, are deliberate. The sins of those guilty of offenses inflicted on innocent souls are being used, as an excuse, to change laws governing the Church.

Many are being misled out of a false sense of loyalty to God's children.

How I suffer when I see the walls of the Catholic Church being taken apart, brick by brick, to make way for a new church.

The new church, which will emerge soon, will not be acceptable to my Son.

Instead it will abolish the Presence of the Holy Eucharist and my Son will suffer the pain of His Crucifixion once again.

The Sacrifice He made, to present the world with this Gift, will be ignored and rejected soon.

Instead, they, the new church, will not tell God's children that The Eucharist is the True Presence of Jesus, my Son.

They will create a new interpretation of the Holy Eucharist and will fail to call down the Presence of my Son. The Food of Life will die. God's children will not be nourished with the Real Body and Blood of my Son.

Their souls will become barren, empty of the Presence of my Son, and the graces He bestows on those who receive Him.

There is a duty on the part of priests to defend the Holy Eucharist. They must be strong and never dilute this Precious and Holy Gift.

My Son loves the Catholic Church and knows how it suffers right now. He feels its pain.

My Immaculate Heart is torn in two, in pain, to witness this Sacred Temple being deliberately destroyed.

Pray, pray, pray to The Father in the Name of His beloved Son to show Mercy on those within the Holy See who want to divide the Church, and scatter God's children into an abyss of desolation.

Please recite this Crusade Prayer to pray for the Catholic Church

Crusade Prayer (53) Prayer for the Catholic Church

Oh God, the Father, in the Name of Your beloved Son, I beg You, to give strength and the graces needed to help priests withstand the persecution they endure.

Help them to adhere to the Truth of the Teachings of Your Son, Jesus Christ, and to never waiver, weaken or submit to untruths about the Existence of The Holy Eucharist.

Amen.

Your loving Mother
Queen of the Earth
Mother of Salvation

Preparations are very much underway for My Second Coming.
Friday, May 11, 2012 20:38 hours

My dearly beloved daughter, preparations are very much underway for My Second Coming.

Many people in the world can and will be saved now because of the prayers of My beloved followers and chosen souls.

So many more than would have been, were it not for the sacrifices of those close to Me.

I yearn to take all of you into the New Era of Peace, the New Paradise on earth.

If only those stubborn souls, who refuse My Call of Mercy and who need to redeem themselves in My Eyes, would listen.

Many believers are lukewarm and are not fit to enter My New Kingdom. Their closed and hardened hearts reject Me now, as I speak.

They pay lip service to Me, in the churches, yet claim to follow Me.

Now that I reach out and stretch My Hand of Mercy, to take their hand in Mine, they push Me away.

So suspicious, so lacking in true understanding as to how I communicate to the world from Heaven, they claim to believe in My Divinity.

Yet they fail to accept that I have the Power to speak to the world through Divine Revelations.

They are missing the chance to grasp the extra graces I desire to give them, in order to bring them to My Sacred Heart.

It is a little like a village suffering in a famine with nothing to eat while they slowly starve.

Yet I stand next to them and can offer them all the nourishment and food to sustain them for Eternal Life. But, they cannot see Me.

Many do not want to see Me, for they doubt that I could be speaking with them now.

For those in the world who have no belief or interest in a world outside of this one you, My followers, must help Me to save them, to cover them.

Soon they will understand that they have a soul. It will be then that I ask all of you to proclaim My Word, so that all of humanity can live in My New Paradise.

Please spread My Word, My Prayers, My Messages and My Warnings, to all souls, especially those who have no faith, belief or knowledge, about My Promise to return to Judge the living and the dead.

They don't have much time so I urge you to pray for their souls.

Your Jesus

Virgin Mary: Go and open your eyes, children, and listen, question and contemplate all that is presented to you, in the Name of God
Saturday, May 12, 2012 10:00 hours

My child, as the roar of Satan and his demons get louder, and the pitch of their screams, heard in the Heavens, I must warn God's children to open their eyes.

Look around you and what do you see?

Unrest, arguments, despair and fighting, all this has been ignited by the evil spirits, that surround humanity.

Released from Hell, their numbers are great. Not for one moment will they ease their torment, spewed out by the hatred they have for all of God's children.

These fallen angels were jealous when my Father, God the Most High, Created mankind and the universe.

Their pride and disgust led to their downfall and they were cast out into Hell.

Led by Satan, their hatred was manifested when I brought the Son of Man, the Saviour of mankind, into the world. Their hatred of me surpasses anything known to humanity.

As Queen of all the Angels, this drove them into turmoil. They knew there would be no return to the Divine Hierarchy.

To hurt God, my beloved Father, they want to destroy that which is closest to His Heart, His precious and beloved children.

By seducing His children, through the temptations of sin, they steal souls.

My Father will not tolerate this wickedness, and the time is close for these fallen angels to be finally cast into the furnace. They know this.

Under the direction of Satan they now increase their plans and every second of the day they cause havoc in the world.

God's children must know that their plan is to snatch everything, which is precious to God, the Almighty Father.

This is why they target His Holy Churches on the earth first.

When they infiltrate God's Churches, they infiltrate God's children.

Wake up, children, to what is happening before your eyes. You must stay alert at all times.

Pray, pray, pray that you are blessed with the graces to recognise evil when it is presented to you as being part of God's plans, when it is not.

It will take strong faith and acceptance of the Truth, contained within these Messages from Heaven, to stay on the True Path to eternal life.

Eternal life is to be welcomed, children, and must never be rejected in favour of false promises.

These false promises are presented to the world in these times by those who lead your nations, and who may be influenced by the king of lies.

Go and open your eyes, children, and listen, question and contemplate all that is presented to you, in the Name of God.

Your beloved Queen of Peace
Mother of Salvation

My New Kingdom: You will be lavished with great abundance and will want for nothing
Sunday, May 13, 2012 16:00 hours

My dearly beloved daughter, it is time to understand that My Messages are not to bring fear.

They are to bring love. They are also being used, to tell those who commit sin or wrongdoing, that they must redeem themselves in My Eyes, or be lost to Me forever.

How could I not tell humanity the Truth?

I realise that you, My daughter, feel a burden from time to time as the recipient of these Divine Messages. You must never allow fear to enter your heart, for it does not come from Me.

Have I not told you that there is a wonderful New Era of Peace ahead for all those who love Me? What is there to fear?

Is it worry over your future, your family or not knowing what lies ahead? If so then you must know this.

I love you all. I want all of God's children to unite as one holy family, together in love.

This is why I am communicating now, in plenty of time, to draw you all closer to Me.

To ensure that you will all turn and open your hearts to the love that I have for every single soul on this earth, I must warn humanity of the dangers they face.

If I did not love you, as I do, I would not warn you.

My Love is so powerful that it is a Love unknown to any human being, for not one of you could have the capacity to feel the Love that I hold for you.

My Love means that I do not want God's children to suffer.

I will take all of you, who will see the Truth, after The Warning, and show you the Love I have.

You and all of those who belong to Me in mind, body and soul will be given the most exquisite Gift, beyond your comprehension.

The New Paradise awaits you, and the earth, that you may think you will pine for, will mean nothing, when you see the Kingdom that has been prepared.

My children, there is much to look forward to. Fear is unnecessary.

Instead consider that you will be given eternal life.

You will be lavished with great abundance and will want for nothing.

The colours, the scents, the love you will feel for all those around you, the peace within your families, lack of fear, your souls full of the Love of God and your perfect bodies – how could you not desire My Kingdom?

My Kingdom will become your new home, when heaven and earth will merge as one, and the dead, who accepted Me as their Saviour, will be resurrected to join with their families, their brothers and sisters in love and happiness.

The relief you will feel when the world of sin, in which you live now, is no longer there, will bring joy, calm and contentment.

No more worries, fears, anxieties or sin.

You will still have free will, but it will be different. You will be living in complete union with Me, according to the Holy Divine Will of My Father. He has waited patiently for this moment.

I am patiently preparing all of God's children, so that not one soul is lost.

So, My dearest daughter, fear not.

Suffering will not last long. In its place will be the home to which each child of God belongs.

That is My Promise to all of you. Do not feel sad, frightened or worried for it is completely unnecessary.

Just learn to love Me more. The more you love Me, the more you will trust in Me.

Only then will fear leave you.

Only then will you truly be free.

I love all of you. Never forget this, especially when you may be worried about the future.

Your beloved Saviour
Jesus Christ

Prayer Requests: Go now and call this request: My call to Jesus
Monday, May 14, 2012 18:00 hours

My dearest beloved daughter, your gift to Me is accepted and as a result will save a further 5 million souls. *

It is My dearest wish to bring an end to your suffering, but, this precious gift you bring Me will now mean I can save more of God's children.

Never forget that this Mission is to save mankind from Hell. I need your help and the help of others to do this.

Never feel alone, for I love you and am with you the entire time. So many more of God's children are beginning to hear My Voice at last.

The Work of the Holy Spirit will bear fruit and very soon the Love of God will be felt in the hearts of even the most barren.

Those lost, empty and barren souls will feel a Flame of Love and witness a familiar yearning to be part of My New Kingdom on earth.

Many will not understand why, but they will be unable to deny their feelings of warmth, love and peace.

So many will be surprised and will want to speak with Me. You must now unite people everywhere to request the Gift of My Love. They must ask for special favours to be granted. You, My daughter, must designate one day a week to this. Each lost soul must ask Me to help them. If their request is according to My Holy Will, then I will answer their prayers. This will instil in them a stronger link to My Sacred Heart and My Great Mercy.

Go now and call this request "My call to Jesus." My daughter, do this as soon as you can as I wish to ensure that those souls, especially those who do not accept that I speak now, they will finally realise how close I am to each single soul. Tell them that I love everyone and don't exclude one single sinner no matter how grievous their sin.

All I ask is for them to come to Me and ask Me to help them.

Your Jesus

Second Seal: World War 3
Wednesday, May 16, 2012 03:10 hours

My dearest beloved, I must inform you that a Third World War is about to unfold in the world.

My tears flow this morning, as you can see.*

The Second Seal is about to unfold as foretold to John the Evangelist in the Book of Revelation.

It will start in Europe.

Your banking system will be the cause and Germany, once again, will be involved in this tragedy as it was on the last two occasions.

When it commences, much will be over saving the economy, and catastrophe will affect Greece, with much fallout in France.

The Middle East will also be involved with Israel and Iran at war and Syria will play a serious part in the downfall of Egypt.

My daughter, I wake you to tell you this, not to frighten you, but to urge much prayer for Europe at this time.

Because of war and lack of money, much of the harvest will be lost and this will lead to the opening of the Third Seal, which means famine.

This is why I now urge all of God's children to try to stockpile dried and non-perishable food to feed your families. It is important to grow your own harvest if possible.

Remember, however, that prayer can mitigate much of this suffering.

The effect of this war will be that My Catholic Church on earth will be sucked into a one-world church, in the name of unification.

This unification, or false peace, will become a reality after the antichrist appears to create a false peace and a so-called end to the war.

This peaceful pact will involve the Western world, until China and Russia become involved with world matters.

They will pose a threat to the '**Beast with the Ten Horns**', Europe, and will overcome them to introduce communism.

The '**Red Dragon**', China, already gains a strong foothold in the world because of their control of the world's finances.

The Red Dragon and **"The Bear"** which is Russia do not love God.

They are being led by the antichrist, who is from the East, and who hides behind closed doors.

When these prophesies unfold the whole world will believe in these Messages. There will be no doubts then.

Please recite this Crusade Prayer, as it will help dilute the impact of these events.

Crusade Prayer (54) Prayer to the Father to dilute impact of World War 3

O Heavenly Father, in the Name of Your beloved Son, Jesus Christ, Who suffered greatly for the sins of mankind, please help us in these difficult times we face.

Help us to survive the persecution being planned by greedy rulers and those who want to destroy Your Churches and Your children.

We implore You, dear Father, to help feed our families and save the lives of those who will be forced into a war, against their will.

We love You, dear Father.
We beg You to help us in our time of need.
Save us from the grip of the antichrist.
Help us to survive his mark, the Mark of the Beast, by refusing to accept it.

Help those who love You to remain true to Your Holy Word at all times so that You can bestow on us the graces to survive in body and soul.

Amen.

My daughter, I realise that this news may come as a shock, but, remember that prayer and the Seal of the Living God Crusade Prayer number (33) will protect My followers, My Remnant Church. You, My children, will survive although it will not be easy.

You will be bullied because of your Christianity, but you will never denounce Me or reject Me.

For this you will be given Gifts. My Gift of the Seal of the Living God will render you invisible to your enemies.

Recite it every day from now on. Keep it before you in your homes and have it blessed by a priest.

Begin your preparation soon for the day of the fallout in Europe is not far away.

Your Jesus

Virgin Mary: My visionaries in the world will be instructed to pray in order to avert the dangers associated with a World War
Wednesday, May 16, 2012 09:00 hours

My child, please try to remain strong in this Work for my Son.

It is important that all those who believe in the Truth of the Holy Word, being given to the world at this time, remain calm.

Your duty is to respond to my beloved Son's instructions. Prayer, and trust in my Son, will bring about your salvation.

The Gift of the Seal of the Living God will be your biggest protection at a time of war or strife.

By pledging allegiance to God the Father, through the acceptance of this free Gift, you will remain free.

Never forget the power of prayer and how it can dilute the impact of such events.

Sadly, many of these events must come to pass for they have been prophesised.

Children, I call on all those who revere me, your Blessed Mother, to understand that this is a calling from Heaven.

All my visionaries in the world will be instructed to pray, in order to avert the dangers associated with a World War.

You must persevere in your suffering and offer it as a gift to God the Father.

My daily Rosary is important at this time no matter what Christian Church you belong to.

You must recite it, because it offers protection to those nations who say it daily, and in great numbers.

Pray, pray, pray for Europe at this time and turn to my Son and ask Him for the strength, courage and perseverance required to retain your trust in God.

Your beloved Mother
Queen of Heaven and Earth
Mother of Salvation

Set up prayer groups devoted to Jesus to Mankind
Wednesday, May 16, 2012 17:38 hours

My dearly beloved daughter, I must emphasise, to all those who believe in Me, that is important to pray for each of your nations.

To do this effectively you must set up prayer groups, devoted to "Jesus to Mankind".

Use this group to recite all the Crusade Prayers given to you.

My daughter, Maria, will arrange to have those put up in a way which will allow you to print them off anywhere you are in the world.

Please spread My Holy Word to all members of the clergy.

Some will reject My Messages.

Others will embrace them with love in their hearts.

However, for the most part, you will be ridiculed and rejected in My Holy Name.

You will suffer as My apostles suffered and will be made a laughing stock in some quarters of My Church on earth.

These verbal and abusive insults will be intense and you will be hurt. But, I say this.

Remember the hatred shown to you will prove that it is, indeed I, Your Jesus, speaking to you from Heaven.

For this suffering I will make you rise again and again every time you are kicked to the ground.

I will raise you up and make you stronger than before.

Why do I do this? I do it so that you will become fit and stronger to spread My Holy Word.

For only then will you receive greater Gifts, which I will provide you with through My Holy Spirit.

So rise and move to prepare your nation, so that it will receive the armour it needs to avoid the Mark of the Beast.

Never forget the importance of the Seal of the Living God.

It will offer you and your family protection, not just in spirit, but a physical protection also.

You are blessed to receive the Seal and it is your duty to ensure that as many of God's children everywhere receive it.

Remember I stand by all of My followers, every minute and when they carry out My Work, they will receive special Graces to make them brave, strong and determined to save the souls of every man, woman and child in the world.

Your beloved Saviour

Virgin Mary: This Seal was foretold in the Book of John
Thursday, May 17, 2012 08:50 hours

My child, God's children will be able to protect their faith, their courage and their safety, during any war, if they continue to pray the **Seal of the Living God Crusade Prayer.**

This is one of the last, and the Greatest Seal of Protection, sent from the Heavens, of all prayers given to humanity.

It is to help sustain all during any future persecution, especially at times of domination and war.

This Seal was foretold in the Book of John and has many Divine Powers associated with it.

Cherish it and use it to protect, not only yourselves, but, your families.

This reminder is needed at this time.

Go in peace.

Your beloved Mother
Mother of Salvation

The One Remnant Church, which will stand, undefeated, until the rise of the New Jerusalem
Friday, May 18, 2012 10:48 hours

My dearly beloved daughter, know now that the spread of My Holy Spirit is about to become rampant in the world.

The Flame of Truth will enrapture the world and fill the souls of many with the simple wonder of My Great Mercy.

Much conversion will take place and it will be then that My Remnant Army will rise to become a powerful force in the battle against the antichrist.

My Remnant Christian Church will spread the Holy Gospel into every corner of the earth.

Fires will pour forth upon those who try to harm My Remnant Church.

For few will be able to withstand the Truth of My Holy Word when it is shown to them.

So many will there be that it will amount to over 20 million.

Leaders will spring up among you and you will have to practice your faith hidden in certain quarters.

You will lead a Crusade of My Teachings and My Crusade Prayers will be your weapon to defeat the enemy.

Strangers will become close, people from different countries will join together. and religions torn apart in the past through their differences, will all join as one.

The One Remnant Church, which will stand, undefeated until the rise of the New Jerusalem.

This is when My Second Coming will take place.

When My New Jerusalem rises from the ashes, from where all those who opposed Me thought that My Church on earth had been burnt to the ground.

And then that will be it.

The New Beginning.

The New Era.

The New Heaven and the New Earth.

The time for the Divine Will of My Father to be realised, finally.

Rise now My army. Diversify and spread your wings. Never deviate from the Truth contained in the Holy Bible.

Never doubt the Words contained in Holy Scripture.

For those among you, including members of My Church on earth, who do, then you must open your heart to the Truth.

The Bible contains the Holy Word of God. The Bible contains the whole Truth.

It does not lie.

If you deny the Truth contained therein you deny the Word of God.

Your Saviour
Jesus Christ

God the Father: Fear not My Hand, but the hand of those who are your enemies
Friday, May 18, 2012 15:20 hours

I speak with you today, My dearest daughter, to bring comfort to those who fear for the future.

The future, dear children, lies in My Holy Hands.

The time has come for the New Kingdom, the Kingdom over which My beloved Son will Reign, to come to pass.

This is the final stage, when earth is being prepared to bring forth the multitudes, who love My Son, and in time, who love Me.

Much must happen for My Divine Will to be done and prayer, patience and courage are needed.

Fear not My Hand, but the hand of those who are your enemies.

Much wickedness is rampant in the world and the time has come for Me to punish those nations who torment My children on earth.

As the battle begins, the houses that honour Me, God the Father, will be renewed.

Soon they will realise how they rejected the One True Messiah I sent to earth, in My Son, Jesus Christ, to give the world salvation.

Then those who believe in My Son and Me, God, the Most High, will rise in unison to prepare the ground so that the Second Coming of My Son can take place.

Only when the Purification is complete will My Son return.

The Purification I speak of is when the good will be separated from those who are evil. Those who live their lives filled with the lies planted in their souls by Satan still have time to repent.

Every attempt will be made by Me to salvage them from the beast for I do not give up on My children that easily.

I will, through the various Divine Interventions, sanctioned by Me, try to take them into My Merciful Arms, to save them.

Trust and belief in Me, is the pathway to Eternal Life.

Only through My Son, The Saviour of the World, can you come to Me, The Father of the Universe, for to come to Me, you must be saved from Sin.

To be saved from Sin you must redeem yourselves, in the Eyes of My Son.

Just as I sent My Son the first time to grant you salvation, so too, do I send Him once more, to save you one last time before the New Heaven and the New Earth merge to become one.

Those who refuse to accept My Son's Great Mercy, after this last Crusade, to bring all of My Children into Paradise, their rightful inheritance, will be lost forever.

There can be no going back after this.

Never forget Who I Am.

I Am God, the Father and I Created you.

I love you.

I desire to bring all of you home, but how My Tears flow so.

This is because there will be so many that I will not be able to save unless they turn and ask Me to help them.

This call from the Heavens has been foretold.

Only The Lamb of God, My Son, has the Authority to reveal to you the events, which lie ahead.

Only He can open the Seals.

He does this now with the help of the Seventh Angel, the Seventh Messenger.

Open your eyes and accept that, at last, the Book of Truth prophesised is now being opened Chapter by Chapter before your eyes.

Accept it as a Gift, because it will bring you eternal life.

Your beloved Father in Heaven
God the Most High

Virgin Mary: The evil one attacks those who love God the most
Sunday, May 20, 2012 12:15 hours

My child, just as more of God's children embrace these Holy Messages so, too, will more people reject them.

All those closest to my Son will be tempted by the evil one to turn their backs.

They will suffer the most, and doubts will block their minds to the Truth.

The evil one attacks those who love God the most.

When he blinds them to the Truth he wins.

Those, who revere me, the Mother of God, will also be a target where the evil one will pull them away from the Book of Truth.

Never does he, the evil one, give up. He inflicts terrible torture on those loving souls so that they will deny the Word of God.

I beg all of those who love my Son to hear my call. You must listen when my Son speaks to you.

Do not denounce the chance to help your brothers and sisters to obtain the eternal life promised to them.

Do not allow doubts planted by the deceiver to prevent millions of souls from being saved.

This is the fierce opposition that will assail you from this day.

You must call on me, your Mother, to help you, guide you and lead on to the True Path.

Your beloved Mother
Mother of Salvation

Pray that you can recognise the true prophets from those who do not speak in My Holy Name
Sunday, May 20, 2012 18:10 hours

My dearly beloved daughter, tell God's children that My prophets in the world today will be rejected, just as they were in the beginning.

Those who profess to come in My Name today, but who do not receive messages from God, will be embraced and accepted.

Those who proclaim My Holy Word and who prophesy in the Name of My Father, will suffer the biggest rejection.

Priests and clergy will attack My prophets today, because Satan blinds them to My Holy Word.

Let any man who tries to stop the true prophets of God know that they will commit a grave sin in the Eyes of God.

Sacred servants and those who proclaim the Truth of My Teachings will be punished should they try to sabotage this Holy Mission.

To those, who do not believe in My Holy Word given to the world at this time, you must keep silent.

For if you don't and denounce Me, you will be held responsible, and you will weep and beg Me to forgive you.

By then the damage you caused will have been felt where souls will be lost.

Never reject My Holy Word given to you through the prophets.

Embrace it and accept it for much work is needed to prepare all of mankind for My New Kingdom.

Remember this.

When Man denies My Word, that is to be expected, when Satan roams the earth.

When a faithful servant of God rejects Me, this is like a sword cutting through Me.

It is the most painful rejection of all.

Come to Me all of you. If you do not believe, then pray that you will be shown the Truth soon.

If you are in any doubt, turn to Me and ask Me to open your heart. Let me fill you with graces, so that you will help Me gather souls in every part of the World in time.

Do not believe that The Second Coming can or will take place without the help of My prophets, sent to prepare you so that you are fit to enter My Kingdom.

Pray that you can recognise the true prophets from those who do not speak in My Holy Name.

Woe to those who tear apart My prophets, for they will have to answer for their offenses against My Holy Father, God the Most High.

Go open your eyes.

Look when I reveal to you the Truth.

Do not turn your head.

Do not close your eyes.

It is time for you to choose.

Follow Me, and help lead My children to Eternal Life.

Turn your back and you deny those souls the chance of redeeming themselves in My Eyes.

Your Jesus

The time is drawing closer for The Warning to take place
Monday, May 21, 2012 20:15 hours

My dearly beloved daughter, the time is drawing closer for The Warning to take place.

Still there is so much work to be done to prepare souls for My Great Mercy.

I call on all those who love Me to pray hard for the global conversion I desire.

So many will come running into My Arms, relief flooding their souls, because they know it is I, their beloved Jesus, who beckons them.

So many will fight the Truth when it is presented to them. The proof I will reveal will not be enough to ignite a single flame of love in their souls.

They have been stolen from Me, and yet they do not want to be set free from their captor, the beast who has devoured their souls.

Spread My Word as quickly as you can, My daughter.

Ignore the taunts, the sneers and the ridicule from those who try to stop you.

Rise and proclaim My Most Holy Word at all costs.

Those who profess to speak in My Name and try to demean you, are crucifying Me. It is not you they torment, but Me, their beloved Saviour.

Human opinion is not important. All that matters are those souls that I yearn to save.

Pray this Crusade Prayer (55) to Prepare for The Warning

O my dear Jesus, please open the hearts of all God's children to the Gift of Your Great Mercy.

Help them to accept Your Divine Mercy with love and gratitude. Enable them to become humble before You and beg for the forgiveness of their sins so that they can become part of Your Glorious Kingdom. Amen.

Soon many millions in the world will hear My Call and more souls can and will be saved.

Never forget the importance of the daily recital of My Divine Mercy Chaplet to save souls.

Go in peace and love.
Your beloved Jesus

My Book of Truth, like a Flame, will spread quickly over the whole world.
Tuesday, May 22, 2012 15:20 hours

My dearly beloved daughter, the next stage in this Holy Mission is about to unfold.

My Book of Truth, like a Flame, will spread quickly over the whole world.

Conversion will be quick and My Holy Word, in all tongues, will be heard.

All of God's children, in turn, will spread My Messages and they will be filled with the Holy Spirit.

Their lips will impart the Truth, and all will prophesy in tongues, so that the Truth can be heard quickly.

The thirst of God's children, who wander in a confused state, because their souls are empty, will be quenched.

The hunger pangs for My Presence will be satisfied when I bring those souls the nourishment they so desperately need.

When this happens very few souls in the world will be unaware of My Great Mercy.

Take My Gift, My Holy Word, My Book of Truth and devour it. For without it you will be like a body without a soul.

When you swallow My Words of Wisdom, you will become whole again.

When you become whole again, you will be ready to come with Me nto the New Era of Peace on earth.

Await now, My beloved followers, for My written Word will be with you soon and you will rejoice with love and peace in your souls.

Go forth all My followers.Let you, your loved ones and all believers, prophesy in My Name.

Walk with Me while I lead you to Eternal Life.

Your beloved Jesus
Redeemer of all Mankind

God the Father: The suffering in the world has been united to the suffering of My Son, Jesus, at this time
Wednesday, May 23, 2012 15:38 hours

My dearest daughter, tell all My children of the love and protection I offer those who call on Me.

My Holy Word on earth is, at last, being heard and many souls are ready to make the greatest leap of faith to embrace the Divine Mercy of My Son, Jesus Christ.

Little do they know that to enter the New Paradise, the New Era of Peace, is but a simple thing.

Look up and accept that you are a child of Mine, first. Acknowledge that I Created each of you, not one of you an accident, and that you are My children, My family, My loved ones.

The tenderness in My Heart is full of Love for each of you.

Many think that because I Am, The Alpha and The Omega, the Beginning and the End, that My Power makes Me proud.

This, of course, can never be.

How can the true love of a parent for a child be clouded by pride?

I suffer for each of you. I weep for those lost to Me. I will use every Power to bring My lost children back into My family, My Kingdom.

Imagine a parent who is rejected by their child. The hurt I feel is not for Me, their Father, but for them and the torment they will suffer if I cannot save them.

The suffering in the world has been united to the suffering of My Son, Jesus, at this time.

Why do I do this? Why do I allow suffering? It is because of sin.

Sinners who won't come to Me willingly can only be saved through the suffering of others.

Those who suffer in this life will be rewarded with My Gifts in the next life.

Help offered freely by those children who love Me, is a powerful weapon against the power accorded to Satan. Those who fight alongside My Son to save the souls of others can save the whole of humanity.

Satan has power, but, only that given to him – a power, which cannot be taken back until the Day of Judgment.

Many of you, dear children, do not understand the Divine Laws that permit these things. But, trust in Me as I reveal this.

Satan will steal the souls of My children who do not believe in Me, or the Goodness, which I provide My children.

He becomes powerless when sinners make sacrifices, through suffering, to save their brothers and sisters from going to Hell.

He is rendered impotent when My children pray for those sinners to be saved.

Prayer is the armour of My children who want to help Me to save the whole of humanity.

Gather together, My children, with My Son and help Me unite My family at last.

Help Me to bring you all into the new wonderful Era of Peace.

Only then can My Will be done on earth as it is in Heaven.

Go, children. Unite in prayer.

Work with Me, your Father, to help save My family.

Your beloved Father
God the Most High

During The Warning, those who redeemed themselves in My Eyes will not suffer pain of Purgatory
Thursday, May 24, 2012 18:30 hours

When the time comes, My dearly beloved daughter, for The Warning, a number of signs will be revealed.

I tell you this to remind all God's children that they must prepare themselves beforehand.

The two stars will collide and many will be fearful.

There is nothing to fear because this is the Greatest Gift I bring so that not one soul is lost to the fires of Hell.

Then, My Cross, will appear in the skies and not one person will fail to notice.

Many will fall down in fear and a great shaking like an earthquake will be felt.

Then will come the silence.

Always prepare for this day as if it were tomorrow. Seek redemption now and reveal to Me your sins.

Catholics must go to Confession. For those who are not Catholics, they must recite the Crusade Prayer (24) I give to the rest of the world for My Plenary Indulgence.

This Gift of My Plenary Indulgence is for all of God's children, of every creed, and offers a great cleansing. Do not reject this Gift. Accept it.

For Catholics who question My Gift and who have begrudgingly criticised My Gift I say this.

Do you believe that I would not bestow this Sacrament on all of God's children?

You must be generous of heart and happy that I do this. Do you think that they should not be given such a Gift? If you do. then you don't truly love Me.

Bow your heads and praise God for this wonderful Gift given to mankind to save their souls.

Then, during The Warning, all those who have redeemed themselves in My Eyes will not suffer the pain of Purgatory.

Those who see their sins unveiled before them, as seen through My Eyes, will be shocked.

Many will find it difficult to accept how blackened their souls are.

Those who do, and show remorse, will ask Me to pardon them. And I will.

But, some will not be sorry and will defend, in their heart, the atrocities they committed as they appear before My Eyes. They won't repent and will slap Me in the Face.

Either way, the fires, of the purification and suffering will be felt by all sinners.

The length of time will depend on the gravity of their sins.

Those who pull away from Me need your prayers. They will be given more time to turn back to Me and ask Me to forgive them.

But, that time could be as short as a day or as long as a few years.

No one, but, My Father knows the date of My Second Coming.

The time between the two events will not be as long as you may think.

Finally, My children will realise the time they are living in and accept the Truth.

For those who know the Truth now and who believe in Me, you have a duty to pray for the souls who will not accept My Mercy.

My daughter, My greatest desire is to save the entire world, including those who are lost to Me.

All the prayers of My followers, who unite as one voice, can help Me to do this.

Go in love. Trust in Me, always, for the time is short and the plans for the salvation of humanity rest in the Hands of My Eternal Father.

Your beloved Jesus

They intend to oust Pope Benedict XVI from the Seat of Peter, using devious means
Saturday, May 26, 2012 16:00 hours

I am delighted to have you back with Me. It is important to keep close to Me now, My daughter. The time is short and you have much work to do.

Today I ask of My followers, My dearest daughter, to pray hard for My beloved Vicar, Pope Benedict XVI. He, My Holy Servant, is under terrible persecution behind closed doors in the Holy See.

I have told you before that the Masonic Groups, who have a vice like grip inside The Vatican, want My beloved Pope out.

And they intend to oust him from the Seat of Peter using devious means.

He will, as I have told you in the past, have to flee for he will have little choice.

This time is short. You must pray hard that he can stay as long as possible for as soon as he leaves, the impostor, the false prophet, will take his place.

How My Tears flow for My beloved Church on earth at this time. All those sacred servants of mine, who accept My Holy Word, as it is given to you at this time, hear Me now.

You must remain faithful to the Holy Mass and uphold the daily Sacrifices. For very soon you will be forced to swallow a lie.

The daily Sacrifices, in honour of My Crucifixion and the change of the wine into My Blood, and the bread into My Body, will be changed, twisted and I will be vilified through new laws introduced by the False prophet.

You must never accept anything that is not the Truth. You must never accept heresy from within the walls of My Holy See. If you do then you will remove yourself from Me.

Many of you will have to offer the Holy Mass in secret and you will need all the courage you can get by praying to Me and asking Me to make you strong.

The changes will begin in the Holy Eucharist itself. You will soon be told that Holy Communion, My True Presence is, in fact, something else.

You will be told it means different things. But, this is a terrible lie.

The Holy Eucharist is My Body and Blood, given to you to allow Me to fill you with My Holy Spirit, to give you the nourishment that you need for your souls.

When the time comes and you, My sacred servants, are presented with the new modern interpretation, then you will know that the contamination has already started.

This is when you will need to prepare. Gather together and defend the Truth of My Crucifixion. Do not accept the lies, the changes in the Holy Mass and the Holy Eucharist. For if you do, then My Presence will be lost to all of God's children.

Follow Me. This is the greatest challenge you will ever have to face, but I will give you the Graces to discern the Truth, from the sacrilegious fiction you will be asked to accept in My Holy Name.

You must ask for My Help now through this Crusade Prayer

Crusade Prayer (56) Priests seeking Protection for the Holy Eucharist

O dear Father, in the Name of Your Precious Son, Who sacrificed Himself on the Cross, for the whole of mankind, help me to stay true to the Truth.

Cover me with the Precious Blood of Your Son and give me the Graces to continue to serve You in faith, trust and honour for the rest of my ministry.

Never let me stray from true meaning of the Sacrifice of the Holy Mass or the presentation of The Holy Eucharist to Your children.

Give me the strength to represent You and feed Your flock the way in which they must be fed with the Body, Blood, Soul and Divinity of Your Son, Jesus Christ, The Saviour of Mankind. Amen.

Please know that I walk with each of you, My beloved sacred servants, every day.

I hold you up. Lean on Me and I will keep you close to My Sacred Heart in these times of terrible torment within the Catholic Church.

Your beloved Jesus

Satan will convince you that My Messages come from him.
Sunday, May 27, 2012 18:00 hours

My daughter, so many of My followers question why many of these prophecies cause fear in their hearts.

Many believe that I create fear. But, this is not quite true.

The fear, which floods many souls, is the realisation that what I tell you is the Truth.

Like any good parent a child is warned of the dangers in life.

Sometimes the dangers, which a parent warns about, can cause fear. Yet the fear relates to the evil caused by man, which lies ahead.

The same is true of evil in the world, it is caused by man, who in turn, is influenced by the deceiver, Satan.

The prophecies given to the human race by God since the beginning of time has struck fear in the hearts of some.

Yet they caused much laughter in other quarters. This is what happened before Noah began to build The Ark. While he was laughed at, sneered at and ridiculed, those in fear did what was asked of them. They built The Ark to save themselves.

Those who laughed, ridiculed and dismissed Noah were destroyed.

All prophecies, which come from God, include warnings to encourage humanity to be prepared for such events.

It is only through preparing your souls that you can withstand the torment caused by the sins of man, which lie ahead.

To those of My followers, who question why My Messages may cause fear, I say this:

Do not believe the lies, planted in your hearts by Satan, that God would never give the world Messages, which strike fear in the hearts of His children.

Many of you, now, especially those who love Me, are being turned away from My Holy Word.

One of Satan's favourite taunts is to convince you that Divine Messages do not contain prophecies, which cause fear.

Surely such Messages can only from the evil one?

How Satan laughs at his own cunning deceit.

Satan will convince you that My Messages come from him; so desperate is he to convince you not to follow My Instructions.

You My followers must be told the Truth.

I must prepare you and that means warning you in advance of things to come only to protect you, to save you.

Never listen to this lie.

My Messages are given to you out of My Divine Love for the whole of creation. Allow Me to guide you like any good parent.

By listening to Me, and following My instructions of prayer, I will protect you.

Fear does not come from Me. When you believe in Me, and trust Me, you will not be fearful, no matter how much evil is presented to you through the sins of mankind.

One thing you must never do is to hide and assume that all will be well.

For to do so you dismiss the existence of evil in the world.

Accept that Satan exists. Believe that prayer can, and will, dilute his powers.

Then stand up and take responsibility, as a follower of Me, Jesus Christ.

When you face the Truth, allow Me to lead you and fear will not enter your heart.

Your beloved Jesus

Know that the 1,000 years referred to in the Book of Revelation means just that
Monday, May 28, 2012 20:45 hours

My dearly beloved daughter, when man questions the Teachings contained in the Holy Bible, this is normal human nature.

When man twists the Teachings in the Holy Bible to suit his own agenda, this offends Me.

But, when My sacred servants denounce parts of the Holy Bible, and throw them to one side, as if they are of no consequence, they deny Me, the Son of Man.

Everything contained within the Holy Bible comes from My Eternal Father who has sanctioned every single Word through His anointed ones.

Believe that the Holy Word of God is contained in My Father's Book, not one Word a lie.

Why then do those who profess to be scholars and experts in the Truth contained with the Holy Bible, question My Holy Word as I present it to you, in these Messages?

My Truth is being given to you now, once again, to refresh your memories, to remind you of the Teachings contained therein.

To My children on earth, know that prophecies contained in the Book of Daniel and the Book of Revelation still have to take place.

Know that the 1,000 years referred to in the Book of Revelation means just that.

If it was meant to be something different, then it would have been given a different time.

My Church, the Catholic Church, has not declared their beliefs, because they have not done this yet.

My Remnant Church, the remaining tendrils of My Catholic Church on earth, will understand the true meaning of My Era of Peace on earth.

You are in the end times, but the earth will be renewed.

I call out to all of you, My sacred servants. My Voice is hoarse as I beg you to respond to My Holy Call from Heaven.

I, your beloved Saviour, have sent many seers and visionaries to you up to now. These helped open your minds to those events still to come.

I have waited until now to proclaim to the world the final revelations. I now send My last messenger, Maria Divine Mercy, the seventh messenger, to prepare the final chapter, as it is unveiled to you.

My Voice is like thunder. It will continue to be heard all over the earth. It will not stop until the day I come to Judge.

You may not listen to Me now. Many of you will dismiss My Word with an arrogance, which wounds Me deeply.

Others will, through fear, ignore Me for it is easier that way. But, soon the changes I speak about will come to pass. Then the Truth will begin to dawn on you.

I call you now and tell you this. I await your response whether or not it is now or in the future.

I am waiting. I will continue, patiently, until the day you come running to Me, seeking My Protection.

I never give up on My chosen servants those whom I called out to, in the first instance.

Do you remember the first time I called you? You felt My Voice speaking to your soul, urging you to join in union with Me. Can you hear Me now?

Ask Me to reveal to you now, that it is I, your Jesus, begging you to come, rise and follow Me on this last arduous journey to Eternal Life. Do not fear My Call. Trust Me and say this prayer asking Me to let you hear My call.

Crusade Prayer (57) Prayer for the Clergy – Jesus let me hear Your call.

O my dear Jesus, open my ears to the sound of Your Voice, open my heart to Your loving Call, fill my soul with the Holy Spirit, so I can recognise You at this time.

I offer You my humble allegiance to all that You ask of Me. Help me to discern the Truth, rise, respond and follow Your Voice so I can help You to save the souls of all of humanity.

Your Will is my command. Give me the courage to let You guide me, so I can take up the armour needed to lead Your Church towards Your New Kingdom.

Amen

Remember, I Jesus Christ, will never allow My sacred servants to wander off the Path of Truth. I will stand at every corner, every avenue and point you in the right direction.

You may find this frustrating at times. You may be confused. You may not want to hear the Truth. You may be fearful. But, know this.

I will always love you. I will always be at your side.

I will never desert you.
Your beloved Jesus

Prayers can avert the atrocities being planned urging the use of nuclear bombs
Tuesday, May 29, 2012 17:42 hours

My dearly beloved daughter, My prophets, My messengers, and all the true visionaries, in the world are uniting in spirit to proclaim My Holy Word at this time.

Those chosen for the difficult Mission, to ensure that the souls of the whole of humanity are prepared for My Second Coming, are being instructed to call out to the world.

They will soon urge for urgent prayer to help those who will suffer in the coming wars.

The time is near for wars to break out and many innocent souls will be the victims in these hate filled terrors against God's children.

Many will be torn in different directions in these wars and much confusion will exist in the Middle East.

So many little wars will escalate.

So many sides splintered in all directions at first, will merge into only a small number of sides.

Then the larger armies will become involved with many nations joining in.

How My tears fall over this terrible evil, led through the influence of Satan, who wants to kill as many people as possible and as quickly as possible.

Pray for these wars to be diluted.

Pray that God's children, through their prayers, can avert the atrocities being planned urging the use of nuclear bombs.

My dearest daughter, Satan will do everything in his power at this time to encourage the Catholic Church to denounce you and to declare these Messages heresy.

You must ignore these attacks. All those who follow My Teachings need only follow their hearts for they will find it easy to discern the Truth.

If My prophets were not given the graces from Heaven to withstand such persecution, then My Holy Word, My Instructions to prepare all of God's children for My Second Coming would not be heard.

Were it not for the stubborn persistence of all God's prophets and God's messengers, from the beginning of time, then, God's children would remain ignorant.

Once the knowledge is given to you, My precious followers, you must never be afraid for you are following the path to Eternal Life. Any other path, irrespective of the glorious, but, worthless, temptations, which pull you towards worldly trappings, will not lead you to Me, for if, and when, the lies about My Holy Eucharist begin to emerge, you must be brave and walk away.

Pray for strength, determination and courage to follow me on the final Path to Salvation.

Your beloved Jesus

My Agony in the Garden is being relived once again and I am doubled with the pain of suffering
Wednesday, May 30, 2012 15:30 hours

My dearly beloved daughter, the torment inflicted on you by those lacking in true humility, but who profess to speak in My Name, will intensify now.

Listen to no voice only Mine. Do not engage or respond to those who insult Me.

They have allowed human pride to block Me and then not only is that not enough they persecute Me.

My Second Coming will be similar to events, which took place during My time on earth the first time.

My Holy Word will be questioned, criticised, dismissed and then rejected.

The first to reject Me will be My own, those souls who love Me the most. They will stand front in line to throw the first stone.

My Agony in the Garden is being relived once again and I am doubled with the pain of suffering.

I agonised over the sins of mankind, not only those who lived at that time, but those who reject Me today. Those who reject Me today hurt Me more because I died for their sins. They have learnt nothing.

Then those who mocked Me, and tore My Eye out with the thorn, the sharpest one in the Crown of Thorns, are those representatives of My Church on Earth.

They won't accept My Second Coming or the warnings I reveal to them now.

Every Word uttered from My Lips is being devoured by those humble souls like children in a famine.

Yet those nourished by the knowledge of the Truth of My Teachings, turn their heads and look the other way.

Humility is no longer present in the souls of many of My followers so that they will be unable to benefit from My special Graces.

Until you become little in the Eyes of God you cannot hear Me.

Until you denounce pride and arrogance you will not feel the Power of the Holy Spirit.

When you reject Me today you plunge the first nail into My Wrist.

When you, My sacred servants, denounce My Holy Word, given to you now, you drive the second nail into My other Wrist.

For those poor souls who have no interest in My Teachings, or the salvation I gave the world through My death on the Cross, they have no one to guide them.

They are the victims here. They are not being led towards Me. They are being denied the chance to prepare for My Second Coming.

Now I call all of My followers to prepare. The battle among believers will begin soon. One half will not only denounce these Messages, they will try to ban them.

The other half will use them to convert others.

Those simple lost souls, who don't know Me at all, will know Me as soon as I reveal the Truth to them during The Warning.

It will be easier for them to see the Truth, than it will for those who say they love Me, but who deny Me now.

This is why you need to pray for the graces to allow you to see Me, hear Me and to let Me prepare you for My Second Coming.

Never believe that to truly follow Me, especially in these the End Times, will be easy.

For this time, silent homage to My Holy Word, will not be enough.

You will be like a new recruit in any army. You will need to train, renew your souls and come to Me, through the Sacraments, before you will be strong enough and brave enough to spread My Holy Word.

The spread of My Crusade Prayers will be your first task.

You, My army will lead the biggest Crusade of My Holy Mission on earth ever. You will start small, but will swell to 20 million.

The prayers and suffering of My Remnant Church can be enough to save the whole of humanity. Never forget that your prayers can save the souls of the most grievous sinners, so powerful is prayer. So prepare to gather together. Prepare well, because efforts will be made to stop you. Accept the abusive insults, which will be flung at you.

Know that every kind of argument will be presented to you in order to stop you in your Mission. But, know that I guide you, steer you and make you strong.

Know also that you, My army, will be responsible for the salvation of millions of souls. Souls who would have had no hope at all.

Let My Love touch your soul and bind you together as one, in union with Me, your Jesus.

Allow Me to cover you with My Precious Blood and bestow My Gifts to help you stay loyal to Me so that, no matter how strong the temptation is, you never deny My Call to you now.

I bless you all, My strong army. I will lead you in your march to the New Era of Peace, every step of the way.

Your beloved Saviour
Redeemer of Mankind
Jesus Christ

Virgin Mary: June Crusade of Conversion Month
Thursday, May 31, 2012 21:00 hours

My child, every effort is being made by Satan and those souls he has infected to undermine my Son's Most Holy Word.

Always remember that Satan plants the first seeds of doubts within the hearts of chosen souls.

The worst condemnation will be poured upon these Holy Messages, by those who are intimately united to my Precious Son.

When Satan does this he wins souls.

Do not let him do this, my child. Walk away and do not engage with him.

My Son never defended His Holy Word nor should you succumb to this temptation.

The scale of satanic influence is growing and spreading throughout the world.

My poor children suffer so and I weep tears of sorrow when I see their dismay and sorrow.

Pray, my children for peace at this time so that God's children everywhere will turn to my Son for strength.

Only Divine Intervention, given through the graces provided through your prayers, can ease your pain and suffering.

My Son yearns for souls to turn to Him, for only He can give them the comfort they need. Nothing else will provide relief from the torment you now endure.

I urge you, children, to dedicate the month of June to the conversion of mankind and to ensure that they will seek salvation.

Call this month the Crusade of Conversion month and pray as one, through prayer groups throughout the world.

Here is the Crusade Prayer for the Crusade of Conversion.

Crusade Prayer (58) Crusade of Conversion Prayer

O dear Jesus, I call on You to embrace all God's children and cover them with Your Precious Blood. Let each drop of Your Blood cover every soul, to shield them from the evil one.

Open the hearts of all, especially hardened souls and those who know You, but, who are stained with the sin of pride, to fall down and beg for the Light of Your Love to flood their souls

Open their eyes to see the Truth so that the dawn of Your Divine Mercy will shower down upon them, so they are covered with the Rays of Your Mercy.

Convert all souls through the graces I ask you for know, dear Jesus. (Personal intention here.)

I beg You for Mercy and offer You this gift of fasting for one day every week for this month of June, in atonement for all sins.

Amen

Children you must fast for one day each week in the month of June.

You must recite My Rosary and the Divine Mercy Chaplet daily.

Doing this, children you will save the souls of millions through the Mercy of My Son Jesus Christ.

Your beloved Mother
Mother of Salvation

666 will be embedded, its number hidden, into a chip, which you will be forced to accept just as you would any vaccination.
Friday, June 01, 2012 20:15 hours

My dearly beloved daughter, the antichrist is preparing, already his peace plan, which he will introduce soon after the wars become widespread in the Middle East, and when the pain and terrible anguish means there is no sign of hope.

Then he will appear suddenly and announce himself to the world as a man of peace, a bright jewel, which will sparkle in the midst of darkness.

As he emerges, he will be seen as one of the most charismatic political leaders of all time.

His handsome, appealing and caring personality will fool the majority of people.

He will exude love and compassion and will be seen to be Christian. In time he will draw many followers who will grow in their numbers so that he becomes like Me, the Messiah.

He will be seen to promote unity among all nations and he will be loved in almost every country in the world.

Then he will be seen to have supernatural skills. Many will believe that he has been sent, by My Father, and that he is Me, Jesus Christ, Saviour of the World.

They will pray to him, love him, give up their lives for him and he will laugh and mock them, when they cannot see him.

This will be the biggest deception of all time and the plan is to steal your souls, to take you away from Me.

He and the false prophet, who will sit like a king, in the Seat of Peter, will secretly plot a one-world religion.

This will appear to be a Christian type religion, which promotes love. It will, however, not promote love of one another, which comes from God. Instead it will promote love and allegiance to the antichrist and love of oneself.

The abomination does not stop there, for when they have seduced God's children, the attack will begin.

Suddenly all will be asked to accept the one world Mark of Allegiance, a united world, which all men will have to partake in. It will control your money, your access to food and how you live.

Rules, many of them, will mean that you will become prisoners. The key to your cell, which keeps you under their control, will be the Mark of the Beast.

666 will be embedded, its number hidden, into a chip, which you will be forced to accept, just as you would any vaccination.

Once embedded it will poison, not only your mind and soul, but, your body. For it will cause a plague designed to wipe out much of the world's population.

You must not accept the Mark. Instead I will instruct you what to do.

Many will accept the Mark because they will feel helpless.

The Seal of the Living God, My Crusade Prayer (33) is your lifeline.

When you receive My Seal of Protection, given to you by My Eternal Father, you will not have to accept the Mark.

You will not be touched. Your home will not be seen, searched or a target for it will be rendered invisible in the eyes of Satan's army.

You will need to keep food hidden, which will last a few years. You will need to grow your own crops, store your own water and keep all Holy objects around you.

My Remnant Church will grow and spread out, and you will be given shelter if it is needed.

Much planning is needed now.

Those who laugh at what you do, or say, surely Jesus would not ask you to do this? Does He not supply all His followers at their time of need?

Even one loaf and one fish can be multiplied. So it does not matter if you only have some food, for I will protect you and you will be safe.

Pray hard for those souls who will be unable to avoid the Mark.

Those innocent souls will be saved who are in a state of grace at the time of being forced to accept the chip.

The rest of you must plan to protect your family and your allegiance to the Holy Eucharist and the Mass.

When the antichrist devours all religions the only weapons which he will be powerless against is the Holy Mass and the Transubstantiation of the bread and wine into My Body and Blood, in the Holy Eucharist.

My Masses must continue. Those of you who know this must gather in numbers now and start the preparations.

The sooner you prepare the more graces you will be given to grow your ranks around the world.

The Rock will become laden with a new building, which they say will be My new temple. But, this is untrue.

But, when the persecution ends My Remnant Church and My chosen people will have the Temple rebuilt and My New Jerusalem will come down from Heaven.

She will descend in glory. The trumpets will be heard in Heaven and on earth at the same time.

And then I will come. You, my daughter, will herald my arrival and many will fall on the ground and weep with relief, love and joy in ecstasy.

For, at last, the moment they have been waiting for. The skies will light up, the thunder will peal and the choirs of angels will sing in sweet unison, as all God's children will welcome the True Messiah.

I, Jesus Christ, will come to Judge. And the Heavens and the Earth will become one.

The new glorious splendour, the renewed earth, will emerge and the New Paradise will embrace all those whose names are in the Book of the Living, who will unite as one.

And while the end of the old earth, soiled with the stain of sin, will have come to an end, the New Era is only beginning.

This is what you must strive for. This is what you are entitled to as part of your natural inheritance, only focus on the saving of all souls.

This is why you must ignore the obstacles presented to you, the persecution, the pain, the horror of evil, by the hands of others. All that matters is the saving of souls.

Your Saviour Jesus Christ

Virgin Mary: I revealed these atrocities to the little children, Melanie and Maximin, at LaSalette
Saturday, June 02, 2012 11:00 hours

My child, it is important that all those who love my Son, pray for the graces of strength and perseverance at this time.

The knowledge being revealed to you, children, through these Messages is to help you prepare.

Never feel you, as God's army, will not be able to withstand the evil regime about to show itself in the world shortly.

Always remember the power of my Holy Rosary.

Always remember, the Power of my Father, is the greatest Power of all.

No power is so strong that it can defeat the most Glorious Power of God.

When you are a true child of God, when you come to the Father through my Son, you will be protected.

Fear, is caused by the unknown, but it can also be caused when the Truth is revealed.

Allow the graces, which are being given to you through the Crusade Prayers, to give you the peace of mind and strength of soul to march for the salvation of souls.

The more souls who are converted to the Love of my Son the stronger will your Crusade be.

Love one another and join in prayer to help save God's children from the antichrist.

Pray, pray, pray that every soul will be brave enough to reject his poisonous mark.

I have revealed these atrocities to the little children, Melanie and Maximin, at La Salette, so long ago. The time for these prophecies to unfold is soon.

These children were told of the evil plans and accepted what I told them. Now you, children, must accept that these events must take place.

You must pray hard to dilute and mitigate much of the pain, which will have to be endured by humanity.

Be brave children.

Trust in my Son and allow Him the freedom to guide you, as He must so that souls can be saved from the clutches of the beast.

Your beloved Mother
Mother of Salvation

Jesus: Never falter. Never doubt My Hand of Protection.
Saturday, June 02, 2012 21:00 hours

My dearly beloved daughter, when My followers allow Me to flood their souls with My unconditional Love, I will ignite within them a strength that will startle them.

Come to Me, like trusting children, with a simple and open heart, with no expectations, and I will bring you a peace, which you will not find anywhere else.

While I weep at the way in which evil and greed have gripped the world I am also full of joy because of the pure love My followers show to Me, their Jesus.

How they bring Me solace, comfort and how I wish I could wrap them in My Arms.

How I wish they could hear Me tell them how much I love them.

How I long for the day, when I reach out My Hand, grasp their hand in Mine, and draw them into My New Kingdom when they will come home to Me at last.

That day is not far away.

To all My followers,you must listen to Me at this time.

You must be strong and persevere during the trials ahead and never lose heart.

Walking along the path, carved out for you towards My Kingdom, will hurt you. Many of you will trip and stumble.

Some of you will run back the way you came.

Others will sit down, give up and remain stuck between the beginning of their journey and the Gates to Eternal Life. So weak will their faith become because of the obstacles they will face.

The stronger ones will be fearless. They will want to forge ahead and charge with every ounce of energy into the New Era of Peace.

Nothing will stand in their way. They will know how to withstand the sufferings ahead. They will know how to fight the enemy. With little fear in their hearts, they will listen to every instruction given to them by Me.

They must always strive to go back and carry those who are weaker, those who are fearful. They must carry on their shoulders those who lack the will and the courage to stand up in My Name.

Those who refuse your help will be left behind and will become part of the kingdom of the Beast, from which there is no escape.

Never falter; never doubt My Hand of Protection.

If you submit everything to My Holy Will, I will look after everything.

Trust in Me. Follow Me.

The time is short, yet the time is plentiful in which to prepare for the battle, which lies ahead.

I love all of you. Never forget the Power of My Love.

Your beloved Saviour
King of Salvation
Jesus Christ

Spend the month of June in quiet contemplation, as instructed by My beloved Mother
Sunday, June 03, 2012 15:30 hours

My dearly beloved daughter, My followers must spend the month of June in quiet contemplation, as instructed by My beloved Mother.

This month is the time when, through the Crusade of Conversion, many people can receive the graces of instant conversion through the sacrifices made by those of you who respond to My Mother, the Mother of Salvation.

You need to be quiet this month.

Please, I urge you to visit your churches as much as you can to recite My Divine Mercy Chaplet at 3 O'clock.

Catholics please receive My Holy Eucharist every day, if possible, during this month.

For this month will be the time when the plans, silently underway to increase unrest in the Middle East, are being finalised.

Be strong. Be patient. Be humble of heart.

Submit your will to Me and offer your trials and sacrifices for the conversion of all sinners.

Go in peace, My beloved followers.

My Holy Spirit is covering you all at this time as I beckon you to this special devotion.

Your beloved Jesus

Just as I was rejected the first time I will be rejected the second time
Monday, June 04, 2012 15:20 hours

My dearly beloved daughter, very few of My chosen people, the Jews, accepted Me, as the True Messiah, when I came into the world and died for the sins of mankind.

This time, very few Christians will realise it is I, Who speaks to them now, before I come the second time.

They will believe the lies, which sprout from the lips of liars, the false prophets, whom they will love, while they will reject Me with a hatred that is at odds with their love of God.

Just as I was rejected the first time I will be rejected the second time.

You must not feel sad at the way I am mocked, kicked, punched and My Messages ridiculed. For such hatred against My Holy Word can only come from Satan. If Satan's fury becomes intense as it is now then you can be sure that he worries about the souls I intend to save from his clutches.

Block your ears. Look straight in front of you and focus only on Me.

Every kind of attack will be hurled at you, My followers, to stop you from following Me.

Every argument against My Word by those who boast of their expertise in holy spiritual matters must be cast aside.

They do not have the Holy Spirit in their souls for they are not worthy because of the sin of pride.

Just as I suffered the scourging at the pillar so, too, will I suffer again, as My Holy Word now is torn apart, with hatred, by those who want to ensure that My Word is rejected.

I say to those souls now. If you will not accept My Hand of Mercy, to save humanity, why do you hold such hatred in your hearts?

Don't you know that you are being tempted by the evil one, who wants to blind you to the Truth?

Hatred, calumny and slander do not come from Me. When you allow those vile sins to overcome you, you do not love Me.

You will come back to Me when you come before Me, during The Warning, if you have the humility necessary to ask Me to forgive you.

If you do not remain silent now, you will suffer, and your remorse will leave you weak and trembling before Me.

How you wound Me.

How you make Me suffer.

You scourge Me just as I was scourged the first time, yet you say you are a Holy Disciple of Mine.

You are a cause of great sorrow to Me.

To My followers, I say ignore these taunts.

Do not open your mouths or engage with those who show anger, hatred and who claim, at the same time, to love Me.

How can you love Me when you do not show love or patience to one another?

You are hypocrites if you scourge another in My Name.

Now the time is ripe for the second rejection, no different from the first time.

The ridicule will mean that those self-proclaimed holy disciples, will mock My prophets, by trying to trip them up, by questioning their knowledge of Scripture.

My prophets do not understand Scripture and they will not defend My Word.

Yet these, so called holy disciples, just as it was during the Crowning of Thorns on My Head, will try to make My prophets look stupid and unworthy.

Then they will go to great lengths to name and shame them while professing, at the same time, how knowledgeable they are of My Teachings.

The bullying will continue until it will be relieved, after The Warning, when these souls will realise the error they have made.

They will weep and suffer because of this, but I will forgive them, because I Love them.

But, then many will not repent. They will inflict terrible suffering and persecution on My end time prophets. Not for one moment will they give up.

Every hurt, insult and assault will be hurled at them, in My Name, Jesus Christ, Son of Man.

They will deny Me, through My Holy Word, given to them today, right up to the end.

Then they will be given one more time to accept the Book of Truth. They will either accept Me or reject Me.

Then I will gather all those humble souls who love Me, and the New Heaven and the New Earth will merge.

Those who still reject Me, will be cast into the Fires of Hell.

I come one last time to save you.

Open your hearts and see that it is I, Jesus, who calls you now.

If you cannot see this, then you need much prayer to enable the Holy Spirit to truly enter your souls.

Remember those who are blessed with the Holy Spirit do not insult others, commit calumny or spread hatred against God's children.

They do not want to control God's children.

They do not break the Ten Commandments.

Your Jesus

Satan intends to poison the minds of some of My chosen souls, towards this Mission
Tuesday, June 05, 2012 22:00 hours

My daughter, it is unwise for those who follow My visionaries, all over the world, to succumb to the evil one's new plan. He intends to poison the minds of some of my chosen souls towards this Mission. He will turn one against the other.

He will create doubts amongst them, against these Holy Messages, and it will cause you much grief and sorrow.

The spiritual jealousy will mount like a beast rising from beneath the ocean, and it will pour a terrible deluge of hatred not only upon My Messages, but on you.

You must pray, for it will happen soon.

Await these events in daily prayer and do not allow this series of attacks to discourage you.

My followers must stay alert to this for when it starts, within the next month, you too will be tempted to doubt My Holy Word.

This prophecy will unfold before you and will be the most vicious and hurtful assault on this Mission so far.

Not only will the attacks spring from those who promote the Messages of those they believe to be authentic modern day visionaries and prophets, they will be supported by some of My sacred servants.

The venom will poison many souls and many will reject Me.

Ignore these attacks, My daughter. Move forward and give the world My Messages, as quickly as you can.

It is important that you spread My Holy Word and My prayers, even among those who do not want to listen to Me, for many, when presented with these Messages, will feel a compunction to do so, and they will then be given graces to see the Truth.

Never ever underestimate the power of Satan's influence over you.

He targets, especially, the souls I need to help Me in My Mission to save humanity.

Your beloved Saviour
Jesus Christ

Virgin Mary: Children, when you suffer in this life, you become closer to my Son
Wednesday, June 06, 2012 17:05 hours

Children, when you suffer in this life, you become closer to my Son.

Suffering, hard as it is, brings graces, especially, if it is embraced willingly for the salvation of souls.

When you suffer, always remember how my Son suffered.

His physical torture, remember, would be very difficult to endure by man. Yet mental suffering can create the same pain.

For those who fight suffering, you must ask me, your beloved Mother of Salvation, to help you cope with it.

I will take your suffering and offer it to my Precious Son on your behalf to save souls.

He will only take what He needs and will give you comfort. He will then ease your load.

Suffering can be a form of purification of the soul.

Reject it and fight it and it will not provide relief. It will become a much heavier burden.

When you offer it up with love you will be relieved of your weight and you will become joyful.

Never fear suffering, for it brings you closer to the Sacred Heart of my Son.

Your beloved Mother
Mother of Salvation

600,000 fallen angels were released last year from the pits of Hell. A further 5 million have now been released
Thursday, June 07, 2012 20:00 hours

My dearly beloved daughter, it is time to take up arms in the Heavenly battle, which rages again with Satan and his fallen angels.

Now unleashed in every nation, Satan's army of angels and their devoted disciples on earth, are infesting God's children in every way.

There are the visual signs. The crisis in My Church, the Catholic Church, was created through the forces of evil, whose number one goal, was to bring it to its knees. Not content with this, the forces of evil want to destroy the Holy Eucharist, by defiling it.

By demoralising My Church on earth, the plan by Satan was to destroy the faith of My followers.

Many of My followers no longer pay homage to Me, their Saviour, because they blame the sins of those who represent Me in the Church. How this wounds Me when they forsake Me so quickly.

The apostasy in the world today was also planned by Satan, by tempting God's children to deny their Faith.

Instead he uses a new religion often known as the New Age Religion. Instead of glorifying God, the Eternal Father, they glorify the human being, as spiritually superior and in command.

Like Lucifer who wanted to be not only like God, but, who wanted to become God, this rapidly evolving cult wants to convince God's children that they are in control of their own destiny, that all can be controlled through a false belief in a metaphysical world, which does not exist.

Belief in false gods, such as the Buddha, has harmed so many people and led them into a dark world, which seems to glitter on first inspection, but, which fails to ignite pure love for one another.

Instead all these new age religions amount to one thing, self-obsession and love of one self, at the expense of another.

The wars, which Satan's Masonic orders create, are becoming plentiful and the largest group of all will mastermind control of the Middle East through massacre.

In Europe they will mastermind the introduction of a new one-world currency to make slaves of them.

Satan's grip is so strong that it will take much prayer to topple the power he wields. Then there will be the temptation to turn God's children away from the Truth.

He, Satan, can play havoc with your mind. But, while he does not have the power to know what you think, he can place thoughts and doubts in your mind.

When you resist at first, by praying for the graces to protect yourselves, he increases his activities.

Satan sends his demon angels to believers and torments them. If you could see them it would shock you. Two or three can surround you and can trip you up, cause you to become confused, distressed and your mind filled with uncharitable thoughts against another person.

Anything to do with God, His Churches, His children and those who represent Him on earth are the first targets.

Then he targets those in high places, who have control over the lives of millions. He tempts them with corruption, manipulation of power and the introduction of bad laws, designed to cause pain and hardship.

And then he orchestrates war.

Children, do not ignore the battle for it is real.

600,000 fallen angels were released last year from the pits of Hell.

A further 5 million have now been released. The time for God's army in Heaven, to destroy Satan, has begun. The time for My army on earth, to gather arms, has also begun.

Time is short. We have much work to do.

Prayer is the weapon. Conversion is the goal. I can only achieve the salvation of souls if My Voice is heard at this time.

Satan knows this. He has placed a curse over this Mission and will pull many of God's children away. Yet he cannot win, for no one can stop the Book of Truth being revealed, for it is I, Jesus Christ, who does this.

Yet many poor souls will be convinced to look the other way as I announce the Truth, for all the world to see, as foretold in the Book of Revelation.

Never allow him to engage with you. You can do this by refusing to engage in insults or sneering by others when you proclaim My Holy Word. For to engage with him, you give him the ammunition he needs to wear you down.

Your beloved Jesus
Saviour of all mankind

Free will cannot be taken away from you. I cannot demand that you follow Me
Friday, June 08, 2012 19:05 hours

My dearly beloved daughter, many reading these, My Holy Words given to mankind out of Love, misunderstand My Intentions.

As the Son of Man, My pledge is to save the whole of humanity.

My Crucifixion, on the Cross, was not simply a moment in time, or a moment in history.

It was a Sacrifice, made to offer every single one of you, even today, the Gift of Eternal Life.

This is a solemn Promise. The life of the world to come, My Kingdom on earth, is for everyone.

I come now to prepare you.

I have told you before that while I come to warn you of the dangers in rejecting My Teachings and the Ten Commandments, laid down by My Eternal Father, I cannot command or demand God's children to listen. For the whole of humanity was given a special Gift, as well as, the angels in Heaven, the Gift of free will.

Free will cannot be taken away from you. I cannot demand that you follow Me.

I can warn you, show you the error of your ways, but I cannot demand that you respond to My call.

I can only ask.

Free will, while a Gift, can also be an obstacle, as it will be used by Satan to plant lies in your mind.

He can make demands of a very forcible nature, which you will find very difficult to fight against such is his power.

My patience is being tested, in these, the end times, like never before.

Despite My Death on the Cross, My Life given up with Love, to save each of you, many have forgotten what this Sacrifice really means.

If I gave up My Life for the salvation of mankind, why don't My children listen?

If they do not want to listen to Me now, through these Messages, that is the choice they make of their own free will. Then why do they continue to misinterpret and twist the contents of the Holy Bible?

No matter how much I am rejected, I will never fail in My duty to warn you of the dangers to come.

The dangers I speak of are not just the miseries being planned by Satan's wicked disciples over your nations, control of your money, your food or human life.

No, the dangers you need to be made aware of, most of all are the dangers of losing your soul to Satan and his fallen angels.

Whether you heed My Word now, is entirely up to each and every one of you.

All I ask is that you listen. Failure to listen, to accept the special graces I bestow on your now, means you may not be equipped properly to save your soul from the beast.

I bless you all. To those who are confused, I urge you to select the prayers, given to you through these Messages.

They will help you respond to My Call from Heaven.

Your Jesus

God the Father: I will fight the Battle of Armageddon, with the Hierarchy in the Heavens
Saturday, June 09, 2012 15:45 hours

My sweet daughter, trust that I, your Heavenly Father, will do all in My Power to salvage all of My children on earth.

While I must respect the Gift of free will, bestowed by Me, as one of the greatest gifts, to ensure that mankind would love Me on their own accord, and not by force, I will do wonders and create miracles to bring My children home to Me.

While a God of Justice, I could never condone or accept evil, but, I will forgive all those who turn back to My Son and seek redemption, when they become aware of the contents of the Book of Truth.

I will fight the Battle of Armageddon with the Hierarchy in the Heavens and will, I promise, defeat the enemy and the devils spawned by the hand of Lucifer.

The time is drawing nearer for Satan to be banished for 1,000 years and woe to the man who does not renounce him or his wickedness.

All will be shown the Truth of My Divine Love and My desire for My splendid Kingdom, My Paradise, to be shared with all.

Every attempt, through My prophets, will be made to draw them into the Arms of My Son.

Do not; My children, forsake Me, your Loving Father.

Come hear My Call.

Do not reject your inheritance.

You are now facing the biggest crisis since the Creation of the human race, for the time has come for you to make the final choice.

Be aware that every lie, every temptation to seek solace in the arms of Satan and his devils, will be made to steal your souls.

Only those who spend time protecting their faith, through prayer and the Sacraments, will be strong enough to withstand their power.

Remember that Satan cannot win for he does not have the power. He will now attack all, even holy souls, to reject Me and My beloved Son.

Instead he will suck you into an abyss of darkness and confusion and you will be caught in an intricate web of deceit from which you will be unable to entangle.

Hear Me now. The final battle has begun. Do not make the mistake of rejecting this call, made from the Heavens for it will mean you will be lost for eternity.

O were you to witness the tragedy of souls who will refuse the Cup of Salvation.

They will tumble helplessly, along with Satan, into the depths of Hell, from which there is no return.

I must as your Father, point out the dangers you face.

Why do you not want to listen?

If you believe in Me, then know that I would send My prophets to warn you.

Did I not do this before? Did they listen? No, many did not, and then the prophecy evolved before their disbelieving eyes.

This time I come to announce that the time for My Son, the True Messiah, to come again is near.

Satan knows this. His hatred for Me is so powerful, that he will do everything to snatch My children away from Me.

I am your God, the Beginning and the End.

I Created the world in the beginning and it will be by My Hand that the world, as you know it, will come to an end.

But, for My beloved children, who renounce Satan, the new world, the New Paradise on earth, awaits you in all its glory.

Do not turn your back.

Do not allow flawed human reasoning to prevent you and your loved ones from entering this splendid Paradise, where you will want for nothing.

Choose My Paradise of love, joy and beauty, a special place, where you will live in perfect harmony, in mind, body and spirit.

No corruption. No sin. Just love where you will live in union with My Divine Will.

Your loving Heavenly Father
God the Most High

The false prophet will not only take over the Catholic Church, he will dictate over all Christian Churches
Sunday, June 10, 2012 15:30 hours

My dearly beloved daughter, I call on all My followers to show courage at this time.

This is not the time to fall down and weep. It is the time to fight for your salvation.

I call on all Christian Churches, My clergy and all those who have devoted their lives to Me, their Jesus, to hear My pleas.

Never forsake the Truth of My Teachings.

Never forsake Me.

Never forsake My Church, for I Am the Church.

Never forsake My Body, for I Am the Bread of Life.

Never accept the lies, soon to be implanted among you, to displace My Church on earth.

It is time to prepare.

Soon you will be made to swallow a new religion, which will be manmade.

Soon, you will be force fed, what will seem like the Holy Eucharist, but it will not be My Body.

It will become empty, barren and will yield no real life.

The only Holy Eucharist that exists, is the way in which My Presence is made known in the Holy Sacrifice of the Mass, as it is now.

Never deviate from this, even if you are forced to do so by the heathen who will take over My Christian Churches.

They will desecrate My Churches and turn them into nothing more than places of entertainment and social outlets.

You must always follow the steps I taught My Apostles at the Last Supper.

Now you must ensure that all is in place before the attack begins.

For soon you will find it impossible to follow a false doctrine imposed on you by the abomination that lies ahead.

The false prophet will not only take over the Catholic Church he will dictate over all Christian churches, which he will merge as one.

But, it will not be I, Jesus Christ, that the new temple will be built upon. It will be a temple, to replace the Holy See, to honour the beast.

Heed now My Words, for you will soon see the Truth.

To those brave enough to stand up to this persecution of your Faith you must plan now.

To those who do not have the strength to fight the reign of the antichrist and the false prophet drop down on your knees now and beg Me to help you.

I will guide you through My new leaders who will spring up among you, led by My Two Witnesses.

Enoch and Elijah, present in My Christian Churches on earth and the House of Israel, will influence the preaching's of the Gospels all over the world soon.

Nothing will stop the Teaching of the Truth.

This time will be difficult, but, rise and follow My army on earth, and more souls will be saved. Do not forsake the flock that I have given over to you to lead.

Fear not, because only by following My Path to Eternal Life, can you be saved.

Follow the path of the false prophet and not only will you become lost to Me, but you will lead innocent souls towards the pathway to Hell.

Be brave, My sacred servants.

Accept that the time for My return is imminent. You do not have time to waste.

Your Jesus

Mother of Salvation: Pray for Christian Churches so they will be given the graces to defend their Faith
Monday, June 11, 2012 12:02 hours

All God's children are being called, throughout the world, to gather together as one, to plead for the Mercy of my Eternal Father, at this time.

Children, pour out your hearts to my Father and ask Him to protect you and cover you with the Precious Blood of His Son.

You must pay attention every day from now on to praying to God the Father, in the Name of Jesus Christ, Saviour of the World, for every protection from the evil forces now rampant in every corner.

Pray, pray, pray for the Christian Churches on earth so that they will be given the graces to defend their Faith.

Never give up hope children for once you pledge allegiance to my Son and pray for strength, your prayers will be answered.

Today I ask that you continue with the Conversion Crusade Prayers and the recital of the Most Holy Rosary and the Divine Mercy Chaplet.

This month is designated to the conversion of many nations.

Fasting must continue to save souls and it may be carried out according to each one's means.

Continue, children, to pray for the conversion so needed at this time.

Thank you for responding to my call.

Mother of Salvation

Remember this is a war, which will be won by My Remnant Church on earth
Monday, June 11, 2012 16:30 hours

My dearly beloved daughter, very soon now those souls, inflamed by the Power of the Holy Spirit, because of these Messages, will gather as one in all nations.

They will join together in unison to proclaim My Word so that every lost soul can be grasped from the clutches of the beast.

My Remnant Church will gather quickly and grow through the world and prayer will knit them together as one Holy Church.

I will send help to each of My Two Churches, My Two Witnesses on earth. Then they will rise and with courage proclaim the Truth in every corner of the world.

My Voice will peal like thunder and those who truly love Me, will not fail to recognise Me.

The graces of the Holy Spirit will fire the souls of My soldiers, and they will march forth and help Me save humanity.

Rejoice, My army, for you are blessed to have been chosen for this glorious task.

Through your love for Me, your Divine Saviour, you will help save your poor brothers and sisters from being lost to the evil one.

Come now, My followers, and allow me to lead you through the dense and thorny jungle into the Light of My New Kingdom on earth.

Never fear My Hand as I now lead you fearlessly into the battle against the antichrist.

Remember this is a war, which will be won by My Remnant Church on earth.

Also remember that the number of souls, which can be salvaged, will depend on the strength of your Faith, your generosity of spirit and your willingness to suffer in My Holy Name.

I Love you.

I Bless you.

I give you the graces you need now to pick up your armour and march to Eternal Life.

Your Beloved Jesus

The test of an authentic prophet lies in the prayers given to them for humanity
Tuesday, June 12, 2012 17:58 hours

My dearly beloved daughter, know that I would never condemn those who say they come in My Name, but, who don't.

I love all of God's children, including the false prophets, sent to confuse humanity at this time.

Many such souls are full of love for Me and feel a need to become closer. They can, through no fault of their own, imagine they are receiving Divine Messages. You must pray for such souls. You must never judge them.

Then there are those who say they come in My Name, but who wear the badge of the beast. Wolves in sheep's clothing, they set out to snare the pure souls and stain them with the sin of deception.

These are the dangerous false prophets, whose goal is to twist the Truth of My Teachings, in such a way that they do not appear noticeable.

They will, through an external façade of false humility, have you believe a lie in My Name. They will present a tolerant mask of deceit and you will be convinced that they are spreading the Truth.

The test of an authentic prophet lies in the prayers given to them for humanity.

Conversion spreads quickly by the Power of the Holy Spirit when Messages come from Heaven, and they cover all religions, all faiths, to unite them as one.

I urge for prayer at this time for such souls who have been deceived to believe they speak with the voice from Heaven. Pray for them so that they will be given the strength to seek humility in order to allow them to see the Truth.

Pray that they will not allow their souls to be used by the deceiver to cause confusion among God's children.

Pray, too, for those who do not speak in the Name of God, but who knowingly speak with the tongue of Satan. They also need your prayers, for they are being used mercilessly, by Satan, as a means to spread lies.

Your beloved Jesus

A Pledge of allegiance to the Divine Will of God the Father
Wednesday, June 13, 2012 16:00 hours

My dearly beloved daughter, just as My Eternal Father bequeathed the Great Gift to humanity of His Seal, so, too, must His children pledge their allegiance to His Divine Will. I ask all of God's children who will march forth in His army, to help save the souls of all God's children, including hardened sinners, to take this pledge:

Crusade Prayer (59) A Pledge of Allegiance to the Divine Will

O God the Most High, O Heavenly Father, I pledge to You my firm allegiance to honour and obey You in all things united to Your Divine Will on earth.

I, through the Sacred Blood of Your only beloved Son, the True Messiah, offer You my mind, my body and my soul on behalf of all souls so that we can unite as one in Your Heavenly Kingdom to come, so that Your Divine Will is done on earth as it is in Heaven.

Amen.

You must pledge your souls to My Heavenly Father, as a token of your Faith, and in memory of My Death on the Cross, so that each of you will drink from the Cup of Salvation.

Your Jesus

The Warning, while not to be feared, will cause pain, in those not in a state of grace
Thursday, June 14, 2012 18:15 hours

I, your beloved Jesus wish you, My dearly beloved daughter, to ask all of My followers to heed My Instructions.

Look to each member of your own family; those among your midst, who do not follow My Teachings.

Look amongst you for those souls lost to Me, who outwardly reject Me. Then I ask that you pray hard for them at this time.

You must beg for Mercy for their souls. Your prayers and sacrifices can save them from a terrible suffering during the Purification at The Warning.

The Warning, while not to be feared, and must be welcomed as My special Gift, will cause pain in those who are not in a state of grace.

Prepare your souls beforehand, for healthy souls will find The Warning a joyous event. They will not suffer because they will be in a state of grace, especially if they receive the Sacrament of Confession regularly. Their strength will help those who must go through the pain of Purgatory after The Warning. Help those who will not listen, through the daily recital of My Divine Mercy Chaplet. Offer a sacrifice, to Me, your Jesus, in reparation for the sins of your families.

I will show Mercy to everyone who accepts the black state of their souls, when they are shown their sins during The Warning. Only those with genuine humility and a pure heart will be forgiven.

Those, including children, who forsake Me, are in desperate need of your prayers. Here is the prayer, which you must recite for their conversion during The Warning:

Crusade Prayer (60) Prayer for conversion of families during The Warning

O dear Sweet Jesus, I beg for Mercy for the souls of my family (name them here). I offer you my sufferings, my trials and my prayers to save their souls from the spirit of darkness.

Let not one of these, Your children, denounce You or reject Your Hand of Mercy. Open their hearts to entwine with Your Sacred Heart so that they can seek the forgiveness necessary to save them from the fires of Hell. Give them the chance to make amends so that they can be converted with the Rays of Your Divine Mercy.

Amen.

Children of God, prepare every day for The Warning for it can happen at any time.

Your Jesus

The Skies will be peeled back, as if a roof has opened
Saturday, June 16, 2012 19:40 hours

My dearly beloved daughter, My Word is being heard by millions, throughout the world, as I prepare all of God's children, for My Divine Mercy.

There are those blessed with the Holy Spirit, who will know instantly, upon reading My Messages, that they come from My Divine Lips.

Those who say they know Me, but who fail to recognise Me, still cannot resist reading My Word, although they fight against Me.

They reject Me, yet they are still drawn to My Messages.

Don't they realise that this is the Holy Spirit, which although dormant in their souls, still draws them to Me?

I say this to them. The time has come for soon your grievances will be shown to you during The Warning.

Your hatred of My Word will be revealed to you and then you will know the Truth.

When that happens you must then join your brothers and sisters and fight for the right to defend My Church on earth.

The skies will be peeled back, as if a roof has opened, to reveal the Fires and the Flames of My Divine Mercy.

The earth will be shaken with such force that no man will escape My Eyes, My Spirit or My Gift,

Many will tremble with fear, because it will only be then that many will become aware of their souls, for the very first time.

They will know that their love of their bodies, all the senses they seek to nurture, is meaningless.

They will see every part of the soul, but it won't be through their own eyes, in which they will see it. They will look at their souls through My Eyes.

They will feel ill and nauseous, as I do, when I see the ugliness of their wretched wrongdoings.

They will see how rotten their behaviour was towards others and the evil they did onto their fellow human beings, their brothers and sisters.

Then they will see their love of self, the vanity and love of false idols and will know how this offends Me.

For those, whose sins are so black, they will feel ill, in pain and will not be able to stand the horror of what they have to see. They will need every strength, to withstand the purification needed, to enable them to survive and follow the path of the Truth.

It is important to understand that The Warning is just that. I come to warn God's children, that their sins can and will be forgiven.

I come to show them what the Day of Judgment will be like. This will mean that those who ask for redemption at this stage will be saved.

Those who still reject Me, will be given time to repent, but not much. If they still forfeit My Hand of Mercy, then I will have to withdraw.

Then I will divide the just into one side and the unjust into another. One more chance then to seek redemption and those who refuse My Hand of Love and Mercy will be cast into Hell.

This prophecy has been foretold since the beginning.

Heed The Warning and save your souls while you can.

Your Jesus

Their wicked plans also include a new global vaccination, which will create disease, all over the world
Sunday, June 17, 2012 20:15 hours

My dearly beloved daughter, the plans of the Masonic groups to take over the world currencies are getting close to completion.

Their wicked plans, also include a new global vaccination, which will create disease, all over the world, to cause suffering on a scale never seen before.

Avoid any such sudden global vaccination announced, for it will kill you.

Their evil schemes would shock all those innocent souls who have no idea how powerful they are.

Driven by a lust for power, wealth and a desire to be godlike in all they do, they believe they are invincible.

They control banks, governments and are responsible for causing terror in the Middle East.

They control much of the world's media and the truth of their wickedness is hidden behind so called humanitarian organisations.

Sadly, very few of God's children know of their plans.

Know that the Hand of My Father will fall so suddenly and swiftly on those nations, who protect such evil leaders.

They will be struck with tsunamis and earthquakes of such a magnitude, that they will be wiped out.

Those who believe that they are so powerful, will see fire falling from the skies, just before My Second Coming.

The seas will become lakes of fire and they will find it hard to hide from the hand of punishment poured out upon those wicked souls, who will refuse My Cup.

Defiant up to the end, they will fight My Eternal Father and the Power of the Heavens.

Siding with the antichrist, from the groups from which he evolves, they will realise the error of their ways, when it is too late for them.

Many of these groups, including leaders of banks, governments, heads of large businesses, all of them interlinked, and working together to make paupers out of ordinary people, will convert after The Warning. So this is good.

The time for Me to separate those souls who love Me, from those who side with the evil one is not far away.

Be warned. There will only be so much time in which to convert. The souls most in need of My Mercy, belong to these wicked groups, who have no respect for the Laws of God.

You must pray that they will see the Truth.

You must pray that they stop inflicting hardships through the terrible laws they mean to bring about.

You must pray to stop the genocide they plan, worse than what Hitler did in World War 2.

This group, the largest in number, since their formation in the Middle Ages, are Satan's army. They will be led by the antichrist. They have been planning to bring about their control of banks for decades.

They have been planning the introduction of the Mark of the Beast, a chip which every man and woman will be forced to have implanted in their bodies to access food, for fifteen years.

Now that the time has come for them to unveil their New World Currency, know that prayer, and much of it, can help mitigate much of their plan.

Here is a prayer to avert One World Control.

Crusade Prayer (61) Avert One World Control

O dear Heavenly Father, in memory of the Crucifixion of Your Beloved Son, Jesus Christ, I beg You to protect us, Your children, from the crucifixion being planned to destroy Your children, by the antichrist and his followers.

Give us the graces we need to refuse the Mark of the Beast, and bestow upon us the help we need to fight the evil in the world, spread by those who follow the way of Satan. We beseech You, dear Father, to protect all of Your children in these terrible times, and make us strong enough to stand up and proclaim Your Holy Word at all times.

Amen.

My daughter, I am saddened to have to reveal these things. My followers need to understand what is happening.

Those who do not believe in these Messages, will be in no doubt when the antichrist presents himself, as I have foretold.

You must unite in groups around the world in prayer,

The more of My followers who do this, the stronger will the Presence be of the Holy Spirit, and the weaker then will be the army of Satan.

Try not to be fearful, for such a persecution can be faced fearlessly.

Once you prepare well, by following My instructions, and keeping in daily prayer the time will be swift.

Trust in Me always.

Remember I died for your sins. It is only fitting that you allow Me to lead you in this time towards the New Kingdom on Earth.

Only I, Jesus Christ, can lead you. Remember that without Me you are nothing.

Your Jesus

No prophet has been given Messages by My Beloved Mother and the Holy Trinity, in such abundance
Monday, June 18, 2012 20:36 hours

My dearly beloved daughter, you must not allow the cruel rejection of My Holy Messages, by those followers of Mine, whom you know are especially devoted to My Holy Will, to distract you.

Expect this kind of rejection to increase in intensity, as My Word will be torn into shreds and discarded, as if it is nothing.

The pain of rejection you feel, is My pain. The humiliation and ridicule inflicted upon you is My persecution. Instead of allowing such disapproval to hurt you, you must accept it in silence.

By joyful amidst your tears, for you know by now, that I have always been rejected, even by My own disciples.

If you are to allow rejection of My Word to delay you in spreading My Messages, then fewer souls will be saved.

Always remember that My greatest desire is to save souls.

My Mission must not be sullied by human opinion designed to undermine you.

The Words I give you this evening are not to provide comfort, but to emphasise the urgency of My warnings to the world.

Many of God's messengers have come before you, My daughter, to prepare humanity for My Second Coming.

No prophet has been given Messages by My Beloved Mother and the Holy Trinity in such abundance.

Only these Messages can reveal the secrets of times to come, and offer the blessings needed by all of God's children, up to the last day.

Grasp the Gift of My Word, given to all of humanity, to give you life.

Without My help, you would find it very difficult to withstand the trials, which lie ahead.

All My true messengers are preparing God's children for the Second Coming. Know that this will take place during the lifetime of this generation.

Take My Cup, drink from it, let it fill you with the gift of discernment, so you can help Me save souls.

Your Jesus

Virgin Mary: I can, with my Son, give you the graces and the circle of protection, which no fallen angel can penetrate
Wednesday, June 20, 2012 19:46 hours

My child, how my Son suffers at this time, and how my own suffering is entwined with His.

Those who cause suffering to others, crucify my Son.

When they do terrible things, which cause hardship, pain and death, to God's children, they re-create the Passion of my Son.

Those who follow the path of the deceiver are being tempted every second by the fallen angels led by Satan.

Many of them do not know this, so you must pray for them.

Many of them do not realise that they are being used by the evil one, to achieve his destruction of the human race.

Very soon, they will be discarded, by Satan, when they serve no further purpose.

My Son will be waiting to welcome such sinners back into His Sacred Arms, so Merciful is He.

The wicked plans being perpetrated by Satan, invisible to all, are to bring about grief to my Eternal Father. By hurting their brothers and sisters, those hardened sinners, hurt God.

Never think that they will achieve all that they set out to do.

I, the Mother of God, as Co-Redemptrix and Mediatrix have been given the graces to destroy the serpent. By asking me to help you I can offer you protection, children, from fear.

I can, with my Son, give you the graces and the circle of protection, which no fallen angel can penetrate.

Satan cannot harm or attack all those who say my Holy Rosary every day.

By reciting three or more Rosaries you can extend this protection for others. If even a hundred people could do this, they could save their nation from the contamination spread by the evil one.

You must gather together, children, and pray to protect yourselves.

You must be generous of heart and pray for your enemies, for many of them do not realise what they are doing.

By trusting in my Son, completely, and accepting the Gifts He now brings you, through His Teachings and prophecies, you can wipe out all your fears.

Satan preys and feeds on fear. Face the Truth and use prayer to mitigate the evil plans underway by those evil groups, who want to destroy humanity.

Feel the Love of my Son, by opening your hearts. Hand me, the Mother of Salvation, your worries and I will take them to my Son.

Then I will cover you with my Most Holy Mantle and you will feel a strength, which can only come from Heaven.

Only then will you be filled with peace, courage and the determination to become part of God's army. This army, already forming, is made up of the multitudes across every nation.

They will march to the end and cannot be defeated.

Thank you, my child, for responding to my call.

Your beloved Mother
Mother of Salvation

Come to Me, all of you who feel unworthy. I am waiting for you
Thursday, June 21, 2012 00:05 hours

My dearly beloved daughter, My followers must understand that like any good parent, I will always want what is best for them.

I will never give them everything they ask for, unless it is according to My Most Holy Will.

I will never let them wander off the path of Truth, without coaxing them back to Me.

I will always try to protect them from all harm.

I will also chastise them for any wrongdoing.

I will, and can, become angry when they do evil onto others.

I will also forgive them when they do wrong, if they are truly sorry for the error of their ways.

I am patient. I am not easily shocked and never, nor could I, hold a grudge.

This is why even those who have wandered off lost and who feel empty inside should ask Me to hold them, love them and bring them the Divine Love, that will bring them true peace.

So many people are lost and have forgotten Me.

Many, because of the sinful lives they have led, are reluctant to turn to

Me. They feel awkward, don't know how to pray, and believe wrongly that it is too late for them. How wrong they are. They must never forget that I offered up My Life on earth for each one of you.

I don't give up on souls that easily. I love all those who, through their actions, deeds and thoughts, break My Father's Laws. You are precious to Me. I love you, just as I love all of God's children.

Never believe you are loved less because you sin. Sin, while abhorrent to Me, is the stain with which you were born.

It is almost impossible for any soul on earth not to sin.

Never feel I could never help you or welcome you into My Arms.

You will stand first in line to enter My New Paradise on earth, which will last 1,000 years when you turn to Me. All I asked is that you speak with Me in these words:

Crusade Prayer (62) For Lost and Helpless Sinners

O Jesus, help me for I am a sinner, lost, helpless and in darkness. I am weak and lack the courage to seek You out. Give me the strength to call You now, so that I can break away from the darkness within my soul.

Bring me into Your Light, dear Jesus. Forgive me; help me to become whole again and lead me to Your love, peace and eternal life. I trust You completely and I ask You to take me in mind, body and soul as I surrender to Your Divine Mercy.

Amen.

Come to Me all of you who feel unworthy. I am waiting for you. All it takes is to hold out your hand and reach Me.

I listen. I see. I weep. I love you.

I will never give up until you are in My Arms and My Divine Mercy floods your soul.

Soon you will finally see the Truth of My great Mercy. Your doubts will fall away like an outer shell, to reveal your soul, which will be filled with the Light and you will come running towards Me. I await that day with great hope and joy. Only when every poor lost soul knows that only I, Jesus Christ, can save them, will My Heart be healed. Remember I may condemn the sin, but I love every sinner, no matter what they have done. Never be afraid to come to Me, to talk to Me, for I love you too much to reject you when you show true remorse.

Your beloved Jesus

Man did not evolve from animals, but that is what those, who do not believe in God, would have you believe
Thursday, June 21, 2012 17:30 hours

My dearly beloved daughter, since time began, and when the world was created by My Eternal Father, there has been much confusion about the origin of the human race.

When My Father created the world so that He could have a family, much preparation was made.

He Created the earth, the seas, the plants, the trees, the mountains, the rivers, the animals and then, on the second to last day, when all was in place in Paradise, He Created man. Man while stained with sin is a sacred creature. Animals are there to serve mankind.

Man did not evolve from animals, but that is what those who do not believe in God, would have you believe.

Evolution theories, which claim that man came from animals, are lies. They can never be proved.

Satan, his fallen angels and every devil, which springs from the enemy of God, has convinced man of this terrible lie.

Man is a child of God, but in order to demean the human child of God, Satan wants to create confusion in the hearts of humanity.

Why does he promote this lie through false teachings? So he can prove that man evolved from apes, and then convince them that they were not created, by the Hand of My Eternal Father.

This is one of the greatest lies, perpetrated by the devil, using the souls of those men who claim they are more intelligent than the rest of their brothers and sisters. Scientists declare that man evolved from animal, but they are being deceived.

Science is flawed when it attempts to declare the truth about the creation of the universe.

No man understands the miracle of Divine Creation.

If man believes he knows all the answers about the origins of humanity, based on human reasoning, then he deceives not only other poor souls, but, himself.

When there is no love of God present in such souls who believe in the superiority of human intelligence, then atheism spreads like a weed.

This weed, which grows in every direction contaminates and destroys every crop in sight and creates disease.

The only cure is to seek help from God through humble prayer and ask that the Truth be revealed.

So many untruths spread by atheists, who try to prove that God does not exist, have destroyed millions of souls. Their victims need your prayers.

Atheism is the biggest religion in the world and those who have devoted their lives to this deceit are lost for eternity.

They will face the fires of Hell.

Unless they turn to Me, during or after The Warning, they will suffer a terrible chastisement.

Pray for them.

Your Jesus

When you spread hatred about prophets sent from Heaven, you are guilty of a sin, which has enormous consequences
Sunday, June 24, 2012 17:30 hours

My dearly beloved daughter, how My Heart breaks when I see those who say they are followers of God, but who flaunt His Laws. They are hypocrites.

It is they who say they follow My Father's Commandments yet feel they can condemn others who sin.

First to take Sacred Scripture as a means to proclaim a lie, by promoting so called tolerance, they offend Me greatly.

These are the people who say that it is wrong to believe in Divine Providence.

These are the people who question the seers sent by Heaven throughout the centuries and then try to disprove them, by the use of My Holy Word, laid down in Sacred Scripture.

Any man, who denies My Word, is disloyal to Me.

Any man who sets himself apart from his brothers and sisters, as spiritually and intellectually superior, needs to very careful.

Any man who uses Sacred Scripture to present a twisted version of the Truth, will be punished.

Any man who stands up and proclaims the Truth, yet dismisses My Word given to the world in these, the end times, will be cast aside by Me.

You are guilty of spiritual jealousy and for this you will face punishment.

When you spread hatred about the prophets sent from Heaven you are guilty of a sin, which has enormous consequences.

Because by doing so, you not only proclaim a lie, you obstruct the Word of God.

I ask that you stop your campaign of torment and calumny now. You will never prevent My Word from being heard.

Why do you keep trying to torment this Mission? Don't you know by now that the Fire of The Holy Spirit could not have spread in the way that it has were My Messages not from Heaven?

You are being used by the evil one who will stop at nothing to prevent these, My Holy Messages, from being given to the world.

Message for the Clergy: For those among you who have pledged a vow, as a sacred servant of My Church on earth, hear Me now.

When you publicly denounce My Messages and prevent Me, your Jesus, in this Mission from saving souls, you commit the greatest sin of all.

You will suffer for this and your Purgatory will be experienced on earth. Every man, woman and child will witness your offence against Heaven.

Your flawed assessment of My prophets, will render you spiritually empty and your soul will suffer a torment like no other.

If you are a sacred servant of Mine, and you are unsure of My Voice, as I speak to you now, then you must remain silent. You must pray for discernment before you consider rejecting My Holy Word.

Thousands of My sacred servants will fail to recognise My Word, sent through this prophet for the end times. How this breaks My Heart.

Many will fall under the reign of the antichrist and desert My Church on earth.

Many of My sacred servants will side with the persecutors of My Church. The seduction has already begun.

You are being prepared by the deceiver to reject Me and your pride prevents you from seeing this.

Many of My sacred servants will not be courageous enough to uphold My Church on earth. Many will side with the false prophet and reject My flock whose faith will enable them to seek the Truth.

Don't you know that I am the Church?

Don't you know that the Church will suffer its own crucifixion just as I did?

It will be tormented. It will seem to have been crucified and many will think it will be dead. But, like My Resurrection, it will be raised to life again for you see it cannot be destroyed.

I warn all of My sacred servants who do not recognise the times that you are living in to be alert now as My Church on earth suffers the greatest persecution since the beginning.

You must prepare and open your eyes.

When did you think I would come and warn you? Did you think that it would be some time way into the future? That it would never happen in your lifetime?

The time for My Second Coming is very close.

I will soon divide the good from the wicked after every attempt has been made to convert most of humanity.

It is your duty and responsibility to keep an open mind, heart and soul.

I need you to respond to My pleas to help Me save as many souls as I can.

Follow Me. This is your calling.

This is why you pledged allegiance to Me, your Jesus.

You did not make your vows on your own terms.

You must allow Me to guide you and help defend My Church on earth.

Much damage has been inflicted on My Church. My Church consists of all those who love Me including all of My sacred servants.

You must be strong, brave and loyal. You must not allow fear or the beast to devour your soul.

Listen to My Word before you condemn My prophets.

Never denounce any of My Messages, without praying for discernment. Even then you must be careful that you do not deny God's children the gift of the graces I now bestow on those poor souls who are starved of the Truth of My Teachings.

To those who openly reject My Word, given to this prophet, know that you will beg Me for forgiveness, when the Truth is revealed.

By then, for those who are responsible for turning souls away from My Word, it will be too late.

Those souls lost to Me, because of your wicked tongue, will have no eternal life.

Reject My Word now, or denounce My Message for having errors and you will be cast aside. You are not fit to lead My flock.

Your Saviour
Jesus Christ

I know My own and they know Me
Monday, June 25, 2012 11:50 hours

My dearly beloved daughter, you must never forget the enormity of this Mission.

Many times you will be drawn into traps laid down by the deceiver to trip you up.

Ruthless, he and all those who are easily led by him, will do all they can to discredit My Word, given to you.

You must rise and ignore such taunts.

As you have surrendered your free will, all that matters now is your total obedience to Me.

Allow Me, in My Divine Wisdom, to lay out before you My perfect pathway to Paradise on Earth.

My followers must heed My warning also. You will come under fierce attack, each and every one of you, for proclaiming My Word.

This is a Mission like no other. You, My army, will lead the flock of My Remnant Church to the gates of Paradise.

This will cause you much personal persecution and it will not be an easy journey.

You must unite together and give each other strength, for in numbers, you will find comfort in each other. In all corners of the earth, My army gathers now.

All seers who are communicated with the Divine Truth, through My Mother, will ignite the Flame of the Holy Spirit along with My prophets, so that the remnant army is adequately prepared for the battle ahead.

Never doubt My Love. Remember that only those who follow Me can enter the New Paradise. When those who come to you torment you, remember your duty is to forgive them and then pray for their souls.

Show love to those who torment you, in My Name. This way you can defeat Satan and he loses his power over you.

I will instruct you every step of your journey. I walk with you always. I know My own and they know Me.

Your Jesus

New Paradise: You will be made of a pure body, incorruptible, free from disease, physical death and aging
Tuesday, June 26, 2012 20:00 hours

My dearly beloved daughter, the New Paradise has now been completed in its full glory, ready for all of God's children on earth.

It will be presented, in all its glory, just like the Paradise created by My Eternal Father for His children in the beginning.

How the angels sing and rejoice for the time to unveil this great splendour to a disbelieving world is very close.

It will be presented by Me, when the New Jerusalem descends upon the earth, at the ringing of My Second Coming.

You, My daughter, will be told to announce this just before I make Myself known.

Only those who accept Me, as the Messiah, will be able to enter its magnificent gates.

Every call from Heaven will be made to reach out to all those who will still reject My great gift right up to the very last trumpet.

Then it will be too late for those poor souls. They will be beyond help after that, as My Mercy will have been thrown back in My Face, in outright rejection.

All that matters now is to warn all those who are in danger of losing their souls to Satan.

Gather them up, My followers. Coax them gently into My flock. Never give up your prayers to salvage them.

O My beloved followers, if you could see the New Paradise when Heaven and Earth will merge as one, you would drop down on your knees and weep with joy and relief.

For those of you frightened about the end times, when the earth as you know it will change, then you must allow Me to ease your worries.

You will take your family with you and all will rejoice in pure utter love and harmony.

You will be made of a pure body, incorruptible, free from disease, physical death and aging.

You all will have your own dwelling with grass, trees, mountains, rivers, streams and flowers surrounding you in all their glorious beauty.

Animals will be tame and live in peace and in harmony with all of God's children.

You will see your children marry, have children and the miracle of families, risen from the dead, will be witnessed by all.

This resurrection will be like no other joy imaginable.

You will be reunited with your loved ones who passed away in this life and went to Heaven.

You will have nations, twelve in total, all signified by the twelve stars in the crown on my My Mother's Immaculate Head, all of which, will be governed by Me with My Apostles and Prophets.

This is My Kingdom, promised by My Father, since He created Paradise on Earth. Anyone who rejects it will perish.

Pray that all of God's children will have the purity of soul to enable them to come home to My Father's Kingdom on Earth, as it was in the beginning, is now and ever shall be world without end, for ever and ever.

Your Jesus

God the Father: I reveal My future plans for the New Heavens and the New Earth
Wednesday, June 27, 2012 20:00 hours

My dearest daughter, today I reveal to all My children My future plans for the New Heavens and the New Earth

When they merge into one glorious Paradise there will be twelve nations.

These nations will consist of some nations in the world who have shown allegiance to Me, God the Father, My Son Jesus Christ and the Mother of God, Queen of Heaven.

Those scattered will be brought together to join those other nations as one, united as one Holy Family.

My Will, will be honoured. You will all have the gift of free will, but it will be entwined with Mine. Only then will the truth of Paradise be truly revealed.

My Twelve nations are signified in the twelve stars on the woman in the Book of Revelation.

The woman is the Mother of God and she wears the twelve stars to signify two things.

The twelve apostles helped My Son to set up His Church on Earth.

The twelve specially chosen nations will form the One True Apostolic Church on the New Earth, when Heaven and Earth merge as one in My New Glorious Paradise.

This is the moment I have been waiting patiently for.

My Divine Will, which created Paradise for Adam and Eve and which was thrown aside caused by temptation by the evil one, will now be done, and this time Paradise will be perfect.

My Son, King of Mankind, King of the Universe, will reign over My New Paradise on Earth.

He will appoint leaders in every nation all joined together by My Divine Will.

The people of those nations will honour My Son in the way in which He must be, the only way, in peace and love for one another.

His Blessed Mother, the Mother of Salvation, was crowned Queen of Heaven and will also reign as Queen of the New Paradise.

Her Coronation in Heaven was a very special Divine Manifestation of her role in the future of the salvation of the world.

She was crowned in great honour and splendour for the role she played, not only as the Mother of God and as spouse of the Holy Spirit, but, as the Mother of Salvation given the power to destroy Satan.

It was My Beloved Son who lovingly placed the crown of twelve stars on the head of the Mother of God at her Coronation.

It will be My Son who will place the crown on her head in the New Paradise as Queen of all God's children.

My Divine Plan to save humanity has already begun.

It is My desire that this Mission will help Me gather lost souls in every corner of the earth and save them from the enemy before it is too late.

My Divine Intervention will prove My Love for all of My children.

Nothing is impossible. Nothing is hopeless in My battle against Satan's army.

I will bring you a new world that will astound you in all its magnificent glory. It is ready.

Its beauty and splendour is beyond your human capacity to envisage.

When you do witness it, you will have eternal life.

Pray that those poor children of mine who do not believe in Me, God the Most High, who do not obey My Laws and who commit terrible atrocities against each other, repent.

I do not want to lose one child of Mine.

Help Me to bring them this wonderful glorious inheritance. Unfortunately it must be by their own free will.

I love you, children, with a passion unknown to humanity.

Come to Me through My Son as one.

The time for the New Paradise on earth is very near, but, you have been accorded the time to help convert humanity through this Mission of the 7th Angel on earth, who works with My Son to bring My family to Me.

Your Loving Father
Creator of all things visible and invisible
God the Most High

My Church must trust Me. They must remove their shackles of fear and doubt and allow Me to make Myself known
Thursday, June 28, 2012 15:00 hours

My dearly beloved daughter, it must be known that those who profess to come in My Name, as prophets, but who do not speak in the tongues from Heaven, are increasing in numbers.

So many of these souls are being infected by fallen angels and speak in carefully constructed, but, loving tones, reminiscent of what you would expect to be My Sacred Voice.

Oh how My poor devoted followers are being deceived now and how confused they will be. Who to trust? Who to follow? Who to believe?

Did I not say that many will come in My Name, but few will speak with My Voice?

There are fewer than twenty who have permission to impart to the world the Word of God and this includes those who are given Divine Messages from Heaven by My beloved Mother.

Many other seers are also present in the world, but their mission is different.

Their role can be one of daily prayer, to help save humanity or one of personal suffering, offered up as a gift to me, to save souls from Satan. Suffering in this way, willingly, crushes the power of Satan, over many, many souls.

My prophets are few and you will know them by My true Voice, which will strike the hearts and souls of God's children, in a way, which is impossible to ignore.

My Messages to the world for these times will be detailed and will unveil Truths not revealed before.

Much of what I give you now is simply to remind you of My Teachings.

Much of what I present to you now is the food of life, given to you through My Crusade Prayers, to help save your souls and those of others at My Second Coming.

Many other Messages given to others will be similar, but will not go into as much detail.

Their missions are just as important as they will convert souls.

Always remember this. I am trying to show you how much I love you and wish to reveal the Truth of My Existence.

The proof of this will at last be revealed to all of God's children soon.

Please do not fight amongst each other trying to outdo each other in terms of your spiritual knowledge.

The Truth is this.

No man knows the Truth contained in the Seal hidden in the Book of Revelation.

As I have told you before, they were sealed up, in the Book of Truth, until now, the end times.

I, Jesus Christ, the Lamb of God, now open these to prepare you for My New Kingdom.

You have been given the Holy Scripture to prepare you and now you must allow Me, the King of all Mankind, to tell you the Truth of what is to come.

By doing this I will be able to lead you through what will be a minefield of deceit, persecution and hatred.

Allow Me, all of you, including all members of My Church on earth, to bring you over these last hurdles to eternal life.

My Church must trust Me. They must remove their shackles of fear and doubt and allow Me make to myself known through these Messages.

Recognise My Love in its pure and simple form.

My Love is not sophisticated and shrouded in mystical syllables.

It is plain for you to see, but full of such compassion that it will cut through you like a flame of recognition when you drop your armour of pride and fear.

When you do this it will become easier for you to follow Me, Your Jesus.

I came as Saviour the first time.

I come, once again, as Saviour, this last time. Only this time My task is even heavier.

The Love of God has died in the world. It is only a flicker.

Were My Second Coming to take place now few would enter Paradise.

The Warning, My Gift of My Divine Mercy, will help convert most of humanity.

Help Me prepare My flock. I need My Church on earth, both clergy and laity, to help Me save all of God's children.

Please accept My Hand, as I reach out and stretch My Call to all nations.

Come with Me, your beloved Jesus.

Follow Me this time.

Do not reject Me like the Pharisees did. This time, you should recognise My Voice.

You should know how I speak by now for you have been given the Holy Scriptures.

Your Jesus

Virgin Mary: So many false religions and false doctrines, created out of the imagination of humanity, now infest the earth
Friday, June 29, 2012 09:20 hours

My child, a terrible darkness descends over the world as the apostasy, which grips it, deepens.

Love for God has been cast aside.

Love for my Son has dwindled and, in its place, is a love of oneself.

Greed and a love of power, infests souls everywhere and the pursuit of self-love has been admired and accepted as being the correct way to live your lives.

Children, it is at this time that you must pray to help enlighten those souls who are in the dark.

They do not know the Truth of my Son's Sacrifice or what His terrible Crucifixion meant.

His Gift of Salvation has been cast aside as if it never happened. Then those who are aware of what His Death on the Cross meant have decided to look to different false gods in order to bring them peace. They will never achieve such peace.

Peace of soul can only be brought about through allegiance and prayer to my Son. Only the pure and humble of heart, who place their full trust in Him, can have eternal life.

So many false religions and false doctrines, created out of the imagination of humanity, now infest the earth.

So many are being guided by dangerous false beliefs that they will lead lost souls to Hell.

The fallen angels are everywhere, children. Be on your guard for they will target, especially, all those who honour me, your Beloved Mother, in order to confuse you.

They will prevent you from praying. They will plant constant doubts about the Love of God in your minds. They will distract you with temptations of the senses. It will take much prayer to keep them away. My Rosary is your most important protection.

My Son, at this time, is granting many graces to those who listen, hear and accept His Holy Messages to the world.

He does this to give you strength and perseverance in this Mission to save humanity from eternal damnation.

Accept these graces, Children, with love for you are very special to have been chosen to follow Him at this time.

As His Remnant Church on earth you will need the Bread of Life at all times for you will not find this journey easy.

Here is a special Crusade Prayer to help keep you strong in your Mission.

Crusade Prayer (63) Preserve me on this journey

My beloved Mother of Salvation, I ask you to pray that I am given the Food of Life to preserve me on this journey to help save all of God's children. Please help all those who are being deceived by false idols and false gods, to open their eyes to the Truth of your Son's Death on the Cross, to save every one of God's children and to bring each one eternal life.

Amen.

Your beloved Mother
Mother of Salvation

The Sacraments of the Holy Confession, Baptism, Marriage and the Holy Eucharist must be preserved
Sunday, July 01, 2012 15:45 hours

My dearly beloved daughter, how sin crushes Me at this moment, and how I suffer the torment of rejection.

My Head is being crushed like the thorns in My Crown just as the Head of My Church, My Holy Vicar on earth, suffers the pain through the persecution he endures at the hand of his enemies.

My Church on earth, My Body on earth is one. The crucifixion is being prepared.

The doctrines of My Church, just as My Teachings on earth were torn asunder by those Pharisees and those who thought they knew the Word of My Father, more than I did, will soon be thrown asunder.

You must all pray for My Church on earth. You must always remember that no other doctrine exists other than that proclaimed by Me, during My time on earth.

All that is the Truth will never be changed for if it is you will be forced to swallow a lie.

My daughter, never allow those who continued to reject My Word at this time to discourage you, or My followers, from helping Me to salvage My Church on earth.

For once the enemy attacks My Church you must join together and ensure that the Gospels are spread to the ends of the earth. The Sacraments of the Holy Confession, Baptism, Marriage and the Holy Eucharist must be preserved. Even these will be made difficult to access.

My sacred servants who love Me must begin preparation now. Very soon you will be forbidden to offer such Gifts to God's children.

The time for preparation has begun.

Allow Me to instruct you, lead you and help you bring My Remnant Church to the gates of Paradise.

Your beloved Jesus

My Word is My Word. No man can defend My Word for it is cast in stone
Monday, July 02, 2012 18:00 hours

My dearly beloved daughter, it is important that My followers remain patient.

The future must never be hurried.

The plans, determined by My Eternal Father, will evolve naturally, by Divine Providence.

Time afforded to you, to help Me prepare humanity for My Great Mercy, is very precious. It is a time in which many will be saved through your prayers.

Hope, faith and love for Me, your beloved Jesus, will sustain you in your Mission.

When you witness the atrocities before you, when everything, which stands in honour of Me is destroyed, you will know then that the time is getting closer.

You must remember that these things must come to pass and that your duty is to fight and resist the enemy as part of My army.

My army will be equipped with Divine Gifts and it will sweep along with it those who are in darkness.

Preparation takes time. Prayer brings you closer to My Sacred Heart and floods your souls with the oxygen it needs to survive the battle ahead.

As you grow stronger with the graces I give you, it will become very easy to identify your enemies who hate all that I stand for. This will cause you pain, hurt and anger, but you must remain dignified in My Name at all times.

When you are challenged in My Name you must respond with love. Never try to analyse My Messages for you do not need to do so.

My Word is My Word. No man can defend My Word for it is cast in stone.

Any man, who tries to break My Word or cast aspersions on it, will fail for they are powerless against My Holy Word.

Now that you know My Voice, you must know the pain you can expect to endure when you proclaim My Word, in these times.

Mention My Name today, even among so called Christians, and there is an uncomfortable silence.

Talk openly about good and evil and you will be sneered at. Point out how sin can destroy your children and you will be asked – what is sin?

Today many do not know what sin is. Many accept sin as a normal part, an acceptable trait, in their lives.

They are happy to condone sin because it gives them the freedom to pursue other pleasures, idolise false gods and satisfy their lusts.

No they do not want to listen for it does not suit them.

You, My beloved followers, will be seen as being obsessed with a love for religion and a love of God, which today bears little fruit in the eyes of the blind.

This is why you must prepare. This is why you must be strong. It will be for these very souls that you will need to pray and help Me salvage.

Allowing such souls to upset you, hurt you or insult you, is a waste of time.

Respond with love and a dignified silence.

Never be afraid to proclaim Me, but never force Me upon souls in such a way where they will run away from you. Instead bring them to Me through your prayers and sufferings.

I bless you My strong brave army.

I love you.

I walk with you every step you mount to bring Me souls.

Your beloved Jesus Christ

The worst suffering of all is the spiritual emptiness where you cannot feel one ounce of love for Me, your Jesus
Tuesday, July 03, 2012 20:00 hours

My dearly beloved daughter, when I send you trials, such as spiritual dryness, you must learn to recognise them as such.

You must also accept that when you endure such dryness of soul, that it is for a reason. The reason is to save souls through such suffering.

Many victim souls believe suffering is one of two things. Firstly, there is the external persecution, which you will suffer because of your work. Then there is the physical suffering, offered freely to Me, as a Gift, to save the souls of millions.

Then the worst suffering of all is the spiritual emptiness where you cannot feel one ounce of love for Me, your Jesus, where no amount of praying releases you from the prison of desolation.

Try, as you will prayer will become tortuous.

Try, as you will to feel love and compassion for Me and you will struggle. This is a form of spiritual abandonment, where I seem to be so far away that you can no longer reach out to Me. What you do not know is this. This is a Gift, a grace from Me. It raises you up in My Eyes, and the trials and sufferings you endure, are allowed by Me because of your generous and pure love, to save blackened souls.

It may seem unfair, but, the closer you come to My Sacred Heart, the more you suffer My own persecution, because of the sins of mankind.

Only those with pure humble hearts, with no personal regard for themselves, when they place Me before all that is of this earth, can endure My pain.

Such souls are chosen carefully by Me and will work with Me, through their gift of suffering, to help Me in My Plan of Salvation.

Never fear, My daughter, that I am not there. You may not feel My Presence, see Me or feel a deep love for Me, as you would normally do, but I am by your side.

Always trust in Me, My beloved followers, even when you find it hard to pray.

Trust in Me when you feel a longing for Me, which cannot be satisfied or quenched, no matter how hard you try to communicate with Me.

Know when this happens that I am much closer than you realise.

Know that it is at these times that I elevate you to become a true solider, a true fighter in My battle to save souls.

I love you. Never give up. Never feel disillusioned for I walk with you always.

The day will come when the suffering will be forgotten. In its place will be a joy which will surge through the world and which will only be possible because of your sacrifices for all of God's children who need your help.

Your Jesus

Virgin Mary: Whatever happens in the world children you must know that God, the Most High, is in command

Wednesday, July 04, 2012 12:50 hours

My child, those who have witnessed the miracles of my appearances on earth will know that the time for the secrets and the prophecies foretold will unfold soon.

Children I have made myself known in the world for some time to help prepare you for the glorious return of my Son.

My Son is preparing all of you, through the visionaries and the prophets, so that you will be made worthy to receive His Gift of eternal life.

You must never be fearful of the future if you believe in my Son, because He is the Bread of Life, and you will have a wonderful new future.

Whatever happens in the world, children, you must know that God the Most High is in command.

The serpent has little power against My Father.

The serpent's power is only strengthened, by those who fall prey to sin, and the temptations he puts in their way.

Man becomes a prisoner when he sins, because his power to resist other sins and offenses against My Father weakens.

Then he continues to sin, until he is engulfed with a darkness, which is so thick that he cannot escape from it, no matter how hard he tries.

Children you are now obliged, out of your love for my Son, to help those poor souls.

Only you can help them and save them because many will not be able to help themselves.

You are the soldiers my Son needs at this time. It will be through your love for Him, that He will grant graces upon lost souls, when you invoke His help, through your prayers.

Here is the Crusade Prayer to save sinners.

Crusade Prayer (64) Save my brothers and sisters

Oh my dearest Saviour, Jesus Christ, accept my gift of prayer and sacrifices to help save my brothers and sisters from the prison of darkness they are in. Allow me to help salvage their souls.

I beg You to forgive them for their sins, and I ask that You flood their souls with the Holy Spirit, so that they will run into Your Arms as the refuge they so desperately need, before they are lost forever. I offer You my gift of surrender for such souls, in humble servitude and thanksgiving.

Amen.

Children, you are one with my Son.

Your love brings Him great comfort and your sacrifices and prayers will help Him to bring all of humanity into the safety of His New Paradise on earth.

Only then can the Holy Family of God the Most High re-unite and live in peace forever and ever.

Your beloved Mother
Mother of Salvation

God the Father: No man can explain how I Created the universe or humanity, no matter how they try, for it is impossible
Thursday, July 05, 2012 15:30 hours

My dearest daughter, help Me in My grief as I weep for all of My children, who refuse to accept that I Exist.

How I yearn for them.

How I weep for their poor souls.

So intelligent and smart in the way of human understanding, they fail to grasp the Truth of who I Am.

I Am the beginning.

I Am the Creator of all that is.

I Am their Father, although they reject Me.

If they could only see the Truth.

If they could only allow Me to touch their hearts so I could show them My wonderful and glorious plans which await them.

Many of these souls do not know Me, through no fault of their own.

Those souls will be shown the Truth so that they will choose My Path.

Then those who were given the Truth, but, who allowed human reasoning and the glorification of human intelligence to blind them, are now lost to Me.

Many such souls will convert, but many will refuse the Cup of Salvation presented to them by My Beloved Son.

Children of My Heart, I beg you. Help Me save My precious children.

My tears flow at this time and I ask you to bring them to Me through the Divine Mercy of My Son.

So many of these souls include young children, who defiantly and publicly reject Me, in order to show others how smart they are.

An exaggerated respect for human intelligence is a temptation driven into the souls of My children by the enemy.

The beast devours My children's souls and they have no idea what he is doing to them.

So many fallen angels convince humanity that human intelligence is faultless. When mankind believes, or convinces himself, that he knows the Divine Law of Creation, he has fallen into a deceitful trap.

No man can explain how I Created the universe or humanity, no matter how they try for it is impossible.

When will they learn?

When will they see that those children of Mine, pure, simple and humble souls who accept Me, understand the simple truth?

They do not need proof because they feel My Love in their pure hearts, which they leave open, so I can flood their souls with Divine Graces.

I Am your God, your Creator and your Natural Father.

My children must come to Me through My Beloved Son and through their own free will. I cannot force them. You, My children, have been given the power to help save their souls.

All of you who respond to My plea to save your brothers and sisters through prayer and sacrifice will be granted special graces. My Power is infinite.

My miracles, aligned with the suffering and prayers of My children, will be used to save lost souls from eternal death.

I love you, My beloved children. Come and help Me unite My cherished family and help My Son to defeat the beast, before it steals any more of My children.

Your Loving Father
God the Most High

One third of the earth will be destroyed as the angels pour fire from the four corners of the Heavens
Friday, July 06, 2012 16:15 hours

My dearly beloved daughter, the time has been set aside so that these, My Holy Messages to the world, are heard by every soul, young and old, throughout each nation.

Many of God's children will sit up and listen to My instructions, if they are given access to these Messages.

Know now that changes have already begun as prophesied where the crops will no longer yield their fruit as before and when the seasons will no longer be the same.

These changes are by the Hand of My Eternal Father as He brings in new laws of the earth, which no man will fail to notice.

Nothing in the world by the laws of nature will remain as they once did.

The seas will rise, the waters will pour, the earth will shake and the soil will become barren.

My Father will impose a great chastisement to stop the spread of sin, which is a source of great sorrow for Him.

Those nations, which defy His Laws, will suffer much. They will soon understand that their sins will no longer be tolerated and they will be punished.

Their punishment is to prevent them from infesting other souls and unless they change their wicked ways they will be forced to do so through Divine Intervention.

My daughter, you must spread My Word quickly now as The Warning draws closer.

Many nations must be given the Book of Truth so that they can prepare themselves for My Second Coming.

The time for My Second Coming will be after The Warning.

Chastisements, handed down by the angels in Heaven, by the command of My Father, have commenced in stages. These will continue to escalate as sin continues to surge.

The battle has begun and the early stages can be seen in many countries.

You will all bear witness to climate destruction, which will rain upon the earth as it groans in pain because of the degradation of sin.

The shaking will increase and nation after nation will suffer according to the stain of sin, which corrupts its core.

Leaders who follow the antichrist will not escape the Eye of My Father and they will be destroyed.

My Father punishes those who lead wicked governments now, in order to salvage His children from their wicked grasp.

He will not stand back and watch as these leaders who follow the antichrist, who remains hidden at this time, destroy His children.

One third of the earth will be destroyed as the angels pour fire from the four corners of the Heavens.

Then many will know that something is wrong and that is caused because of the Anger of My Father.

Yet many will still not learn. After the Warning, many will convert. Yet many won't even when they are all given the proof of the state of their souls.

They will still idolise the false allure, which they think the earth has to offer. Only this time their lusts and those material idols they worship will become even more obscene and wicked. All their sins, visible to all those who can see them for what they are, will become so ugly that few of God's children will be able to bear to watch.

Every abhorrent sin will be publicly displayed with contempt for God. Every action will degrade the sinner to such depths that they will behave like animals.

All respect for the human body will disappear and every evil lust will be flaunted for the world to see without any shame in their souls.

These are Satan's prisoners. All of them are children of God, but they will lose their souls to the beast.

Chastisements are part of God's plans to cleanse the earth in order to purify both the sinner and the ground you walk on.

Only when the earth is purified can My Second Coming take place.

Pray, My followers, for the courage and the fortitude to deal with these chastisements.

You must never fear them for you, My army, will pray for those nations and help in the purification needed for the conversion of humanity.

The Seal of the Living God will protect each and every one of you.

It is because of the Love My Father has for all of His children that He must chastise them for if He doesn't they will march forward, unwittingly, towards the gates of Hell.

Your Jesus

They may not listen, but, they must be given the Word of God
Saturday, July 07, 2012 15:30 hours

My dearly beloved daughter, when I ask humanity to listen to My Voice, it wounds Me when those who love Me say, I would never speak in this way.

If only they would listen, then My Heart would be lifted and so many more souls would be saved.

The preparation for My Second Coming is being imparted by My Divine Lips through these Messages. The preparation for My birth was also made known through the prophets beforehand to alert God's children to the coming of the Messiah.

Why do My disciples on earth refuse to accept that My Father would send His prophets to herald My Second Coming?

How little they really know about the way in which My Eternal Father prepares humanity for great events.

My clergy, My sacred servants, need to hear My Call now for I need their help. Yet many will fail to respond. They will reject Me, through My Messages.

They will realise the Truth, but, only when it is too late.

My daughter, never be afraid to publish My Messages, including those you find strange or frightening.

They may not listen, but they must be given the Word of God.

It is not for man to dictate that you stop imparting the Holy Word of God.

Close your ears and ignore the scorn of opinion, for it is not important.

To those of you who call yourselves Christians and who pour scorn on My Message I say this.

By tearing My Word asunder, by finding My Messages offensive and by ridiculing My Word you have cut the cord, which binds you to My Heart.

You cannot accept My Messages because you think you know Me and recognise My Words when they are spoken. Instead, you have fallen prey to the deceiver who blinds you to the Truth.

I call on all of you, once again, to call on Me, your beloved Jesus, and allow Me to open your hearts.

Let Me fill you with the Power of the Holy Spirit, so that you will recognise Me.

To priests, I urge that you understand that the time has come for the prophecies of Daniel to unfold and for the Seals in the Book of Revelation to be opened by Me, the Lamb of God.

Remind yourselves of My Promise.

I will come again to judge the living and the dead.

My Promise to bring eternal life to all those loyal to Me is about to unfold.

You must ensure that you have prepared adequately for this Glorious Event.

Your Jesus

Be warned. The New World Religion will seem, on the outside, a good and holy organisation, full of love and compassion
Sunday, July 08, 2012 17:17 hours

My dearly beloved daughter, the great apostasy I spoke of is now gathering pace in the world.

This time it spreads like a veil over My Holy Church on earth and clouds its vision like a deep fog.

This is the time for the great separation of My Church into two camps.

On the one side you will have My beloved loyal sacred servants who follow My Teachings and who never deviate from them.

On the other side there are those priests and other leaders in My Christian Churches who are influenced by modern life and who will desecrate My Laws.

They bow to the pressures from people who demand that they show tolerance in the Name of God by changing God's Laws to suit human demands.

They are full of pride, arrogance and worldly ambitions. Not to them will it matter if they change the Holy Sacraments to suit a sinful agenda.

No they will facilitate acts of abomination to be committed in My Father's Churches and all in the name of civil rights and tolerance.

They will condone sin and will insult Me by parading such sins in front of My Sacred Tabernacles expecting Me to swallow such vile acts. Soon they will abolish the Sacraments to suit all.

In their place there will be held celebration parties and other forms of entertainment.

This will become a New World church which will boast an impressive building in Rome, but which will not honour God.

It will be built with secret satanic symbols for all to see and it will idolise the beast.

Every sin, abhorrent to My beloved Father will be publicly honoured and millions of people will accept their laws of depravity as being worthy in the Eyes of God.

My sacred servants who remain loyal to me will have to hold secret Masses or face imprisonment.

They will gather in force and, filled with the Holy Spirit, they will continue to feed God's children with the Food of Life.

They must ensure that all those they lead are offered the protection of the Seal of the Living God.

The time is very close now for the new temple, to be built in honour of the beast.

This will be built under the dictatorship of the antichrist who will enter the world stage shortly as the man of peace.

Gather together all My followers as soon as you can. My priests who recognise My Voice, you must begin your preparations to ensure that My Church on earth can endure, with strength, the forthcoming persecution.

In time, the refuges will be ready for you to use, for I have been instructing My followers for some time to ensure that they will serve your purpose.

This persecution will be short and you will get through it, painful though it will be.

Be warned. The New World religion will seem, on the outside a good and holy organisation, full of love and compassion.

It will exude a magnificent image of tolerance and will extol every sin know to God. It will twist each sin so that it appears to become acceptable in the Eyes of God.

But, you must know that such abomination sickens Me, and woe to those who follow this dangerous path to eternal damnation.

Sin will always be sin in My Eyes.

Time does not change this. New rules, to suit man's craving for sinful pursuits, will never be accepted by Me.

Prepare now for this great deception for it will take place very soon.

Your Jesus

Every person alive in the world will see their souls and know, for the first time in many cases, that they have one
Monday, July 09, 2012 23:00 hours

My dearly beloved daughter, I wish to prepare all of My followers now, in a way which will not only help them, but, all their loved ones, for The Warning.

It is not enough to repent because of fear. A penance is required.

For all of you My followers hear My instructions now to prepare your souls for The Warning.

You must begin by meditating on all the wrongdoing you are guilty of against yourselves and your neighbours.

For Catholics among you, you must receive the Sacrament of Confession every two weeks, if you wish to remain in a state of grace.

In this way your pain, during The Warning, will be mild and you will have the strength to help your brothers and sisters who will suffer a terrible pain and guilt as they try to come to terms with the illumination of their conscience.

For those among you, who are Christians or other creeds, and who believe in these Messages, you must recite the prayer given to you through **Crusade Prayer (24) Plenary Indulgence for Absolution**

You must say this prayer for seven consecutive days and I, your Jesus, will grant you pardon.

O My Jesus, You are the Light of the earth. You are the Flame that touches all souls. Your Mercy and Love knows no bounds. We are not worthy of the Sacrifice you made by your death on the Cross, yet we know that Your Love for us is greater than the love we hold for You. Grant us O Lord the gift of humility so that we are deserving of Your New Kingdom. Fill us with the Holy Spirit so we can march forth and lead Your army to proclaim the Truth of Your Holy Word and prepare our brothers and sisters for the Glory of Your Second Coming on earth. We honour You. We Praise You. We offer ourselves, our sorrows, our sufferings as a gift to You to save souls. We love You Jesus. Have Mercy on all Your children wherever they may be.

Amen.

I now bequeath a special prayer also for you to say for those poor souls who may die of shock during The Warning and who may be in mortal sin.

Crusade Prayer (65) For those in mortal sin

Oh Dear Jesus, Saviour of mankind, through Your Divine Mercy I plead for clemency for all those poor souls in sin who may be taken from this earth during The Warning. Forgive them their sins and in memory of Your Passion, I beg You to grant Me this special favour in atonement for their sins. I offer myself to You in mind, body and soul as a penance to salvage their souls, and to bring them eternal life.

Amen.

My followers, The Warning will be a great event of Salvation where I will prove to the world My Divine Mercy.

Every person alive in the world will see their souls and know, for the first time in many cases, that they have one.

The time is short now and you must start preparing.

Do not forget My instructions to have food, which lasts ten days, candles, which are blessed and holy objects in your home.

Trust in Me and rejoice because many souls will be saved.

I will not reveal a date, but you know what must be done.

When your sins are revealed you must ask Me to forgive you and bow in humble thanksgiving for this Divine Gift, which is your passport to eternal life in the New Paradise on earth.

Remember there is not one sin, no matter how serious, which cannot be forgiven once true remorse is shown.

Your beloved Saviour
Jesus Christ

They will deny Me by saying that My Holy Word contradicts the Word of God
Wednesday, July 11, 2012 21:30 hours

My dearly beloved daughter, you are enduring My pain at this time, as I weep because of the number of God's children who are dying in a state of mortal sin.

It is so painful that I am enduring, yet again, the terrible wounds inflicted on Me during My Crucifixion.

My daughter, it is important that you understand what is happening to you for you must prepare how to deal with this Mission when it causes you such suffering.

The abuse you endure, in My Name, is to be expected.

When any chosen soul imparted My Holy Word to the world, in the past they suffered mortification just as you do now. They were ridiculed, abused, made to look foolish and, even worse, accused of being deceitful as if they were telling lies.

I too, was called a liar. I, too, was laughed at. They said that I was a fraud, an imposter and against the Word of God.

They found every excuse to prove that I was a fraud.

They even used the Holy Word of God, My Eternal Father, to try and prove that what I spoke about denied Holy Scripture.

Any one can say they represent the Word of God. Very few who say they receive the Word of God are taken seriously. They are usually ignored.

But, those who say they speak in My Name, but who do not, and who deliberately spread lies, are usually applauded and accepted through the deceitful influence of Satan.

In the case of the genuine prophet, such is the power of My Voice, that it will provoke a very strong reaction. In such cases people will either embrace My Word with love for the Truth or they will deny Me outright.

Those who accept Me will feel My Love touch their souls in a way, which will enflame their hearts so that there can be no turning back.

Those who reject Me will not ignore Me. Instead they will ridicule Me and vilify My Holy Word with viciousness, which is at variance with the Christian virtues they profess to have.

They will deny Me by saying that My Holy Word contradicts the Word of God just as they did when I walked the earth.

They fail to understand why My Word creates such a powerful reaction. They have been tempted by Satan and don't know it. They have let their guard down and allowed him to cloud their love for Me.

No one will ignore My Word. They can't. For either way it provokes a reaction whether it is one of love or one of hate.

Your Jesus

The Warning for many will be a frightening event, when it will seem like the world has come to an end
Thursday, July 12, 2012 10:50 hours

My dearly beloved daughter, let no man underestimate the impact that The Warning will have on the whole of humanity.

The Warning for many will be a frightening event, when it will seem like the world has come to an end.

Many will witness what will seen to be a catastrophic occurrence when two comets will appear to collide and explode close to the earth's surface.

The flames of fire will seem as if a volcano has erupted in the skies and many will be fearful.

The rays of red fire are the Rays of My Blood, the Rays of My Mercy, given to all of you as a Gift of such magnitude that no man will be able to comprehend what is happening.

Many will feel a fire burning through their bodies, as if the heat of the sun is overpowering them.

Inside they will feel a burning heat, until the sense of realisation enables them to witness the spectacle of their souls.

Many will feel the earth shake as if there is an earthquake.

The ground will shake, groan and many will fall down clutching whatever they can for shelter.

Yet the ground will not open up and swallow them. For this is not a physical earthquake, but a supernatural one.

Before this happens the weather patterns will erupt.

My Cross will appear after the explosion in the skies.

Many will weep bitter tears of remorse and sadness and will endure the pain of humiliation because of their sins.

Others will scream and curse because they will not be able to withstand the illumination, a Divine Sign, because of the darkness of their souls and they will resist the Light of My Mercy.

They will howl with the pain of the fires of Hell, as My Sign of Mercy will show them the fate, which awaits them unless they repent and change their ways.

Those good souls who love Me will also suffer, for many of them will also be stained with sin, but they will receive instant Absolution. They too, will be humbled, when their sin of pride is shown to them.

Many will stay indoors for some days afterwards and many will have to fend for themselves because of the lack of services. This is why you need to prepare.

It will also be a period of suffering when souls will endure the pain of Purgatory as their purification takes place. In this way many will experience a revelation of the state of their souls and become humbled in a way in which they have never experienced before.

So many people will accept what has happened and will know that they have been given a great Gift of My Graces and My Divine Mercy.

The conversion will be global and on a scale not witnessed since My death on the Cross. Billions will turn to God because the Truth will become apparent.

They will know exactly what will happen on the Day of Judgment and they will know how to save their souls because My Love will have enveloped them.

They can become whole again of mind, body and soul.

My Cross will be the proof of My manifestation of My Divine Mercy, promised to mankind for so long. It will be seen in the skies all over the world.

A calmness will descend throughout the earth as a result of this act of Divine Intervention given to God's children to awake them from their slumber.

But, the fallen angels will attack all God's children through their dedicated army who will refuse My Cup of Salvation.

So bitter, with hearts of stone and infested with the stain of Satan, they will fight those who love God.

Their numbers will not be a match for those who follow the Truth, yet their hatred will inspire them to plot evil acts which will destroy this peace and calm.

This will orchestrate a plan to convince the world that this event was, indeed, a cosmic accident, which they will say that scientists can prove.

Many, sadly, will then believe this to be the case and many of God's children will fall back to the old sinful lives they once led.

The battle for souls will then commence and it will take some time for this to reach the final confrontation when My Second Coming will bring to an end the wickedness.

My dear followers, do not allow these revelations to bring fear.

Instead prepare for this glorious event and allow your souls to embrace it.

Accept this wonderful Divine Act to strengthen your resolve and to spread My Love further amongst your family and friends.

Be proud of your ties to Me, your Jesus, and help Me salvage those souls who will refuse to accept My Mercy. Go. Prepare. Rejoice for the time is close. I love you.

Your Jesus

After the world war will come the famine and then the plagues. Yet, prayer can mitigate the Chastisement
Friday, July 13, 2012 16:25 hours

My dearly beloved daughter, My followers need to know the sequence of events for, by understanding this, they will be empowered with the knowledge so that they can help to mitigate the Chastisement.

The Warning is taking place as a last resort by My Eternal Father in order to plunge the Light of God, the Light of the Truth, into the hearts of mankind.

Without it most of humanity would be cast into Hell for they would not be worthy of My Father's Kingdom.

This is a Divine Act of Great Mercy to pluck all of God's children from evil and to take them into their rightful inheritance.

Because of the great darkness covering the earth at this time, where the Light of God is but a glimmer, this Act of God is necessary.

It will divide the good from those drowning in sin, but who will stubbornly cling to the beast and all the glory he promises them on this earth. It is a waste of time for such poor souls because they must know that their time on earth is short.

The earth will be replaced by a New Paradise to which they will be refused entry if they reject My Act of Love and Mercy.

Many will stay in the dark. Many will convert instantly. If most of humanity repents, then the Great Tribulation will not be as difficult.

The World War will not have the same impact if the majority of people repent after The Warning.

After the world war will come the famine and then the plagues. Yet, prayer can mitigate the Chastisement.

Pray hard so that the War, and the Chastisement which will follow it, can be diluted and averted. Only the faith of humanity and allegiance to Me, your Divine Saviour, can achieve this.

My daughter, it is not I, your Jesus, who will bring about these terrible sorrows. It will be created by the wicked sins of man, whose lust for power; money and control of the world for his own gain, are insatiable.

While many of My followers will be waiting patiently and eagerly for My Second Coming there will be more confusion.

Many will come forth and claim to be Me, the Messiah, and people will be fooled.

Remember what I told you I will return to earth just as I left it when I ascended through the clouds.

Ignore any one who claims to be Me, in the flesh, for this will not happen.

My followers will be strong because of their love for Me and they must focus on the one desire that, if fulfilled, will bring Me joy and comfort. That will be the Mission to save souls, all souls, before I come again.

Remember that allegiance to Me will be the key to salvation and the world of the future, which will have no end, for it, will be the New Paradise, which offers each of you eternal life.

Your beloved Jesus

So now you should understand why you are different to visionaries. It is because you are a prophet, the end time prophet
Friday, July 13, 2012 23:05 hours

My dearly beloved daughter, you must know that the role of the prophet differs to that of the visionary.

A prophet will always be an outcast, hated, feared and isolated.

A prophet will always work alone as if he is cast into a desert. The only fruit within the barren desert will be the Voice of God.

My daughter, when you feel alone and abandoned, know that this is how the prophets felt, in the past. Many prophets felt the weight of this task laid out before them.

Most of them knew they were not worthy to impart the Holy Word of God, but they accept the Divine Calling from the Heavens because they were sent.

Because they were sent into the world they knew, instinctively, the obligations they had to fulfil, yet it was not easy.

Every word they uttered was thrown back in their faces.

Every word torn asunder in the synagogues and the temples set up to worship God. Many were cast out by their own people and could not return to their birthplaces.

Many became nomads and never found a place where they would be welcomed as a lost son. Instead they worked, lived and stayed alone with no one to turn to.

Yet they knew, in their hearts, that they were being guided by God and felt no fear as they spoke with His Voice.

The graces given to them enabled them to be strong. They never faltered in delivering the warnings to God's people, the prophecies and the Word of God.

It did not matter to them that they were laughed at because they knew the Truth of God was the food of life.

Without the Truth, God's children would not have had the means to recognise the prophecies as foretold. Nor would they have been able to accept the Laws laid down by God for the good of mankind.

Rejected, ridiculed, cast aside and deemed as eccentric, just as I was during My time on earth they still delivered the Word of God. Their words live forever. They will never die because they spoke the Word of the Lord, God the Most High.

And so it will be with you. You will remain alone like a voice in the wilderness.

You will be ignored in many quarters of My Church on earth.

The difference this time, is that these prophecies will unfold in your lifetime, and the Truth will be proved to this generation.

They will believe then when the proof of The Warning is witnessed.

The prophecies of the Seals, as I open them and reveal the contents to you, will also prove that I am speaking to the world through you, the 7th Angel, the 7th Messenger.

You will be listened to yet I urge you to remain silent and not to comment to those who question you or challenge you.

You do not understand the meaning of the Messages yet. In time you will. In the meantime you do not have the authority to defend My Word.

Every attempt will be made to trick you into responding in the hope that you will trip yourself up through your lack of knowledge. So you must remain quiet, isolated and anonymous until I give you the instruction.

So now you should understand why you are different to visionaries. It is because you are a prophet, the end time prophet.

This Mission is protected by the Heavens and cannot be destroyed.

Go in peace and understanding, My daughter.

Your Jesus

It is not enough to believe in the Father, for those who reject His Son, reject salvation
Saturday, July 14, 2012 15:15 hours

My dearly beloved daughter, so many religions in the world follow the wrong path thereby making it difficult for God's children to obtain eternal life.

Eternal life, was only made possible by My Death on the Cross.

My Father who sent Me, His only Son, as the sacrificial Lamb, made it possible for the whole of humanity to obtain salvation and eternal life.

Eternal life was given as a gift to Adam and Eve. Then, because of the stain of sin and disobedience, it was taken away.

In its place, man became mortal; his body impure, his life in the physical form imperfect and the earth became a poor imitation of the rich and splendid earth Created for Adam and Eve in the Garden of Eden.

God, My Eternal Father, then granted salvation to those who accepted Me, His only begotten Son, as the way to His New Paradise.

Only through Me can you be accepted by My Father.

It is not enough to believe in the Father, for those who reject His Son, reject salvation.

Remember that so many of God's children who, through ignorance, do not acknowledge Me, the Saviour of Mankind. But, because of My Great Mercy, the Truth will be revealed to them by Divine Intervention.

They are all equal in My Father's Eyes and He wants to unite all such souls into His bosom. He loves them all.

When they see the proof they will accept that God, the Most High, gave them the gift of eternal life through My Sacrifice on the Cross. In this way all will adore the one God.

For there is only one God who Created each of you.

Now go, My daughter, and help ensure that My Messages are given to every creed, every nation and every one of God's children.

I include those Pagans and those with hearts of stone.

It does not matter if they spit at you, or refuse to listen; you must give them the Messages.

Any man, or follower of Me, Jesus Christ, who cannot accept that I wish to communicate the Holy Word of God to all religions is not a true Christian.

So many have rejected these, My Messages to the world, because I embrace all of humanity and every other religion including that of atheists.

You have no right to assume that only you, the true Christians, are loved by God, My Eternal Father.

You are blessed and loved, but without the conversion of the whole of humanity My Father will not achieve the victory He wants to unite all of His children.

You, My followers, have a great responsibility because of the Gift of the Truth given to you.

It is your duty to spread My Holy Word in order to bring those poor souls who are ignorant of My Existence into the Kingdom of God.

Your Jesus

Virgin Mary: My Son's Church on earth will not listen this time, yet they know how my Son was treated the first time

Sunday, July 15, 2012 15:45 hours

My child, the pain endured by my Son and His disciples during the time of His Mission on earth, is identical to that which is to be endured by His followers as He prepares to come again.

During my Son's time on earth He faced huge obstacles. Very few were prepared to listen to Him in His own community.

He was treated with contempt and looked down upon by those who were in charge of the temples and the synagogues.

Yet, He was welcomed by the simple people, and His Word was accepted because they could see the Truth that He spoke.

His Word created fear and uncertainty in many quarters, but few could ignore the Wisdom of His Teachings.

My Son created division although that was not His intention.

His simple demeanour meant that few could accept the fact that He was the Son of God.

Many asked how could the Son of Man be such an ordinary simple man?

They denied Him, for they thought that the Messiah would be majestic, proud and would command attention in the highest echelons of the Church.

My Son could not get those in charge of the church at the time to listen to Him. Their pride prevented them from listening to the Truth.

The same will happen now as my Son prepares the world for His Second Coming.

My Son's Church on earth will not listen this time, yet they know how my Son was treated the first time.

This time His Holy Word, given to you, the end time prophet, will not be accepted in my Son's Church on earth.

My Son's Church turns a deaf ear to the gift of prophecy. They deny prophecy because they do not want to listen.

My Son's disciples will be turned on by those in charge of the Catholic Church on earth and accused of being false.

Although my Son's Teachings have never changed they will find fault with His Holy Word given to them now.

They will declare these Messages to be in contradiction to the Word of God.

You must, children, always remember that my Son could never contradict His Church on Earth, for He is the Church.

The Truth is still as it always was.

You must follow the Word of God for my Son's Voice is being cast aside and ignored just as it was the first time.

Do not allow yourselves to be denied the Gift of His Salvation, the last act of His Mercy on earth.

So patient has my Son been, for such a long time. The Truth was given to humanity at my Son's Passion on the Cross.

It was reinforced through all those chosen souls who were enlightened by the Power of the Holy Spirit down through the centuries.

Now the time has come for my Son to come again and only those who recognise His Voice, because of the Gift of the Holy Spirit, will follow His instructions.

The Church will, just as they did during my Son's time on earth the first time, reject His Word, as He prepares for His Second Coming.

They will fail to recognise Him or accept Him.

They have learned nothing.

Pray that those brave souls within the Church, who do recognise His Voice, will have the courage to lead all of God's children to eternal life at this crucial time in history.

Your beloved Mother
Mother of Salvation

God the Father: I will wipe out their false churches, their wicked cults, their false idols, their cities and their nations
Sunday, July 15, 2012 17:45 hours

My dearest daughter, it is difficult for My children to remain free of sin because of the curse inflicted upon them by the hand of the serpent.

Never do I expect My children to be completely free of sin at all times for this is impossible.

It is important that anyone who knows the Teachings of My Son's Church on earth to seek repentance for your sins as often as possible.

Through repentance it will be easier to remain in a state of grace and this will create a barrier to further temptation.

My children, you are now about to witness great everlasting changes in the world. They will happen after The Warning takes place.

While many will ignore these Messages from Heaven, it is important for those who accept them as the Word of God to prepare.

You are the link in My armour against the enemy and through your faith I will lift you up and protect you against the persecution.

It will be your love for My Son, Jesus Christ, the Saviour of the universe, that I will be able to salvage those children who cannot abide the Light of God.

Your consecration of love, suffering and prayers will be their saving grace from the fires of Hell.

Be not afraid for yourselves, but, for those who not only cannot see, but, who refuse to see, the times in which you are living today.

The preparations are complete and the time is ripe for the changes to commence for I will not allow the beast to steal souls.

This Intervention, promised to mankind for so long will take place very soon and then the battle will begin to save My children.

Do not fear My Hand for, when it falls, it will be used to punish those who are trying to destroy My children.

I will stop them from deceiving souls.

I will stop them from their murderous intent and I will wipe out their false churches, their wicked cults, their false idols, their cities and their nations, if they continue to reject the Hand that feeds them.

They have been warned. You, My beloved children, will help My Son to save them.

Never fear because those with the Seal of the Living God are not only protected, but, are given the graces to defend the Word of God so that as many souls as possible will be given the Gift of Life.

Your beloved Father
God the Most High

The time is near for the persecution of My Beloved Vicar, Pope Benedict XVI to reach its pinnacle
Monday, July 16, 2012 15:15 hours

My dearly beloved daughter, it is time to prepare all of God's priests, bishops and all those who run My Holy Catholic and apostolic Church on earth.

For the time is near for the persecution of My Beloved Vicar, Pope Benedict XVI to reach its pinnacle.

Very soon he will be forced to flee the Vatican. Then the time will come when My Church will divide, one side against the other.

I call on all of My sacred servants to remember your most holy vows.

Never forsake your mission. Never forsake Me. Never accept lies in lieu of the Truth.

You must ask Me to help you in the difficult times ahead. You must rise, unite and follow Me.

Pray for the strength you will need through this special Crusade Prayer.

Crusade Prayer (66) For clergy: Help me to remain true to Your Most Holy Word

O Dear Jesus, help me to remain true to Your Most Holy Word at all times. Give me the strength to uphold the Truth of Your Church in the face of adversity. Fill me with the grace to administer the Holy Sacraments in the way in which You taught us.

Help me to feed your Church with the Bread of Life and remain loyal to You even when I am prohibited from doing so. Free me from the chain of deceit I may face in order to proclaim the True Word of God. Cover all Your sacred servants with Your Precious Blood at this time so that we will remain courageous, loyal and steadfast in our allegiance to You, Our Beloved Saviour, Jesus Christ.

Amen.

Do not be disheartened, My beloved sacred servants, for the discord has been prophesised and must come about in the final battle for souls.

I love you and I will be with you now as you walk with Me the thorny road to Calvary so that Salvation can be achieved once more for all souls.

Your Beloved Jesus

Young souls are dear to Me and I weep with the way in which many of them were never taught the Truth
Tuesday, July 17, 2012 19:50 hours

My dearly beloved daughter, your Mission must embrace all of God's children. I especially yearn for the souls of the young and those who allow human intelligence to block their ears to the Truth of My Being.

Young souls are dear to Me and I weep with the way in which many of them were never taught the Truth.

They were led by their parents, many of whom do not believe in God, into an abyss of darkness.

The light they seek is that brought to them by the false light of all that glitters. They are seduced by music, clothes and entertainment, all designed to stimulate the senses.

They do not know Me. Many never heard of Me, or what hope I represent in their quest for future happiness.

Lucifer, the fallen angel in My Father's higher Seraphim Hierarchy was a talented musician.

As Satan in the world today, he tempts My young tender souls through music.

Music is his weapon of destruction and he uses every type to draw little innocent souls into his web of deceit.

Music is a great Gift from God. It is also used to mask the wicked allegiance to the evil one through lyrics, which honour the beast. Very few young souls understand the power of music or when it is used in the wrong way.

Please, I urge you to help me save their little souls. Bring them to Me. Never force them. Instead consecrate young children to Me through this prayer.

Crusade Prayer (67) Keep my children safe from the King of Lies.

Please dear Jesus, I ask You to keep my children safe from the King of Lies.

I consecrate these children (name them) to Your Sacred Heart, and ask that through the cloak of Your Precious Blood, You will enlighten their souls and take them safely into Your loving Arms so that they can be protected from all harm. I ask that You open their hearts and flood their souls with Your Holy Spirit during the Illumination of Conscience, so that they are cleansed of every iniquity.

Amen.

Prayer for atheists during The Warning

To those of you who say you are atheists hear now My promise. I love you and I will never give up My fight to save you from the clutches of the deceiver, Satan, who blinds you to the Truth. When the time comes, and when you will see your sins before your eyes during The Warning please say these words,

Jesus, show me the Truth and save me from evil. I am truly sorry for my sins and I ask You to take me now and show me the Light of Your Mercy.

Amen.

You will never be confused again if you say this prayer. A weight will be lifted from your heart and you will be truly at peace. Remember these words when the day arrives. I will not forsake you. I will hold you and you will feel My Love surge through your body and then you will be given the proof you have been longing for.

Your Jesus

God the Father, Jesus Christ, Virgin Mary:
Once The Warning takes place there will be much confusion
Tuesday, July 17, 2012 19:11 hours

My dearly beloved daughter, time is moving quickly now. I have been preparing all of you now for some time.

You, My followers, know what you must do. Your own Confession is important and you must try to get this once every week from now on.

Be at peace. I am pleased at the way in which you follow My instructions. Please keep going back to My Crusade Prayers and concentrate on the prayers to save the souls of others.

Once The Warning takes place, there will be much confusion. People, everywhere, will be humbled in a way, which is out of character.

Many will be too distressed to go back to their place of work immediately. People in powerful positions, in governments, will question their laws.

Those murderers and criminals, amongst your communities, will feel a terrible sorrow and despair, but many will atone for their sins.

My priests and My other sacred servants will immediately know that these Messages come from My Divine Lips.

Then they will rise and follow My loyal followers to help Me prepare the world for My Second Coming.

Some among them will know that it is I who speaks to them, but will lack the courage to openly proclaim My Most Holy Word.

In time they will be given the graces to uphold My Sacraments, when they realise that they are to be desecrated. Then they will be given the proof of these prophecies.

Many parents will need to instil, in their children over the age of seven years, the importance of prayer and repentance from then on. Parents, you have a duty to teach your children the Truth.

Their hearts will be open to My Love after The Warning and you must keep guiding them in spiritual matters.

Ensure that you keep Holy Water in your homes and a Benedictine

Cross from now on along with the Seal of the Living God hanging in your home. All of these will protect your family.

Follow My instruction and all will be well.

My daughter, you must now go and ensure that the Book of Truth is published as quickly as possible. It is important that those souls who have no access to computer are given this.

Have no fear for I will guide you and send you help to ensure that it is sent all over the world.

Go in peace. Go in Love. I am with you always.

I stand by you every moment of the day guiding you even when you do not realise it. I am in your heart.

Your beloved Jesus

Virgin Mary: It is frowned upon by today's so-called tolerant society to say that you believe in Jesus Christ
Wednesday, July 18, 2012 19:16 hours

My child, I weep at this time because of the way God's children are afraid or embarrassed to declare their love for His Son, Jesus Christ.

So many in the world today, who love My Son, are embarrassed to openly proclaim His Name in public for fear of being reprimanded.

It is frowned upon by today's so-called tolerant society to say that you believe in Jesus Christ, the Son of Man and that you believe in His Teachings.

Yet many never think twice about using His Holy Name, many times throughout the day, when uttering profanities.

His Name is spoken very often, but not in the way it is meant to be.

So many are afraid to be open about their love for my Son in a world, which frowns on Christianity.

Christianity is despised by two-thirds of the world.

Christians are bullied, scorned and often persecuted like no other religion in the world.

God's chosen people, the Jews, also suffer and have been persecuted in the most inhumane manner because of who they are. A chosen race, they will be converted soon and will welcome the Messiah, the second time, although they failed to accept Him the first time.

Children, you must never be afraid to declare your love for my Son. When you express your love for Him openly and fearlessly, many people will listen. Then the more you proclaim His Holy Word the more confident you will become.

Then you will receive more graces to give you the strength to take the next step.

After a while it will not concern you what others think of you. Yet many will be impressed with your honesty and many will want to know more about my Son.

Now is the time to speak about my Son's Mercy to as many people as you can.

They must be told about His Divine Mercy, the greatest Gift of The Warning, which will be seen throughout the whole world. Then, afterwards, they will know the Truth and many more will want to hear these Messages from Heaven.

Thank you, my child, for responding to my call.

Your beloved Mother in Heaven
Mother of Salvation

My Arms were pulled out of their sockets during My Crucifixion and, as such, the Image on the Turin Shroud shows this
Thursday, July 19, 2012 07:00 hours

My dearly beloved daughter, a great plan, to deceive God's children, is being plotted to destroy evidence of My Existence.

Soon many will come forth, masquerading as holy devout servants of Mine, to try and destroy belief in Me, your beloved Jesus.

They will start by questioning My birth, My Mother's purity and My Resurrection from the dead.

They will demonise all of these things as being false and will present, what they call the proof, to ensure that as many Christians as possible will become doubtful about My Life on earth.

They will create lies about My Crucifixion and make claims about My moral character.

Then they will start attacking relics, question them and try to expose them as nothing more than superstition in the minds of Christians.

Then there is the Turin Shroud, the cloth that covered My dead Body in the tomb. They will deny, finally, that it is authentic and promote lies.

My Arms they will say are too long and they will question this. Yet they fail to understand the torture My Body had to endure during My Crucifixion. My Arms were pulled out of their sockets during My Crucifixion and, as such, the Image on the Turin Shroud shows this.

Then they will try to prove that the Resurrection never took place. All lies, they will say, so desperate are they to wipe out all traces of Me.

Then they will try to deprive all of those who convert during The Warning of the Holy Sacraments and the Holy Bible.

They will ban the Bible from most places.

Then they will introduce a new false book, which they will say will proclaim the importance of loving one another.

They will use the love, which Christians have in their hearts, a Gift from God, to manipulate them into accepting a Message of so-called love.

Love one another they will say. Now love one another's religion. Join together as one religion and show true love for your brothers and sisters.

Love of oneself will be the underlying Message.

Love yourself first and you will find it easier to love your neighbour will be their message and this will be the biggest lie they will force you, My followers, to swallow.

Love of oneself ahead of others offends God.

It is selfish. Do not listen to the lies. Yet so convincing will they be that many will believe what they are being told and will follow the leader of this One World religion like lambs to the slaughter.

Infiltrating so many nations, the New World religion will be condoned by many governments.

They will ruthlessly stamp out Christian Laws.

They will then create laws to ban all religions, especially Christianity.

They will impose penalties on those who do not respond to their demands.

Communism will be at the root of all this evil. It is not that Communism promotes atheism. It will be because it will promote hatred of God.

Russia and China will be in power in many nations, starting with Europe.

The European Union, the Beast with the Ten Horns, will be devoured by the second beast, more ruthless and more powerful.

Then Communism will take root, before it spreads everywhere. This period will not last long. It will be short. Your prayers will dilute the impact, but this has been foretold and will unfold.

Pray, pray, pray for the conversion of the whole world during The Warning.

If the majority of souls convert then much of the Great Tribulation can and will be eased.

Your Jesus

The world will soon be presented with the most deceitful lie, which is impossible for mankind to grasp at this stage
Friday, July 20, 2012 17:46 hours

My dearly beloved daughter, the three and a half years remaining in the Tribulation period commences in December 2012.

This is the period when the antichrist will emerge as a military hero.

His soul has been given over to Satan who possesses every part of him.

The powers he will possess means, that in time he, will be seen not just as the man of peace, but, people will think he is I, Jesus Christ, the Saviour of Mankind.

They will also, in time, believe that the antichrist has been sent to herald The Second Coming.

So many poor souls will, therefore, willingly accept his mark, the Mark of the Beast. For he is the beast in every way because of the way in which Satan will manifest himself in his body.

He will perform miracles in the sky.

He will heal people.

He will be head of the New World Religion and he, and the false prophet, who will head up the shell of the Catholic Church on earth, will work closely to deceive all of God's children.

The world will soon be presented with the most deceitful lie, which is impossible for mankind to grasp at this stage.

For those of you who are being given the Book of Truth, these My Holy Messages, to warn humanity of these things, know this.

So sophisticated will their plan be, that many will be fooled by the loving humane exterior which they will present to the world as their wicked plan.

The antichrist and the false prophet, between them, are already finishing planning their wicked reign and the first thing they will bring about will be the escalation of the war in the Middle East.

The antichrist will be the main man pulling the strings in the background. Then he will come forth and be seen to broker a peace plan.

It will be then when the world will fall under his spell.

Meanwhile the false prophet will seize power within the Catholic Church.

Very soon it will be sucked into the New World religion, a front for satanic worship. Worship of self will be the fundamental aim of this abomination and the introduction of laws, which amount to two things, the abolition of the Sacraments and the abolition of sin.

The Sacraments will only truly be available from those priests and other Christian clergy who remain loyal to Me. They will offer these Sacraments in special refuge churches.

The abolition of sin will be introduced through the introduction of laws, which will be seen to endorse tolerance.

They include abortion, euthanasia and same sex marriages. Churches will be forced to allow same sex marriages and priests will be forced to bless them in My Eyes.

During this time they will continue to say their own version of the Holy Mass. Their offering of the Holy Eucharist, when they will desecrate the Host, will be held in Catholic churches.

My Presence will not only be missing in such Masses, but it will be missing in the very churches where they dishonour Me.

All of these matters will be very frightening for My followers. You will no longer be able to benefit from the Sacraments except from the priests in My Remnant Church on earth.

This is why I give you Gifts now, such as the Plenary Indulgence, for the absolution of your sins. It is not meant to replace the Act of Confession for Catholics.

It will be a way in which you can remain in a state of grace.

Although billions of people will convert during The Warning, these prophecies will still unfold. But, much of them can be diluted through prayer to reduce the suffering and the persecution.

You, My followers, remember, are protected at all times by the Seal of the Living God. You must spread the Seal and get it to as many people as possible.

Please understand that I tell you these things to prepare you so that you can prevent as many souls as possible from accepting the Mark of the Beast.

Satan will use the power of possession in those souls who take the Mark and it will be very difficult to save them.

You will be instructed every step of the way, My followers, though this Mission. You must not allow fear to enter your hearts for I will fill you with the courage, the strength, the stamina and the confidence, to rise with your heads held high as you march in My Army.

Remember Satan cannot win this battle for it can never be. Only those with the Seal of the Living God and those who remain loyal and steadfast to God can win.

Your Jesus

The Love of God will shine down on all those who ask My Father to stop the antichrist from inflicting terrible suffering on humanity
Saturday, July 21, 2012 15:15 hours

My dearly beloved daughter, for those among you, My followers, who worry about the times ahead you must know that all Power lies in the Hands of My Eternal Father.

His only wish is to save all of His children from the clutches of the beast.

Sadly, the beast, Satan, is dismissed, by those non-believers, as being a figment of the imagination.

He and his army of demons are everywhere, prompting God's children to sin in their thoughts, actions and deeds every second of the day.

My Father not only wants to save the souls of every single one of His children, He wants to protect them from the persecution of the antichrist.

The power to avert, dilute and mitigate these trials lies in your hands, My followers.

Your prayers can alleviate much of this suffering, which is being planned by Satan's army in the years ahead.

Those who convert back to the ways of the Lord, God the Most High, will be given the graces to help stop much of this ugly and evil plan which is being prepared by this wicked group against their fellow brothers and sisters.

The Love of God will shine down on all those who ask My Father to stop the antichrist from inflicting terrible suffering on humanity.

You must pray hard that he is cut down along with the false prophet quickly.

You, My followers, will be given special Crusade prayer Litanies to break down and weaken his power.

These must be said daily after The Warning and, ideally, during Adoration of the Holy Eucharist.

These Litanies, designed to destroy the antichrist and his army, will be a powerful force and if enough souls join in these prayers they will be instrumental in disrupting much of the plans being perpetrated by the antichrist and the false prophet.

The first litany will be given to you shortly.

Stay strong and trust in My Love for you, for it is not My desire to see you suffer.

All I desire is the unification of all of humanity in the New Era of Peace, which lies ahead.

This is all you need to focus on. All suffering will be wiped out and forgotten when this New Era unfolds.

Be patient. Trust in me and know that the love that My Eternal Father has for His children is insurmountable and beyond your comprehension.

Love and trust in His great Love and know that the Power of My Divine Mercy is so strong that when it envelopes the whole of humanity that billions will convert.

That will be when the Power of the Holy Spirit, which will surge through the majority of the souls of God's children, will become an intolerable burden for the antichrist.

He will find it difficult to penetrate the armour of God's army.

This is why you must never give up hope. The battle for souls could be shortened and mitigated if enough souls convert and do as I instruct them.

I love you all and I hope you trust in Me always.

Your Jesus

You will win this battle for souls and it will not take long before the New World, without end, will emerge
Sunday, July 22, 2012 19:00 hours

My dearly beloved daughter, many chosen souls are enduring a great suffering at this time as their hearts entwine with Mine because of the scourge of sin.

This unification of suffering, now being experienced by many visionaries, seers and victim souls is to salvage the souls of those who will die in mortal sin during The Warning.

It is a suffering like no other and will help defeat the enemy during The Warning.

My daughter, you must continue to publish My Messages although this is painful for you at this time.

The unrest in the world will escalate quickly and not only will wars emerge, but, the global bank will try to seize control over much of the world's currencies.

Chaos will prevail and ecological disasters will rise as the Hand of My Father falls to punish humanity for their weakness and slavery to sin.

My followers, your prayers have staved off many calamities, which would have destroyed cities and nations.

You must never give up prayer. Perseverance and loyalty to Me, your Jesus, will ease the situation.

You must stay strong during this time of strife for very soon everything will change.

Despite the wickedness of Satan's army, the growing faith of My army will stand before them and stop them in their attempts to destroy My Church.

Never feel disillusioned with this work even when sometimes it seems hopeless. My Mercy is great. My Love covers all of God's children.

You will win this battle for souls and it will not take long before the New World, without end, will emerge.

This is your future, the future of the world which you must strive for. Satan's days are almost over.

Rejoice because soon the suffering will have been forgotten.

Your Jesus

Virgin Mary: As the Mother of Salvation, my last title from Heaven, let me help you
Monday, July 23, 2012 16:36 hours

My child, the valley of tears flooding every nation in so many ways has been foretold many times.

Yet they have not listened to the warnings I gave to visionaries over the centuries.

Some of those who know the promises of the Lord, who said He would come again to rule in a world without end can recognise the signs.

Most people will not because they do not know the Gospels.

Children, these times are very difficult and confusing. I, your beloved Mother, offer you protection against Satan, if you would only ask me.

I have been accorded the power to crush him. If you invoke my help I can ease your torment.

My child, his influence is becoming clear to many of you who open their eyes.

His wickedness has manifested in many of God's children.

Murders, senseless killings, wars, greed, persecution, immorality and rampant sins, which break every one of God's Commandments, laid down by Moses, are there for all of you to see.

For those who have little faith and say what does it matter, you must know the damage which Satan inflicts upon your soul.

He is like a disease, which is difficult to cure. Once it grips you, it leads to other diseases even worse than the first so that one cure is not enough.

He poisons the soul, the mind and the body so quickly that it is very difficult to disengage yourself.

Children, you do not realise how powerful and vindictive he is. Once he infests a soul he will not leave it alone so that the soul in question nearly loses his mind.

In some cases these souls no longer control their own impulses.

As the Mother of all of God's children, I have the power to help salvage your soul.

As the Mother of Salvation, my last title from Heaven, let me help you.

You must say my Holy Rosary every day for protection and Satan will leave you and your loved ones alone.

Never underestimate this prayer for Satan's power diminishes as soon as you say it.

Children, the Power of God is bequeathed to those who call on my Son, Jesus, to give you the strength to live through these times. It cannot be given to you unless you ask for it.

Here is the next Crusade Prayer you must recite in order to seek protection from Satan.

Crusade Prayer (68) Protect me from the influence of Satan

Mother of God, Mother of Salvation, cover me with your Most Holy Mantle and protect my family from the influence of Satan and his fallen angels.

Help me to trust in the Divine Mercy of your beloved Son, Jesus Christ, at all times.

Sustain me in my love for Him and never allow me to wander away from the Truth of His Teachings no matter how many temptations are placed before me.

Amen.

Pray, pray, pray always for protection against the evil one for he causes terrible hurt, harm and misery in your lives.

If you do not ask you cannot receive these graces.

Trust in me, your Mother, at all times for it is my role to help my Son to salvage the souls of all of God's children.

Your loving Mother
Queen of the Earth
Mother of Salvation

Love is a sign from God. No matter what religion or creed you follow love can only come from God
Wednesday, July 25, 2012 23:30 hours

My dearly beloved daughter, I wish to discuss the importance of love and how, without love, the world could not survive.

God is Love. Love comes from God.

Where you find love you instantly feel the Presence of God.

Nearly everyone in the world feels love at some stage. Love frees the soul and its purity gives you a glimpse as to the depth of the Love that God has for every single one of His children.

Love defeats death.

Love defeats evil.

Love is everlasting. It can never die for it comes from God and will last for eternity.

When love is attacked in this life by the evil one, who acts through souls, it suffers, withers and can be replaced by indifference or, at times, hatred.

It is only through love, especially for each other, that peace in the world can evolve.

Without love people would die and become barren.

When you love a child you are feeling the same kind of love that My Father holds in His Heart for each child born in the world through His Creation.

Imagine a parent's anguish when a child goes missing.

The grief, the worry and the anxiety are identical to that felt by My Father when His children wander and become lost to the Truth of His Existence.

Then imagine the horror, which a parent has to endure if their child cannot be found.

What if they become lost forever? This is the heartbreak My Father endures when He loses His children.

Nothing consoles Him until He can find them again or when they turn and come running home to Him again.

The whole of Creation was founded through the Love of My Father.

His Love floods the Heavens and the earth and is intensely powerful.

All was created by His Divine Love and His generousity of Heart, so that He could share all the wonders of Creation with His children.

His Love for His children will never die.

His betrayal by Lucifer, to whom He gave everything, has meant that His Love for humanity has not been reciprocated by much of mankind.

But, as an ever-loving Father, His Love is so powerful that nothing can ever kill His Love for His children.

His Love means that every person has been given a second chance.

The Warning, a great Gift, sanctioned by My Father, is a special calling from Heaven.

This calling, a great supernatural miracle, will give each of you the chance of being saved; of being called and of being given the key to open the door to the New Paradise on earth.

For those of you who accept the Key to Paradise you will, in effect, defeat the beast.

The world will be finally rid of evil, sin, suffering and every pain.

Peace will reign.

Love for My Father will flourish finally and you will all live according to His Divine Will.

Love is a sign from God. No matter what religion or creed you follow love can only come from God.

It is the Light present in every soul, even those who are hardened sinners, for God does not extinguish His Light ever.

Grasp it. Embrace it. Cling on to love for it will lead you to Him.

Love will save you from the dark.

Your Jesus

The pact with Satan is almost over and two events must soon take place
Thursday, July 26, 2012 23:55 hours

My dearly beloved daughter, many people do not really understand the mystery of My Second Coming.

My Second Coming is the fulfilment of a New Covenant.

It will be the Creation of the perfect Paradise, which was lovingly brought to fruition for Adam and Eve by My Beloved Father. At that time all things on earth were in perfect harmony and according to the Will of God.

The time since My Crucifixion on earth has been painful for humanity because of the reign of Satan who has ruled the earth during this period.

The pact with Satan is almost over and two events must soon take place.

The redemption of the human race will occur during The Warning. From then onwards people, including those who are ignorant of the Existence of God, will embrace the Truth.

Others, who will respond slowly to this great miracle, when the proof will be presented to them, will convert in time. They too will seek forgiveness for their sinful lives.

Then comes the final stage, the sanctification – the final purification so that the whole of humanity is fit to enter the perfect Paradise.

This is the Paradise inhabited originally by Adam and Eve. It will only be then, the Divine Will of My Father, where all people will love and respect the Will of My Father, is to be accomplished at last.

Before this all comes to pass there will be much opposition to the Will of My Father being finally realised.

God's children will be pulled in every direction. Although the Holy Spirit will be poured out over the whole world during The Warning, every effort will be made by Satan to stop this global Confession.

He, and his wicked followers, are also preparing for The Warning. Their goal is to convince everyone that it did not happen.

So many people will find it difficult to openly accept God's Love and the existence of the New Paradise as long as Satan walks the earth.

Freedom will only come when he is banished.

Sadly, those who will fail to see the Truth, and who will stubbornly refuse to accept God, will never see Paradise.

Please say this Crusade Prayer to accept the Divine Will of My Father.

Crusade Prayer (69) Prayer to God the Father to accept His Divine Will

God, the Almighty Father, I accept Your Divine Will. Help Your children to accept it.

Stop Satan from denying Your children's right to their Father's inheritance.

Never let us give up the fight for our inheritance in Paradise.

Hear our pleas to banish Satan and his fallen angels.

I ask You, dear Father, to cleanse the earth with Your Mercy and to cover us with Your Holy Spirit.

Lead us to form Your most Holy army, laden with the power to banish the beast forever.

Amen.

Go in peace.

Your Jesus

When the 20 million in My army has been reached I will multiply this number into billions
Friday, July 27, 2012 18:30 hours

My dearly beloved daughter, My wish to unite My followers as one army is already bearing fruit through these Messages.

My army has already formed and is united through the Power of the Holy Spirit, which is spreading like wildfire across the world.

For those of you who now accept My instructions, although you may think you are working together in small groups, you must know that My army now consists of over 25,000 dedicated soldiers who recite My Crusade Prayers each day.

Your dedication to Me, your beloved Jesus, brings Me so much comfort and joy for your prayers are saving millions and millions of souls, every second of each day.

Were you to witness their gratitude you would never cease to continue to pray, such is its power.

Satan is suffering because of this Mission and he will do everything possible to sabotage it.

This is why you must not allow outside bullying by those who accuse you of heresy to delay you with the spreading of My Messages.

If you allow others to confuse you, those who try to humiliate you or who sneer at your faith, then fewer souls can be saved.

Think of this Mission as the same as if you were working for an overseas aid agency, those groups of people who go into ravaged countries to save the lives of those suffering from famine.

It is vital that you overcome all obstacles to get aid to the victims. One hour's delay can mean the difference between life or death. The same is true of this Mission.

Look in front of you, ignore the interference of who will try to pull you back and then march forward.

Gather others in your path and lead them towards victory. The victory of salvation.

Your army swells every day. Hold on to My Hand until we reach the army I desire of 20 million which will spearhead the battle against the antichrist.

When the 20 million in My army has been reached I will multiply this number into billions. And when this happens the beast will finally be destroyed.

This is My promise. For in great numbers God's children, filled with His Divine Love will destroy evil.

Love, remember is stronger than hatred. Only love, in abundance, can wipe out evil.

Your Jesus

It is the sin of abortion, which will be the downfall of many nations and for this they will be punished severely
Sunday, July 29, 2012 20:10 hours

My dearly beloved, the apostasy in the world has God's children confused about the existence of sin.

Many souls, when they think of Sin, instantly think of the most grievous of sins, such as murder.

Sin takes many forms. Sadly because sin has been dismissed as faults or traits it is now deemed to be simply a natural weakness. Many no longer believe in sin.

Abortion, after murder of one's brother, is the greatest form of genocide in the world. Yet it is not only tolerated, but laws are brought in by your nations, which deem it a necessity.

It is the sin of abortion, which will be the downfall of many nations and for this they will be punished severely.

Abortion is a despicable act and it wipes out generations of God's children who cannot defend themselves.

No one will kill a child of God and avoid severe punishment.

The Anger of My Father will be witnessed by those nations, who have legalised abortion, during the Chastisement.

They will be wiped out and no compassion shown to them just as they showed no remorse for this mortal sin when they condoned the killing of God's children in the womb.

I call out to those who cunningly try to dismiss abortion as something, which is needed to protect the rights of a mother.

Lies are used to camouflage the atrocity of abortion, which defies the Law of God.

For this sin, any lawmaker, doctor or any person who contributes in any way to this abominable act, is guilty in the Eyes of God and will suffer the punishment, which lies ahead.

To those who condone execution I say this.

You, who condemn a man to be killed, are guilty of the same crime he may be guilty of.

You are guilty of murder in this instance and it is a mortal sin. You have not been given the right to take a life or to judge. Only I, Jesus Christ, have the right to Judge.

Anyone who contributes to the death of a murderer, through the act of execution will suffer in the fire of Hell for eternity, unless they repent.

So many of you believe in the law, an eye for an eye. How misguided you are. Do you not accept My Father's Commandments? Thou shalt not kill.

Thou shalt not kill also applies to those aggressive armies who march into lands, which do not belong to them, in order to control.

It applies to armies who shoot and kill innocent souls. All of this is murder. It is against the law of My Father.

Other sins such as greed, lust, speaking ill of others, cheating people out of what is rightfully theirs, revenge and slander all lead to all other sins.

They become acceptable in your world today because your greatest love is for yourselves.

The lie, which you have been forced to swallow by your false teachers, self-gratification, is your path to sin.

You are told that you must spend your time satisfying your hunger for wealth.

You are told that you must look after yourself – that you are the most important person in your life. You must seek out everything to satisfy all your senses. Everyone else comes second.

This leads to greed; selfishness, lust and then you can be enticed to commit mortal sin.

Sin will now be accepted by your nations like never before.

Laws will be introduced which will legalise mortal sin and woe to those of you who object.

Those who will advocate such wickedness will tell you that these laws are to protect the vulnerable when, in fact, all they do is to legalise murder, abortion, same-sex marriage and the idolatry of false gods.

They will condone the persecution of the poor and cast them out onto the streets to make paupers out of them.

They will bring in laws to force you to stop practising your religion. By doing so you will be breaking the law – a sin in their eyes.

As I told you before your world is so full of untruths that good is presented as evil and evil presented as good.

Your world is back to front and, as a result, sin flourishes.

I urge you to go back and study the Ten Commandments. Obey them and live as you are expected to, in the Eyes of My Father.

Break the Commandments and you sin. Argue that certain sins are okay and you defy My Father.

Obedience to the Laws of God is weak and fragile in the world at this time. Many of God's children have not been told firmly, by My sacred servants, of the consequences of sin.

Tolerance of sin is the greatest sin of all.

Tolerance is a cunning lie planted in the minds of humanity by the king of lies, Satan.

Tolerance is another way of justifying sin to suit man's weakness for succumbing to the temptation of Satan.

Wake up and accept sin for what it is.

Argue amongst each other and defend sin all you like, but, it will never be acceptable in the Eyes of My Father.

To enter Paradise you must be free from sin.

To become free from sin you must repent.

To repent you must first of all accept the Ten Commandments.

Then you must show true remorse.

True remorse can only be felt by those who humble themselves before Me.

Only then can sin be forgiven.

Only then are souls fit to enter My Father's Kingdom.

Your Saviour
Jesus Christ

My Catholic Church has been torn into shreds, yet the soul of My Church will never be taken or consumed by Satan
Monday, July 30, 2012 01:00 hours

My dearly beloved daughter, when I endured the Agony in the Garden the greatest abomination, shown to Me by Satan, was the disloyalty of the Catholic and Apostolic Church in the end times.

This is where Satan, who tormented Me with visions of the future, showed Me the lukewarm servants of the Church in these, your times.

They have allowed pride and false truths, dominated by their tolerance of sin, to blind them to the Truth of God.

Their allegiance to worldly pursuits means that many of My sacred servants do not have the compassion or humility in their souls to lead My followers towards the sanctity required to save their souls.

So many have turned against me although they say they love God's children.

By promoting tolerance in the Name of God, they present a false doctrine, which masks the Truth.

Those dissidents in My Church on earth, who claim to be creating a new type of following, in the name of the Catholic Church, but who deny My Teachings, are being tempted by Satan, who wants to destroy My Church.

He, the evil one, has already caused terrible sin to corrupt My Church and now wants to hammer in the final nails when he will crucify My Church and, in turn, cast into Hell those sacred servants of Mine who desecrate the Word of God by facilitating the acceptance of sin among God's children.

Their sin of slapping Me in the Face, by parading obscenities before Me, which they claim are acceptable and tolerated by God, will be severely punished.

They dare, through the sin of pride and deceit, to mislead souls and direct them into a den of darkness, without understanding how they are condemning souls into the lake of fire.

Many of My sacred servants are being misled and don't know it. Yet many such servants, if they are honest with themselves, are confused.

Then there are those who pose as My sacred servants, but come from the other side. Slaves to the beast, they deliberately present themselves as my anointed priests.

They cause Me such terrible anguish. Not only do they corrupt souls, they have knowingly created a pact with Satan who will devour them.

They perform vile acts on My altars, before the Holy Eucharist, but few know that they commit such acts. Yet I yearn for their souls.

My Catholic Church has been torn into shreds, yet the soul of My Church will never be taken or consumed by Satan. But, the servants of My Church can be seduced and destroyed by the beast.

This is the time for Me to intervene to help them rise above these terrible torments.

I need you, My followers, and those sacred servants among you who understand what is happening amongst you to say this **Crusade Prayer (70) Prayer for Clergy to remain firm and true to the Holy Word of God.**

O Dear Jesus, help Your sacred servants to recognise the schism within Your Church as it unfolds.

Help Your sacred servants to remain firm and true to Your Holy Word.

Never let worldly ambitions cloud their pure love for You.

Give them the graces to remain pure and humble before You and to honour Your Most Holy Presence in the Eucharist.

Help and guide all those sacred servants who may be lukewarm in their love for You and re-kindle the fire of the Holy Spirit in their souls.

Help them to recognise temptation placed before them to distract them.

Open their eyes so they can see the Truth at all times.

Bless them, dear Jesus, at this time and cover them with Your Precious Blood to keep them safe from harm.

Give them the strength to resist the seduction of Satan, should they be distracted by the allure of denying the existence of sin.

Amen.

My sacred servants are the backbone of My Church.

They are the first in line to face a terrible onslaught of attack from Satan at this time.

Help Me to steer them on the path to salvaging the remnants of My Church as it heads into the schism, which will be created by the false prophet shortly.

Gather together and pray for the unification of My sacred servants who are needed to keep My Church strong in the days, which lie ahead.

Your Jesus

Virgin Mary: Failure to proclaim the Truth of my Son's Teachings means that God is being forgotten
Tuesday, July 31, 2012 18:10 hours

My child, the persecution you are enduring is because of the publication of the Book of Truth.

The evil one is placing obstacles along your path and will stop at nothing to wear you down.

It is important to ignore the constant wicked lies with which you are being presented by those who claim to be knowledgeable about the Word of God.

Their dismissal of these Messages is not important. Only the Word of my Son is what you must respond to and nothing else.

You must trust in my Son and remain silent when those, blinded by lies, try to engage with you to trip you up. Do not listen. Do not respond. Instead, simply proclaim the Word of God.

My child, so many followers of Christ are suffering at this time. Their voices are but whispers in a world, which shouts about the glory of earthly wonders.

The True Word of God is no longer declared openly even by servants of God in the Church.

Embarrassed to be seen to openly declare the Truth they wander hopelessly trying to find their way amongst the confusion caused by secularism.

The offense, which is caused when God, or my beloved Son, Jesus Christ, are mentioned is widespread. Very few souls are brave enough to stand up and declare themselves soldiers of Christ.

Even holy souls are frightened to do this for fear of causing outrage amongst the heathen.

Failure to proclaim the Truth of my Son's Teachings means that God is being forgotten.

How I weep when I see poor little children who are being ignored by their guardians in the development of their souls.

They lack the nourishment of the Holy Spirit because they are not taught how to profess their love for God. Many do not believe in God the Father. This saddens Him.

You, my child, have been given a difficult task. When you declare to the world the contents of these Messages from Heaven, you are attacked from three sources.

Those who believe in God, but who refuse to listen to the Word of God, as it is being given to the world now.

Those who profess to be leaders in my Son's Church on earth, who refuse to listen because they do not accept prophecy.

And then those who do not believe in God at all.

Your voice will continue to fall on deaf ears, but you must not let this discourage you.

All you have to do is to obey my Son in all things and leave everything in His Holy Hands.

In time they will listen. When they do many souls will turn to my Son with love and joy in their hearts.

You must never falter or delay in your response to my Son's request to ensure that everyone in the world is given the Word of God at this time.

I ask all of God's children to respond to my call to pay allegiance to my Son's Holy Word now. He loves all of God's children and wishes to prepare every soul for His long awaited Second Coming.

Do not deny Him. Accept His Hand of Mercy before it is too late.

Your loving Mother
Queen of the Earth
Mother of Salvation

Allow Me to lift you, from all harm, to safety away from the Antichrist
Tuesday, July 31, 2012 20:00 hours

My dearly beloved daughter, hear Me now as I inform you that My Time is almost upon the world.

Your time is short as the days of darkness fade and a new dawn, a new beginning, will emerge.

All your tears of fear and distress are almost over with little time left for the Glorious Era of Peace to emerge.

The renewal of the Kingdom of the Earth will shortly take place and My Dominion over all of God's children will replace the seat of Satan.

Your confusion, My followers, over the authenticity of My Calling to you now, will disappear.

All will become clear, like the crystal clean waters of a spring from My Heavenly Body, as it gushes forth now to consume the hearts of all God's children.

The Light of the Truth will inflame the world, despite the ever-growing darkness, which has settled like a festering disease over every corner of the earth.

Soon the Truth will set you free, clear away all your doubts, your fears and will release within you a clarity of mind and soul. Then, filled with My Holy Spirit, a global conversion will take place.

Those whose faith is weak will be renewed and the Truth of a new Christian army will come into being.

Hope, love and prayer will sustain you as I lead the world towards the New Legacy promised to you for so long.

To those of you who are fearful of My Messages, just remember this.

The world, which awaits you, is a great Gift for you and your families. It is a Paradise, which you should be longing for, as nothing on earth, as you know it, can compare.

If you love Me, then trust in My Goodness, My Love, My Promise, to bring you into the Glorious inheritance for which you were born.

Surrender all your worries and fears now.

Allow Me to lift you, from all harm, to safety away from the antichrist.

Recite this **Crusade Prayer (71) Prayer to save us from the persecution**

O Jesus, save God's children from the antichrist.
Protect us from the plans to control the earth.
Lord, save us from the persecution.

Protect dark souls from the antichrist, so that they can be redeemed in Your Eyes.

Help us in our weakness.

Strengthen us in spirit to rise and lead each other as we march in Your army to the Gates of Paradise.

I need You, dear Jesus.
I love you, dear Jesus.
I glorify Your Presence on earth.
I shun the darkness.

I adore You and I surrender myself in body and spirit so that You can reveal to me the Truth of Your Presence so that I will always trust in Your Mercy at all times.

Amen.

Go now and prepare your souls so that you remain strong and loyal to Me, as I lead you towards Eternal Life.

Your Jesus

I ask of all God's children to once again dedicate the month of August to save souls
Wednesday, August 01, 2012 16:45 hours

My child, there is much change, much of which has been disclosed to you in the past, about to be witnessed in the world.

There will be much destruction, much unrest and chastisements, all of which will come about because of the sin of humanity.

I ask of all God's children to, once again, dedicate the month of August to save souls.

This is what you must do. Go to Mass every day and receive the Holy Eucharist.

Then every day at 3 o'clock say the Divine Mercy Chaplet.

For those of you who can, you should fast for one day a week.

My children will be shocked as these changes will come about, but must never fear the Hand of my Father, if you are loyal to the Teachings of His Beloved Son, Jesus Christ.

Please keep the Seal of the Living God close to you in your homes in the coming months for much will unfold.

The Body of my Son, Jesus Christ, present in His Church on earth is being violated and will suffer terribly.

Many plans to topple my Son's Church are already underway and very soon it will collapse.

Other events foretold will now be seen through ecological disasters, as the Hand of my Father will fall in punishment on those nations whose sinful laws will no longer be tolerated.

Pray, pray, pray for souls at this time who may suffer during these events.

Use this month to pray for all souls who may perish in wars, earthquakes or in the forthcoming Confession, The Warning.

My Heart is entwined with you children and, together, we must work hard to save souls.

By praying for the salvation of souls, we are carrying out the Holy Will of my Father.

Your beloved Mother
Mother of Salvation

God the Father: Just as My Son was crucified so, too will His Church on earth be crucified
Thursday, August 02, 2012 22:06 hours

My dearest daughter, the trial of My Son's Church on earth has already commenced.

The scourging, the persecution, is about to begin.

Just as My Son was crucified, so, too will His Church on earth be crucified.

The trial is taking place now.

My Son was sent to save humanity from the fires of Hell.

His Death on the Cross, a terrible cruel atrocity, was permitted, by Me, as a means to offer My children a future. My Son's Body became His Church on earth. His priests and sacred servants took the place of His apostles.

Now, as He returns again to redeem mankind and claim My precious children, so that they can enter My Paradise, history will be repeated.

My Son preached the Truth and He gathered many people who followed His Teachings who did not doubt His Word.

Then He was betrayed by those close to Him and devoted to Him within His ranks.

His Church, the Catholic Church, was also betrayed within its own corridors.

The temptation by Satan brought this about and a great evil was responsible for the demise of My Son.

In His Church today its demise commenced some time ago. As with My Son, many followers loyal to the Holy Word laid down by Me, deserted Him.

Then began the trial where My Son was accused of heresy. So too has My Son's Church on earth suffered the same fate.

Through the wicked amongst them, who committed grave offenses against humanity, many loyal followers deserted the Church.

In turn they deserted My Son and discarded His Teachings.

The trial of My Son's Church on earth has rendered its priests silent, when it comes to defending My Son's Teachings.

They are afraid of offending those who deny My Son, because of the sins of those amongst them. My Son's Church now faces the greatest trial of all, not seen since the Crucifixion of My Beloved Son.

His Church is being mocked unmercifully, not just by its enemies from outside, but from its enemies within.

The Crown of Thorns will now be placed on the Head of My Son's Church and few of His followers will stand by him.

Just as My Son's apostles, with the exception of John, deserted Him during His trial and execution so, too, will those in high places within the Vatican desert My Holy Vicar.

He will, as Head of the Catholic Church, be forced to walk a terrible path in disgrace, through no fault of his own.

While he will be whipped, sneered at and made to look foolish, it is not he they will vent their rage at. It will be against the Truth of the Church, the Christian Church, formed because of My Son's Sacrifice, that they will pour out their hatred upon.

Christianity will be scourged in every crevice, in every nation, in every place of worship, until it is weak with exhaustion.

As it will be led up the road to Calvary, just as My Son was led, it will be tied and secured with ropes, to render it impossible to escape the torment.

Then, as it climbs the hill, it will be pelted with stones, spat upon and jeered at, all the way to the top.

Then it will be nailed to the Cross.

Little sympathy will be shown for it, by those who blame the Church, for its sins against the innocent, when they will condemn the Head of the Church, My Son.

They will blame Him for the sins of others caused by the temptation of Satan.

When they have nailed My Son's Church to the Cross they will send hundreds of guards, just like the six hundred soldiers who stood on

Calvary to ensure that not one morsel of Flesh escapes without punishment.

Not one servant of His Church, who proclaims loyalty to it, will be allowed to escape.

When the Church has been crucified, they will ensure that it is starved of food and water until its dying breath. All its disciples, just as it was with My Son's apostles, will be nowhere to be seen.

They will go into hiding for fear of reprisals.

In what will seem to be its dying breath, all will become silent until the cheer of those who crucified the Church will deafen the entire world with its false doctrine.

The voice of the new head of the church, the imposter, the false prophet, will ring out.

All will fall in thanksgiving to Me, God the Most High, with relief. For this will seem to represent a new beginning.

It will be then that My Son's Presence will no longer grace the altars within this Church for this cannot be.

It will be then that My Hand, in chastisement, will fall in punishment. This is when the Battle of Armageddon will begin.

This is when I will come, through My Son, to save souls.

Do not deny this prophecy.

Do not hide behind false securities, for this day must come.

The Crucifixion of My Son's Church must come about because of the Final Covenant.

But, then the Glorious Resurrection of the Church, the New Jerusalem, will wipe out all the tears; all the suffering and then the New Era will come.

Trust in My Son at all times.

Never fear for I am your Father and I will come to renew the earth and gather all of My children in this final miracle foretold in the Book of Daniel.

The Book of Truth is now being revealed to you, children, as promised.

Do not reject My Divine Intervention for I speak the Truth.

God the Most High

To dissidents in the Catholic Church: Desecrate the Laws of My Church and you will be punished
Friday, August 03, 2012 16:45 hours

My dearly beloved daughter, the earth is about to shake, as My Father's anger will spill over those nations who defy My Father's Laws.

No Mercy will be shown as His patience has been tested to the limits.

Their sins include abortion, murder; laws which try to undermine Christianity, same sex marriage and the adoration of false gods.

Then there are those dissidents within My Church who threaten to disown Me.

When they try to distance themselves from My Church, and try to create new laws in defiance of My Holy Will, they disown Me.

I cast them out now for their disloyalty. Their attempts to introduce laws, based on the sin of pride, lust and worldly ambition, will not be tolerated.

Did they think they would be allowed to distance God's children from My Church on earth and avoid the Hand of My Father?

Did they think that they were above the Laws of God?

They do not love God they love themselves.

Lacking in humility, their public rejection of the Laws of the Catholic Church, disgust Me.

Their shameful demands where they try to force My Church to accept laws, which offend Me, means they have cast themselves into the darkness.

Their religious vows are meaningless.

Their pledge to honour and obey My Church has been broken.

Unless they repent and come back to My Body, My Church on earth, they have no right to call themselves servants in My Church.

You have been warned. I will cast you into the wilderness.

Desecrate the Laws of My Church and you will be punished.

Your Jesus

When they deliberately bribed liars to deny My Resurrection, the Pharisees denied generations of Jews the right to the Truth
Saturday, August 04, 2012 10:35 hours

My dearly beloved daughter, mankind must understand the weakness of human nature before they can truly entrust themselves into the Arms of God.

To those faithful amongst you, your faith and love for Me, your Saviour, brings Me great joy.

But, when you say you love Me, this brings with it a great responsibility.

Never forget the weakness in your nature, though no your fault of your own as you were born with original sin, as it can cause you to sin when you are least expecting it.

When the souls of those who say they love Me reach a stage where they are consumed with love for Me, that is when they have to be careful. Sometimes this makes them feel elevated in My Eyes, which is true, because they are.

But, then comes the temptation to see others in a less than flattering light.

They can be tempted to, not just feel compassion for those poor souls who are in darkness or confused, but, to look down upon them.

Sometimes their strong faith and knowledge of Scriptures gives them a false sense of security.

They believe they know everything regarding the Teachings of the Church, My Church, My Body on earth.

This is what happened with the Pharisees. They thought they knew everything about the Laws of God. The Love of God.

What they failed to understand was the prophesies foretold so clearly about the coming of the Messiah. This meant that they rejected the Christ, the Son of the Living God, when He came as promised.

The cruelty they showed Me, Jesus Christ, Son of Man, was in complete contradiction to the love they claimed to have for God.

If they truly loved God they would never have treated any child of God as they did.

Their minds were closed to the prophecies given to the world through the prophets, which proclaimed the Truth.

The Truth is that all prophecies will be fulfilled as promised by God.

They rejected the Messiah promised to provide the future salvation for the whole of humanity.

In turn, through their lies, when they deliberately bribed liars to deny My Resurrection, the Pharisees denied generations of Jews the right to the Truth.

My Death on the Cross wasn't enough for them. They wanted to ensure that no trace existed of Me, the Redeemer of the world afterwards.

They then went back and led God's children into a false faith in which the Truth became a lie.

Remember the prophecies from God are always fulfilled.My Second Coming is now about to be fulfilled. This time the leaders in the Christian Churches will deny Me like the Pharisees did.

They will torment Me, My prophets, My people and anyone who dares to spread the Truth of My Coming.

Do not deny Me this time. Open your hearts.Listen carefully to Me, as I prepare you for the final chapter in the salvation of the world.

Your Jesus

If you believe in the existence of Satan, then know that everything that is unjust and evil in the world, is caused by him
Sunday, August 05, 2012 17:40 hours

My dearly beloved daughter, I am calling out to everyone, young and old, who is unsure about their faith in God.

I appeal to those amongst you, who do believe in Me, but, who do not speak with Me, or avail of the Sacraments, or who do not attend their churches, to honour Me.

I love you. I will never desert you and you are going to be given a special Gift shortly.

You will experience what it is like when you will come before me on the Day of Judgment. Then you will forget your doubts.

Many of you, despite your lack of faith, honour Me in so many ways, but you do not realise this.

You, in your daily lives, feel love, concern and sympathy for others.

You feel an urge to fight injustice and are repelled when you witness wicked acts, committed by others over those less fortunate than themselves.

You show love for others and look after those who need your help.

You hate to take advantage of others and are sensitive to the needs of those who suffer in this life.

You feel love for your family.

You laugh and rejoice when you are with friends and feel a tremendous love and friendship for those close to your heart.

When you marry you feel an overwhelming love for your spouse. Then, when you have children, the love you feel surpasses anything you could ever have imagined.

You cry tears of remorse if and when you hurt someone. You forgive others when they offend you, insult you or cause you harm.

Where do you think this love and these emotions come from? Don't you know they can only come from God?

Love is difficult to explain. Difficult to analyse and it can never be proved by science for it is a Gift from God.

Hatred, on the other hand, comes from the dark side.

Satan, to many people, may not seem real, but he exists.

Many of you do not believe in evil or the existence of evil spirits, for they are careful not to reveal themselves.

If you believe in the existence of Satan, then know that everything that is unjust and evil in the world, is caused by him.

He is the king of lies and he has the power to blind you to the truth of your existence.

Because of your blindness My Mercy is now going to cover the world to prove to you that I exist.

Be prepared for this day for it will happen soon. When the signs in the skies are shown to you and you witness the clash, the noise and the shaking in the ground know that I have come to waken you up.

When this happens, I beg you to turn to Me then, for I want to fill you with My Love, so I can bring love and joy into your hearts.

When My Mercy comes upon you will you feel peace at last.

I love you and I will never forsake you.

I await your response when this great day comes.

Your Jesus

When such souls attack My Holy Word with such venom, this is a sign of Satan's confirmation that these Messages are authentic
Monday, August 06, 2012 18:06 hours

My dearly beloved daughter, there are many of My devoted followers who are plotting a campaign to destroy this Mission.

To those who believe that it will be the non-Christians and the atheists who will denounce My Word in these Messages then know this.

It will be those who openly proclaim their belief in Me, their Jesus, who will hurt Me the most.

They are being clouded by the deceit of the king of lies, who has sent many fallen angels to such souls. Not content with denying My Holy

Messages, they will set out to gather as much support as they can amongst My priests to try and sabotage this Mission.

Such souls never stop to ask themselves, why they do this. Why they feel such hatred towards you, My daughter. Why My Holy Word disturbs them so much.

When such souls attack My Holy Word with such venom, this is a sign of Satan's confirmation that these Messages are authentic.

For when such strong opposition is shown and when holy people are provoked to attack Divine Messages such as these you can be sure then that they come from God.

When they deny My Word, this cuts Me so that I weep with sadness, when they don't recognise Me. But, that is okay. In time they will know the Truth.

It is when they set out to deliberately drive souls away from My Mercy, that they offend Me greatly.

If they are responsible for souls who are denied salvation they will be punished.

Their punishment will be one of wretchedness when they try to defend their actions, for just one lost soul. Their actions can mean that a soul who, would otherwise have been converted, may suffer the final persecution in the fires of Hell.

It is when they try to sabotage the Word of God that their previous good works will be rendered useless. For what good are they when they counteract such worthy deeds, with deeds of hatred for God?

I say to them. The day you come before Me to answer for such mean spirited actions will be very difficult for you.

Not only will you have to answer for yourself, but, you will have to answer for the lies you spread about Me, My Holy Word, to others.

Is it your fear of My Holy Word, which drives you to such wickedness? Fear comes from Satan. Pride also comes from Satan. Don't you know that it is because you believe that you are so well versed in My Holy Scripture that this causes you to decide that you know more than you do?

You find fault with My Holy Word just as the Pharisees did. By doing so you say that you know more about the Truth than God.

Remember that the more you spread lies about My Holy Word you sin against the Word of God.

This sin, against the prophet of the Lord, is one of the most frowned upon by My Father.

All those who have sinned against the prophets of the Lord were punished. For when they try to stop the Word of God, given to the world to save souls, they are preventing the salvation of souls.

For this they will be struck down, for nothing will stop the Word of God from being delivered to His precious children.

Your Jesus

This is My last Mission on earth where Holy Messages from the Blessed Trinity are being given to the world
Tuesday, August 07, 2012 15:50 hours

My dearly beloved daughter, My Love for you is as strong, as it is intimate, although it does not seem like this to you at this time.

You need to spend more time in My company, for only by doing this, will you find peace in this Mission.

My Graces fill your soul now so that you can communicate to the world My Messages in the fastest time possible.

How weary I am and alone in My Heart right now, My daughter.

I fret for those innocent souls who are ignorant of My Existence. Good at heart and Christian in the way they treat others, yet, they do not believe in My Existence.

I watch each day at the way they live their daily lives with no faith in the Existence of God or their future life in the New Paradise.

Please help Me to tell them I love them.

Spread My Word and I will ignite a sense of recognition in their souls.

It does not matter if they reject you, My daughter, or My beloved followers; all that is needed is to let them read My Messages.

I will send the Holy Spirit so that a spark, albeit a tiny one, will ignite a Flame of My Love in their souls.

This is My last Mission on earth where Holy Messages from the Blessed Trinity are being given to the world.

The Holy Spirit is present in these Words of Divine origin. They are your food to nourish your souls in order to help you prepare for battle.

Listen to the Holy Word of God. Take it, share it and unite all of God's children ready for battle.

Bring all of your brothers and sisters, especially those who struggle to believe in God, towards My Great Mercy.

My Heart heaves with love for them. They, each of them, are God's children.

I need their souls so that I can take care of their future so they will have eternal life and happiness.

I can't bear to think of what will happen to them if I can't save them.

My daughter, while My Divine Mercy will save much of humanity, I need you and My followers, My sacred servants and ordinary people to spread the net and find all those poor, unhappy and confused people in need of God's Love.

Spread the net of My Love, like the fisherman, wide and far and in places where God is completely rejected, despised and hated especially.

Then go and find God's precious young children, who do not know anything about Christianity, yet they live in so called Christian countries.

Go as far as Russia, China and countries where God is not revered and go and capture souls.

Feed them with My Messages. It does not matter how you communicate, but, do it in a way where it does not seem as if you are preaching.

Entice them through what may interest them. Use every kind of modern communications to do this. I need them quickly. I am relying on the spreading of My Word by all of My followers.

I will guide you.

You will know in your hearts what to do. Ask me to help you with this special Crusade Prayer to make you strong.

Crusade Prayer (72) The Disciple's Prayer

Dear Jesus, I am ready to spread your Holy Word.

Give me the courage, the strength and the knowledge to impart the Truth so that as many souls can be brought to You.

Take me into your Sacred Heart and cover me with your Precious Blood, so that I am filled with the graces to spread conversion for the salvation of all of God's children in every part of the world no matter what their creed is.

I trust in you always.

Your beloved disciple.

Amen.

Your Jesus

By declaring the Voice of the Holy Spirit to be evil you are guilty of a blasphemy of such magnitude proportions
Wednesday, August 08, 2012 23:20 hours

My dearly beloved daughter, when people ask what I mean by the Word of God, let Me explain.

The Word of God, as contained in the Holy Bible, both the Old and the New Testaments, the Word of God, the Truth, is being given to the world through these Messages by the Gift of the Holy Spirit.

These Messages are being presented by the Holy Trinity and are the only ones of their kind ever delivered to humanity by a prophet.

The reason is that this is the last Mission, the final form of Divine Communication and Intervention being presented to the world because of My Second Coming.

Never interfere with the Power of the Holy Spirit, for this is a very serious sin.

In these Messages, the Voice of the Holy Spirit is being poured out to save mankind from eternal damnation.

You may deny Me, your Jesus, or the Divine Messages given to you by My Beloved Mother and you will be forgiven.

For all of you have the right to discern such Holy Messages because of your gift of free will.

However, when you reject the Holy Spirit and publicly blaspheme against it, this is an eternal sin and only a miracle, sanctioned by God the Father, can save your soul.

You must remain silent if in doubt about any Divine message given to the world and pray for the seer. Pray and follow your faith and continue in your ways of honouring God. It is very important that you do this.

By declaring the Voice of the Holy Spirit to be evil you are guilty of a blasphemy of such magnitude proportions that this is deemed an unforgiveable sin.

You need to ask God to forgive you now, because should you continue to mount deliberate campaigns to block the Voice of the Holy Spirit, the Voice of the Holy Trinity, and declare it to be an evil spirit, you will not, nor can you be forgiven, for this is a grave sin.

Many well-meaning Christians pull this work apart. The Messages, they say, do not conform with Holy Scripture.

When they say this they do not know the Truth, which is contained in the Holy Bible.

They either attack these Messages based on hearsay by others who claim to know the Truth or they declare them to be untrue based on their flawed interpretation of the Truth.

Worse still, they twist the truth and compare these Messages with new and ludicrous interpretations of the Holy Bible.

Listen to Me now, your Jesus, as I tell you this.

The high priests in My time on earth tried to twist the Truth of God's Laws, in order to justify their rejection of Me.

They used lies to stop people from hearing My Voice.

They declared Me a liar, a false prophet and accused Me of heresy.

I blasphemed against the Laws of the Church, they said, and violated the Sabbath by conducting the Paschal Meal on a different day to the one they deemed to be correct.

They not only misunderstood Me, they out-rightly rejected Me because they were not prepared to welcome the True Messiah, at that time.

They were not ready. They never thought that they would witness the arrival of the True Messiah in their lifetime.

So wrapped up were they in their ceremonies, their hierarchical regulations – which at that time exalted their leaders and placed them on pedestals as the real kings of their church –that they had no room in their hearts for Me, the Redeemer of Mankind.

The same will happen again as I prepare the world for My Second Coming. The Pharisees could not understand the importance of humility.

They could not accept how God works in that He does not exalt the powerful or the most experienced religious leaders in His Church to unveil His plans, or warn His children.

God chose the ignorant, the humble and the generous of heart to deliver His warnings to humanity.

He raised the weak and elevates them, through suffering, to become pure of heart so that He can manage how He communicates with them. In this way, human pride, on the part of the prophet, is unlikely to interfere with the Truth.

They rejected John the Baptist and murdered him. They murdered the prophets of old. They tormented chosen souls, through whom God communicated with.

In your world today, do you think it will be any different?

Will you, devoted followers of Me, and those who claim to be experts in My Christian or other churches who believe in My Eternal Father, accept the Word of God today.

No. You will do exactly onto the prophets, the true prophets as has been done to them since the beginning. You will vilify them in My Father's Name.

But, remember this. When the Truth is finally revealed to you, there will be no turning back if you are found guilty of the one eternal sin. That is if you blaspheme against the Holy Spirit.

Should you blaspheme against Me, Jesus Christ, you will be forgiven.

If you deny the gift of prophecy you, too, will be forgiven.

But, if you block the final plan of salvation by ridiculing openly and gathering believers of My Church to consistently proclaim the Voice of the Holy Spirit to be false and evil you will suffer eternal damnation.

Your Jesus

Don't you know that you are nothing without Me? An empty vessel, which nothing can satisfy
Friday, August 10, 2012 12:45 hours

My dearly beloved daughter, know that when you postpone prayer to Me, Your Divine Jesus, that you become weak and distanced from Me.

You must never postpone prayer or delay the time you need to devote to Me each day.

When you do, the evil one distracts you and fills your mind with worldly matters, which are empty of substance.

Then you will feel an emptiness and a struggle will become apparent within your soul.

Don't you know that you are nothing without Me? An empty vessel which nothing can satisfy no matter how powerful the allure of material wonders seem.

When I elevate a soul it entwines itself within My Sacred Heart.

But, to stay firmly within Me the soul must communicate with Me and declare its love constantly and offer thanksgiving. Otherwise it can become detached just as a baby is separated from its mother at birth, when the umbilical cord is cut.

Do not take your eyes off Me for one minute, for the evil one waits.

Then at the most unexpected moment he moves in for the kill and snatches you away.

He uses the senses to tempt and other souls to torment his victims. He especially targets My soldiers and they suffer the most.

My daughter, while busy with My Work you took your eyes from Me and this caused you to suffer. You became lost and confused. Your agitation increased as every interruption, caused by the evil one, meant you postponed your appointed time with Me, your Jesus.

When this happens you must go to Confession, receive My Body and spend time in prayer.

You must never forget to say My Beloved Mother's Holy Rosary for it offers a ring of protection against Satan.

Go now. Come to Me today in prayer. Then during your day talk to Me as a friend and share all your concerns. Then hand them over to Me and leave all your worries to me.

Your Jesus

The rains, the floods and the destruction of crops to come, will be the result of a Chastisement from Heaven
Saturday, August 11, 2012 20:10 hours

My dearly beloved daughter, the rains which will fall all over the world represent the deluge of tears which fall from My Eyes as I watch God's children wander so far off the path of eternal salvation.

The rains, the floods and the destruction of crops to come, will be the result of a Chastisement from Heaven.

The valleys of tears will spring up everywhere and it will be blamed on climate change and global warming. But, this is not so.

So many people in the world do not believe in God. They do not honour me, His Beloved Son. Instead they are consumed with an obsessive passion for false gods.

What do I mean by this?

These people create heroes and idols in the world of TV, fashion, music and sport. They then elevate them into human idols and they pay homage to them. They then idolise them in ways, which damage not only themselves, but, the person they have elevated.

They believe that these idols are sacred and do all they can to copy their lifestyles, their way of dressing, their personalities and even their physical appearance. It amounts to paganism. All of this has been foretold, My daughter. The world will idolise false gods.

These people are full of love for their bodies, themselves and with little charity or love shown for their neighbour, in their hardened hearts.

Their hearts have turned to stone.

They do not love God. Instead they have fallen under the spell of Satan who has placed these beliefs and thoughts in their minds.

There is no respect for the human body.

The body is created by God, and as such, is a temple designed in which the Presence of God should reside.

When Satan tempts humanity he focuses on the body and the pleasure it seeks through the senses.

This is why mankind now loves his own body to such an extent and he places it on a pedestal.

Never content with the way in which the body was made by God, he continually seeks to improve, change and amend the human body to suit his interpretation of perfection.

The way in which women, in particular, change their bodies and present it to the world in immoral ways disgusts Me.

Those women who have no shame in exposing their bodies commit sin yet they may not realise this. They think it is acceptable to abuse the body they were born with and flaunt themselves in a way, which can be the cause of sin.

Their love of self is one of the greatest sins of pride. They then convince young girls that it is acceptable to present their bodies in public in this way.

So many sins of the flesh are flaunted in the world and deemed to be acceptable.

Yet they are all punishable after death. Not only is sin being committed, but, it is presented as being a good thing.

Adultery is acceptable today and applauded.

Murder no longer shocks and there is no longer respect for human life.

Sexual immorality is rampant and justified.

The days of such sinful behaviour are drawing to an end.

Until humanity accepts that sin will always be sin they forfeit the right to enter the Gates of Paradise.

For every sin you are guilty of, the part of the body used when committing the sin, will be burned and purified in Purgatory.

If in mortal sin, you will feel the pain of the fire tearing through that part of your body used to commit the sin for eternity. There will be no end to this torment.

Why, why do they not listen to their hearts? So many people know that what they do is wrong, but carry on sinning regardless because it is acceptable in the eyes of the world.

The entertainment and media industries have created such a false acceptance of such behaviour that many innocent souls have been corrupted by lies.

Only the Truth can save them now. They are being given the Book of Truth, but will they listen? Satan and his fallen angels will do everything to ensure that they don't.

It will be only be when the chastisements are showered down from the heavens that they will have to discard their empty useless and disgusting habits. For they will be too busy trying to survive and put bread in their mouths.

Sadly it will only be through such chastisements that humanity can be purified on this earth. By being given the gift of purification, while alive, they are being given a chance to avoid the lakes of fire.

Your beloved Saviour
Jesus Christ

The antichrist will claim he is Me, Jesus Christ
Sunday, August 12, 2012 18:00 hours

My dearly beloved daughter, know that just as I instruct you to prepare humanity for the salvation that is rightfully theirs, so too, does the evil one prepare souls.

He prepares false prophets to deceive God's children so that they will accept the antichrist as their Jesus.

This wickedness is difficult for you to comprehend, but with the Gift I have given you to read souls you will know instantly who these false prophets are.

They will always target you, My daughter, in the most devious ways for you will be their number one adversary. Yet, their lies, couched in what will seem to be like the Holy Words of God, hide the biggest lie of all.

They will declare that the false prophet will be the true Pope. They will declare, subtly at first, that the antichrist will be Christ the King.

When they seduce poor souls that their messages come from God, such souls will be none the wiser.

I must warn all of God's children. I will never come in the flesh the second time.

I will not appear in the world as a leader. Nor will I, this time, perform miracles to prove to you who I am other than the miracle of The Warning and the miracle in the sky, which will be seen some time after The Warning takes place.

The antichrist will claim he is Me, Jesus Christ. This abomination has been foretold.

Who to believe children is no easy task for many will come in My Name. But, know this.

The evil one, through his false prophets, will never tell you to pray to the Holy Spirit or receive the Sacrament of the Holy Eucharist.

He will never admit that I, Jesus, the Son of Man, came as the Messiah, in the flesh, to redeem man from sin.

He will never ask or encourage you to say the Holy Rosary or show allegiance to My beloved Mother.

Be on your guard. Stay awake and only follow My instructions.

The evil one is trying to form an army amongst my followers. Although his other army is well established on earth he now targets those who believe in Me, your Jesus, because he wants to hide his evil deeds behind holy people.

He will use their love for Me as a shield to hide the lies he intends to inflict upon the world.

Trust in My Words and do not deviate from the Truth as it is being given to you, through these My Holy Messages to the world at this time.

Your Jesus

Virgin Mary: My child soon many of the world prophets, visionaries and seers will no longer receive Messages
Monday, August 13, 2012 19:45 hours

My child, soon many of the world prophets, visionaries and seers will no longer receive Messages, in order to make way for these most important Messages.

Much of my work, through visionaries, will stop soon to leave room for the Voice of the Holy Spirit given to you, the end time prophet.

Many false prophets, who have come forward, will still shout at the top of their voices and those will be the only other voices competing for attention with these true final Messages from Heaven.

Do not be fearful, my child, for you and this Mission is protected.

It is not just you who works for this Mission. The entire Heavens and all the angels and saints are working with you. This is why you must never feel alone, even when you suffer.

You are being blocked every day by the enemies of God.

Plans have been underway to block the publication of the Book of Truth, but this persecution is almost at an end.

Keep close to me, your Mother, at all times so that I can place my Holy Mantle around you to protect you from the evil one.

You are getting stronger and braver yet you feel tired. This will pass and the world will welcome the Book of Truth promised to them for so long.

Go now and thank God for this great Mission.

All of the Heavens bless you.

We hold your hand every day and all the saints protect you.

The battle begins the moment the first book is sold. It will spread all over the world so you must prepare adequately.

Call for help and you will receive it.

Go in peace and love.
Your beloved Mother
Mother of Salvation

This is My Book. My Word. My Promise
Wednesday, August 15, 2012 03:00 hours

My dearly beloved daughter, I speak with you of this, the most important day, the day, which I chose to launch My Book for the world.

This is the day of the Assumption of My Beloved Mother, Queen of the Heavens, Queen of the Earth, Mother of Salvation.

It is no coincidence that the Book of Truth is being made available on this date for My Mother is the Mother of Salvation. The Book is to help salvage the souls of the whole of humanity.

My Mother plays an important role in the salvation of souls.

She is the Co-Redemptrix, Mediatrix of Grace and Advocate. This means that My Blessed Mother has been chosen by God to help Me, her Son, in the final plan of salvation.

Her role in this significant period of time is not understood.

She gave birth to the Redeemer of Mankind and brought into the world the Gift of Salvation because of her acceptance to become My Mother.

She is the Mother of all God's children now and she has been given the power to crush Satan, as I prepare to salvage the human race from his wicked plan to deceive God's children.

The Book of Truth is not merely a book. It is My Holy Word, the first part of many revelations, to convert the world.

While it may have seemed very difficult to produce, with so many obstacles placed before you, My daughter, this Work is, I assure you, protected from Heaven.

This is My Book. My Word. My Promise.

When I said I would come again, I meant that I would come again.

Just as I came into the world the first time, God My Eternal Father prepared His children, in advance, through the prophets.

Many listened. Many did not.

Either way the world did not fail, afterwards, to understand the Truth. They knew and understood the meaning of My Passion on the Cross, and the freedom it gave the world to be given the Gift of eternal salvation.

The same is happening now. The world is being prepared for My Second Coming. Now.

The Holy Word of God is being given to mankind, through these Messages, as a great Gift.

Many will listen. Many will not.

One thing is clear. Very few will not know about it.

They will either accept My Word as it is being given to them now or they won't.

I have fulfilled the promise of My Father.

My Father promised the world they would be given the Book of Truth at this time.

Many will digest the Truth and accept it. Others will find the Truth too bitter to taste and will deem it to be lies.

Let them know that the Covenant will be fulfilled, as will these prophecies.

No man, no matter how he argues against My Holy Word, will prevent the Truth from being revealed to the world.

The prophecies contained in the Book of Revelation are unfolding before your eyes.

No man understands the full meaning of the Book of Revelation for its contents were not revealed to the world clearly, as they were only guidelines.

Now that I, the Lamb of God, come as promised to open the Seals, few will accept this. Why?

If you believe in Me, in these Messages, why do you deny the Truth, when it is being given to you?

Failure to accept the Truth given to you about the false prophet, the antichrist and other prophecies will mean that you will not allow Me to instruct you in the salvation of souls.

Only by following the Truth can you be safe.

Remember that only the Truth will free you from the lies, which infest mankind, through Satan.

You must continually call on My Mother to help bring you to Me, so that you are protected from the lies, which Satan will use to block you from the Truth of My final Holy Words, given to the world before My Second Coming.

Go in peace and love. I unite you all in the protection of My Precious Blood at this time.

I rejoice at your response, My beloved disciples and I rely on your faith to help Me in this special Mission.

Your Jesus

Paganism is rampant and a fascination with the occult is being encouraged
Thursday, August 16, 2012, 03:15 hours

My dearly beloved daughter, I love all God's children, but, at this time, the level of darkness, which sweeps the world means that I weep with worry because of the state of their souls.

So few understand the Truth of their future life, which awaits them in the New Era of Peace, in the world to come. The world, without end.

If they could only see it, touch it, savour it and witness the love and peace, which lies ahead they would pray to Me every second of the day begging Me for the right to enter this New World, the New Era, the New Beginning.

It is the perfect state of unity for their families and all their brothers and sisters. It is not an empty promise. It is the Paradise created for all God's children.

The fallen angels, which sweep the world, are seeking out souls everywhere in order to seduce them.

They use violence, hatred and other temptations to encourage the widespread sin so evident everywhere.

Pornography is now being spread, in the most subtle ways, to seduce and encourage sin.

Laws are being passed to ensure that sin is accepted everywhere.

Even My Church is endorsing laws, which offend God.

It will continue like this until mankind will behave like animals with no sense of godliness.

Paganism is rampant and a fascination with the occult is being encouraged so that through the world of entertainment it will appeal to young souls.

Wake up now before it is too late to save your souls.

Parents must rise in unison in accordance with My Heart's desire to protect the young whose souls are the number one target of the evil one.

He knows how precious young souls are to Me and he will relentlessly seek them out.

I ask you to say this **Crusade Prayer (73) for Young Souls, Young Children.**

O Jesus, help me to save the souls of young people all over the world.

By Your Grace, help them to see the Truth of Your Existence.

Bring them to Your Sacred Heart, and open their eyes to Your Love and Mercy.

Save them from the fires of Hell and through my prayers have Mercy on their souls.

Amen.

Your Jesus

This time is likened to the calm before the storm. Use it to prepare as many people as possible
Sunday, August 19, 2012 22:56 hours

My dearly beloved daughter, when you suffer because of Me, and when you feel isolated and beyond Me, know that this is when you are closest to My Sacred Heart.

Although this, My Book of Truth, is a Gift to the world from Me, and is protected from Heaven, it does not mean that this journey will not be painful for you.

You will experience a criticism and a new kind of attack now that My Holy Word is printed for the world to share.

You must never respond to those who demand that you explain why this Book was necessary. Remain silent and continue with My Work.

Do not let any one stop or delay the spread of My Book, for every day counts as there is limited time for souls to be granted the time to redeem themselves in My Eyes.

Let me assure you, My daughter, and all of My followers, that you are now setting out on a journey, a pilgrimage, like no other.

This time is likened to the calm before the storm.

Use it to prepare as many people as possible. Spread My Messages, My Crusade Prayers, and pray for your brothers and sisters, so that after The Warning, they will accept My Mercy.

Gather My Church together and pray for strength, for the false prophet is preparing and is already present in the Vatican. But, he hides his true façade very carefully. My beloved Vicar is being isolated and time is short.

I want all of you to begin a new Litany of Prayers for protection against the false prophet and recite them once a day from now on.

The Crusade Prayers may be selected in different lots and recited as you can.

Here is the first Jesus to Mankind Litany Prayer (1) Protection against the false prophet

Dearest Jesus, save us from the deceit of the false prophet.

Jesus, have Mercy on us.
Jesus, save us from the persecution.
Jesus, preserve us from the antichrist.
Lord, have Mercy.
Christ, have Mercy.
Dearest Jesus, cover us with Your Precious Blood.
Dearest Jesus, open our eyes to the lies of the false prophet.
Dearest Jesus, unite Your Church.
Jesus, protect our Sacraments.
Jesus, don't let the false prophet divide our Church.
Dearest Jesus, help us to reject lies presented to us as the truth.
Jesus, give us strength.
Jesus, give us hope.
Jesus, flood our souls with the Holy Spirit.
Jesus, protect us from the beast.

Jesus, give us the gift of discernment, so we can follow the path of Your True Church at all times, forever and ever.

Amen.

My daughter, please do not feel overwhelmed with this Mission for I will send you help soon. You must accept all that I ask of you and remain strong in the confidence that all is well.

The conversion is already obtained through these Messages and amounts to hundreds of thousands of souls already. So do not feel helpless or worried. I am pleased with the loyalty and dedication of those who love Me, without condition.

I am sending you those of Mine with pure hearts to offer you protection.

They will lift you and help you to lead My followers on the entire journey to the Gates of the New Paradise.

I love you, My beloved followers. Persevere with Me on this thorny path. Accept the ridicule you will have to face as you continue to spread My Holy Word.

Know that I am always with each one of you. I know My own and they know Me. Nothing can separate us.

Your Jesus

I am like a storm, which is brewing. My Voice is like thunder in the distance
Monday, August 20, 2012 03:30 hours

My dearly beloved daughter, you must never forget, through the agony, which you endure in My Name, that the Power of God cannot be surpassed.

I am like a storm, which is brewing. My Voice is like thunder in the distance.

As My Holy Word will now cover the earth, like a blanket, a rumbling sound will be heard in the distance.

As My Word spreads from man to man the storm will begin to get stronger and the rumbling of thunder will increase.

Soon the thunder will roar and few will fail to hear the Voice of God.

As the storm increases in strength, many souls, who try to batten down the hatches, will be unable to prevent the storm of My Voice, or the strength of My Mercy, from touching their souls.

The time has begun for the Intervention from Heaven to pour out over a pagan world full of darkness.

My Light will lift the hearts of even the most hardened of hearts, as the Truth will begin to sink in.

To all of God's children reading this Message, please remember My Promise to you now.

I am making Myself known to you in these Messages, through My Holy Word.

My Spirit will invade your souls during The Warning. Then I, your Jesus, will descend from the clouds at the Second Coming.

Then I will raise the New Jerusalem so that peace can, at last, be achieved in the New Era, the New World without end. My Power is Almighty.

Satan may have certain powers, but they are nothing. His power can be frightening, but he cowers in fear before Me in terror.

You must not give him more power by giving into his temptation. Nor should you allow fear of him to block your love for Me.

When you fear Satan you are feeding his power and he can control your senses.

Only prayer, and much of it, can weaken his power and his grip over you. Now that My Word is in print, Satan will raise his army to prepare for a terrible battle.

All of you, My followers, must surrender your will and trust in Me completely, as I lead you through this bloody battlefield.

Make no mistake, Satan and his demons, are furious because of this plan, the final Plan of Salvation.

He will cause havoc with this Work.

He will create debate, cast aspersions on this Work and will do everything he can to stop My Book of Truth, My Holy Messages, from being spread.

You may also expect disapproval from elements within My Church on earth and a raging argument among Christians, as to the authenticity of My Holy Word.

When the storm ahead gathers speed, as My Word is multiplied in every tongue and in every language, the Sound of My Voice will be deafening.

The Power of God must never be underestimated for I am the King of Mankind.

I now come, on behalf of My Eternal Father, to gather all of His children, in the final battle, when I will banish Satan into the lake of fire.

It will be a terrible battle and many souls will reject Me.

No matter how hard I will try, and despite My Power, it will be by their own free will that they will choose the evil one.

Trust in Me and allow Me now to purify your souls so that you will be worthy of My New Paradise on earth.

Link arms, My followers, in union, to protect My Holy Word, so that those who do not know Me can come to Me.

I love you.

I bless all of you.

Your beloved Saviour
Jesus Christ

The Book of Life foretold contains the names of all those who will be saved
Monday, August 20, 2012 15:45 hours

My dearly beloved daughter, the Book of Life foretold contains the names of all those who will be saved.

However, because of My Great Mercy, more souls will be saved because of The Warning.

Even more souls can also be saved because of your suffering and that of all chosen souls alive in the world today.

The prayers of My followers, including the recital of My Crusade Prayers, to save souls, will be a powerful means of salvaging even the most hardened of souls.

Souls who will refuse My Mercy can now be saved because of the generous intercession of those amongst you who offer sacrifice, including prayer, fasting and the acceptance of suffering, in My Holy Name.

This is My Promise such is My Great Mercy.

I bring many gifts at this time because of your love for Me.

Accept them with love and thanksgiving.

I bless you. My Promise to bestow more Gifts, because of your response to this Mission, My beloved disciples, will and can now be fulfilled because of your loyalty to Me.

Your Beloved Jesus

God the Father: Only when I am satisfied, will I bequeath the most spectacular miracles for the world to witness
Tuesday, August 21, 2012 18:00 hours

My dearest daughter, let no man underestimate the Force of My Anger as humanity succumbs further into the depths of sin.

I have sent you the prophets. Then I sent My Beloved Son, whom I sacrificed to save you and then I sent more messengers, all to little avail.

Few souls even looked at such messages from the prophets or accepted the signs given to the world by the Blessed Mother of My Beloved Son.

Because of My great love for you, as a Father, I am giving all of My children the Gift of Salvation, yet again. You must not ignore My prophets, for this could lose you your place in the inheritance, which I have planned for you.

Children, many of you who believe in Me, your Eternal Father, fail to understand the secret of salvation.

This pathway to spiritual perfection lies in your ability to accept the purification needed to ensure that you are fit to stand before Me.

Many souls must be stripped bare of all worldly attractions, distractions and corruption of soul.

For those of you, fortunate enough to have endured such a purification, you will know that until you become, as a baby, little in My Eyes, you will be unable to surrender to My Holy Will.

Struggle against such purification, and you will find it difficult to redeem yourself in My Eyes.

When you are free of all the world has to offer and focus on My Son, you will realise that the only real love and joy that exists comes from God. Nothing else, once you experience this, can satisfy you again.

You may slip from time to time, but this is to be expected. For you cannot be freed from sin until the New World begins and you align your will to Mine.

My Plan of Salvation, which can only be achieved on earth by your allegiance to My Precious Son, has already commenced. It will not take long for the global conversion. This will be achieved through My end time prophet and as a result of The Great Warning.

Feel My Holy Spirit, children, invade your soul as it spreads very quickly across the earth.

I pluck My children from their spiritual darkness in every part of the world.

I need your sacrifice and prayers to help in the salvation of souls.

Only when I am satisfied will I bequeath the most spectacular miracles for the world to witness.

When these miracles are presented they will multiply the conversion

I need to take My children to safety and into the New Paradise. Only then can we become a real family again.

I love you, children. I am pleased with those of you, generous of heart and pure of soul, who recognise this Divine Call from Heaven.

I bless you all.

God the Most High

Virgin Mary: When I waited with the apostles in the Cenacle for the descent of the Holy Spirit, it took ten days of preparation
Wednesday, August 22, 2012 09:18 hours

My child, the wilderness in which My children find themselves in the world today is because they do not know how to be given the Gift of the Holy Spirit.

Just as I taught you, it takes a long time to be given the Gift.

It consists of a very tough journey before any of God's children can be made worthy to receive this special Gift.

When I waited with the apostles in the Cenacle for the descent of the Holy Spirit it took ten days of preparation.

Although these holy, devout and loyal servants of my beloved Son were promised the Gift, they were not fully prepared spiritually to be given the Gift.

I, their beloved Mother, had to help them prepare their souls. It meant teaching them the importance of full surrender of their free will. To become worthy they had to understand the depth of humility, to which they had to succumb, before they were ready. Some of them thought that they had learned everything from my Son.

However, this was a sign of pride and when pride exists in you, you cannot receive the Holy Gift of the Holy Spirit.

To receive the Gift of the Holy Spirit you must become little before my Son, like a small child.

There can be no room for pride or arrogance. Yet, people today who claim to speak with authority about the way in which my Son speaks fall into a trap.

They, when claiming to be knowledgeable about spiritual matters, speak with an arrogance, which does not reflect the graces, which are given to those who genuinely possess this great Gift from Heaven.

Those who have been bestowed with the Gift of the Holy Spirit are submissive to the wishes of my Son.

They are not boastful.

They are not aggressive.

They do not criticise another using the Name of my Son to do so.

They do not mock others, when proclaiming their interpretation of His Holy Word.

They do not preach hatred.

When my Son's disciples were prepared by me, many arguments took place.

It took some time before they finally accepted what was expected of them.

Only then, when they understood how only humility of soul can allow the Holy Spirit to enter, were they finally prepared.

I urge all of God's children, especially those who believe in my Son, to ask me, their Mother, to allow me to prepare them for this great Gift.

My child, it took me a full year to prepare you and this was no easy feat. Do you remember how hard you found it to say my Holy Rosary? How hard you found it to surrender your will and to prove your humility?

Now that you have received the Gift it does not mean that you can take it for granted.

You must continue to pray, remain humble of heart and seek redemption every single day. For just as it is given, so too, can it be taken away.

I ask all those following these Messages to pray for the Gift of the Holy Spirit.

It is not enough to pray just the once and say that you have received the discernment you asked for and to then cast aspersions on these Divine Messages. If you do this then you have not been given the Gift.

Please call on me, your Blessed Mother, to help prepare you through this Crusade Prayer.

Crusade Prayer (74) for Gift of Discernment

O Mother of God, help me to prepare my soul for the Gift of the Holy Spirit.

Take me as a child, by the hand, and lead me on the road towards the Gift of discernment through the Power of the Holy Spirit.

Open my heart and teach me to surrender in body, mind and soul.

Rid me of the sin of pride and pray that I will be forgiven for all past sins, so that my soul is purified and that I am made whole, so that I can receive the Gift of the Holy Spirit.

I thank you, Mother of Salvation, for your intercession. and I await with love in my heart for this Gift for which I yearn with joy.

Amen.

Remember, children, come to me, your Mother, to help you to open your soul to receive this wonderful Gift.

When you receive this Gift, I will take you before my Son.

For only then will you be truly ready for the next step on the stairway to spiritual perfection.

Mother of Salvation

Just as the soldier who pierced My Side was instantly converted, so too, will millions of souls
Wednesday, August 22, 2012 20:10 hours

My dearly beloved daughter, you must not feel isolated from Me because of the enormity of this work.

For although it may seem to be of such magnitude, that you feel you will not be able to cope, know that I only ask of you that which you are capable of.

Rejoice that My Word is being sought out all over the world, for this is My Heart's desire.

I desire that all of My disciples respond immediately to My Call, for I need them to help Me in My Mission to save humanity.

This is only the beginning of a rapid conversion when the Blood and Water will gush forth over every human soul.

My Blood and Water will convert even blackened souls. Just as the soldier who pierced My Side was instantly converted so, too, will millions of souls who, at this time, do not believe I exist.

Have not I told you that My Mercy is endless?

Have I not promised that miracles, sanctioned by My Father, will take place to bring the world together and all souls to their rightful inheritance?

So many souls are now responding to My Call. Their prayers alone will be multiplied and millions more will be saved. All souls are to be included in your efforts to salvage the whole of humanity.

Your goal, My dearly beloved disciples, must be not to allow any single soul to slip through the net. This net will be thrown out and cast into the waters to catch souls and save them. You, My disciples, are the fishermen. I give you the net through the graces I now bestow upon you.

You will help Me to save every living soul and not one single effort will be left undone – not one stone unturned – as I venture forth to save humanity once again.

So, instead of cowering in fear, worried about the huge response to My Call, My daughter, you must rejoice. For at last My Holy Will is being fulfilled. Yet we still have a long way to go.

Your Jesus

Virgin Mary: Conversion can weaken the impact of the antichrist
Thursday, August 23, 2012 12:40 hours

My child, let all God's children know that the more opposition that there is to the Holy Word of my Son, at this time, the more will be the graces poured out upon the disciples of my Beloved Son.

All the prophecies foretold can be mitigated in many ways, were all God's children to accept the grace of conversion.

Conversion can weaken the impact of the antichrist. Your daily prayers, including the recital of the Crusade Prayers, will help bring this about.

To those who oppose my Son's Mission on earth, I ask that you pray for their souls.

This battle for souls is intense and you must rise above the torment and the scourging to ask me to pray for poor misguided souls who believe that they speak in the Name of my Son, but who are, instead, being deceived by the evil one.

My Son will never give up His quest for souls especially those who reject Him, mock His Holy Word and whose souls are blackened by sin.

You must stay strong, children, all of you, and remain firm in your resolution to do the Holy Will of my Son.

This will not be easy, but to gain entry to the New Paradise is not easy.

It requires much patience, much prayer, much love for one another and the ability to forgive all those who cause you grief and who desecrate the Word of my Son. Thank you for responding to my call.

Mother of Salvation

Important Message God the Father: I will grant immunity from the Gates of Hell to those souls for whom you pray
Thursday, August 23, 2012 15:15 hours

My dearest daughter, it has been seldom that the Holy Trinity has communicated to mankind in this way and the first time that I, your Father, have sanctioned a Mission of this kind.

My children, many of whom do not realise the significance of this Divine Intervention, will understand soon why it is necessary.

If the Second Coming of My Beloved Son were to occur, without warning, My precious children would never enter the gates of My New Paradise.

They would never have been able to prepare their souls and would not be fit to be admitted to the New Era of Peace.

This, a communication, which the world will find difficult to respond to.

So dark is the cloud, which covers the hearts of man, that few souls will be able to see the Light of My Divine Promise.

The forces of evil, ever present in the world, prevent My children from reaching out to Me. My determination to bring My family close and to unite them to My Bosom is fierce.

Let no man fail to understand that I will facilitate the rapid conversion of humanity, whatever the cost.

Allowing for the free will of all of My children to remain untouched, the miracles I will command, will turn their hearts inside out.

This is My Promise as I call out to each of you dear little children of Mine.

I, your Beloved Father, yearn to take you, gather you and hold you close to My Heart and take you to safety.

So few of you know the depths of My Love. Once you experience love for Me, your Eternal Father, you could never sever again your link from Me. I want to give you comfort.

I desire to let you know that My Love for you means that, through My Son Jesus Christ, great Mercy will be shown even to those with hearts of stone and to those with souls so black that only a miracle can save them.

To those who love Me, I say this. Your love for Me, your Father, will be given back to you in abundance. Your love for My Precious Son, will be rewarded, in that I will grant immunity from the Gates of Hell to those souls for whom you pray.

Nothing is impossible.

My Love is endless.

Trust in me.

Trust in My Son.

When you do, I will grant great graces for the salvation of mankind.

Your beloved Father
God the Most High

Give My Father thanks for the Gift of His Grace of Immunity from the Fires of Hell
Friday, August 24, 2012 03:15 hours

My dearly beloved daughter, I want you to ask My disciples to begin the recital, daily, of My Jesus to Mankind Litanies as and from now.

These prayers will bring great Graces and will save all those for whom you place within your special intentions for the salvation of their souls.

This second one is in honour of My Eternal Father, who Loves every one of His cherished children.

I lay My Head on His Shoulder, My Arms wrapped around Him every day, to give Him comfort as He frets for all those poor souls who are lost to Him.

Come to Him, My beloved disciples, and give My Father thanks for the Gift of His **Grace of Immunity** from the Fires of Hell to those who respond to His Call.

Jesus to Mankind Litany Prayer (2) For the Grace of Immunity

O Heavenly Father, Most High, I love You.
I honour You.
Lord, Have Mercy.
Lord, forgive us our trespasses.
I adore You.
I praise You.
I give You thanks for all Your special Graces.

I beg You for the Grace of Immunity for my beloved (name all those in a list for the salvation of souls).

I offer You my loyalty at all times.

You, O Most Heavenly Father, Creator of all things, Creator of the Universe, Creator of humanity, You are the Source of all things.

You are the Source of Love.
You are Love.
I love You.
I honour You.
I lay myself before You.

I beg for Mercy for all souls who don't know You, who don't honour You, who reject Your Hand of Mercy.

I give myself to You in mind, body and soul, so that You can take them into Your Arms, safe from evil.

I ask You to open the Gate of Paradise so that all Your children can unite, at last, in the inheritance You have created for all of us.

Amen.

I want all of you to know this.

The Love My Eternal Father has for each of His children is beyond the capacity of your knowing.

It is one hundred times, or more, stronger than that which a parent holds in their hearts for their own child on earth.

So strong is the Love that My Father has for His children, that He has made many sacrifices which you are not aware of.

His Hand has been pulled back from inflicting many chastisements, which He planned in order to punish His children. His patience has been tried beyond endurance.

The insults, thrown at Him, have been ignored by Him.

Instead, He wants to bring His children back to Him, not through fear, but through the love of those children of His, who love Him the most.

He relies on those of you with a deep abiding love for Him and Me, His Son, to help gather His lost children so He can take them to Him.

Bring all those souls close to your heart and place them now before the Throne of My Father and, in His Mercy, He will give you the greatest Gift of all. He will grant their salvation.

Bring the names of dark souls, including a list of those not known to you, and beg for Mercy for their souls.

My Father awaits, with Love in His Heart, for your generous response.

Come. Do not hesitate, for this is the most extraordinary Gift of its kind from Heaven.

You of this generation are, indeed, blessed.

Your Jesus

Virgin Mary: Embrace the Gift of the Grace of Immunity children. Cherish it, for it is a rare Gift from Heaven
Saturday, August 25, 2012 12:00 noon

My child, Heaven rejoices. The Choirs of Angels are singing at the top of their voices in praise of my Father.

His Glorious Mercy, bestowed by Him, through the special Grace of Immunity, is being acclaimed with great love and joy by all the angels and saints in Heaven.

My children, do not, as yet, understand the significance of this great Gift of Mercy by The Father, God, the Most High.

You, my children, now have the power to save the others, the lost souls. This means that the power of the evil one can be conquered in a way, which was not possible up to now.

The lies, the deceit and the hatred, which the evil one plants in the minds of God's children, can be rendered useless, if the prayers given to those who love my Son are presented before the Throne of my Father.

Embrace the Gift of the Grace of Immunity, children.

Cherish it, for it is a rare Gift from Heaven.

It proves to you the Love of your Father for each of His beloved children.

It is one of the great miracles, presented to all of God's children in the end times.

Thank you for responding to my call.

Mary, Queen of Heaven
Mother of Salvation

Hatred is the cause of all evil in the world and it takes many forms
Sunday, August 26, 2012 18:30 hours

My dearly beloved daughter, hatred is the cause of all evil in the world and it takes many forms.

Hostility towards another person springs from fear, the fear that this person may hurt you in some way.

Disagreements with another person can come about because of the sin of pride. This is when you feel that you must prove your worth, at all costs, even if you are wrong.

Jealousy very soon turns to hatred although it can be mild to begin with.

Dislike of oneself begins, because you compare your life with others, whom you feel have better fortune than you.

Very soon this dislike develops into hatred of oneself and one's body. This then leads into sins of the flesh.

Hatred may also develop because of the sin of coveting another's possessions.

This can lead to war when one country covets the riches of another.

Or it can mean allowing greed to consume your soul when you crave the same worldly riches as your neighbour.

Envy also turns into a form of hatred, especially when, no matter how hard you try to emulate another, you fail to achieve what you set out to do.

All sins, if allowed to fester, can lead you towards hatred.

When you feel hatred, you must know that Satan has managed to invade your spirit.

When this happens he will hold you in a vice-like grip and will not leave you alone.

No matter how much you try to release his grip, he will hold onto you for dear life. Your only weapon is prayer.

Pray, pray, pray when hatred surges through you. For until it leaves you, you can never feel peace, love or joy again.

When hatred takes hold of your heart and soul, you become one step further removed from Me, your Jesus.

You suffer terribly and feel an anger and a helplessness, which you cannot control.

Never believe the final lie, which Satan will plant in your soul, when he has cast a cloak of hatred over you. The lie is this. Your hatred can only be dissipated when you seek final revenge on the target of your hatred.

What to do when hatred envelops you? The power of love can evaporate hatred, instantly.

When you pray and ask me to help you My answer will be this.

Forgive your adversaries and those whom you believe are the cause of your hatred.

But, to forgive you must humble yourself before Me and ask Me to forgive you first.

Once you forgive those you hate you must then atone for your sin.

Show your adversaries love. Fight hatred, a wicked and dangerous disease of the soul, with love.

Love is the cure to rid your soul of this infestation.

When you can do this you will have defeated Satan and he will leave you be.

Never be afraid to fight hatred in your soul even though you will find it very difficult.

If hatred could be diluted in this way, through the humility of the sinner, peace would reign in the world.

Your Jesus

This is the responsibility I give you My Disciples, to convert the souls for whom I yearn the most
Monday, August 27, 2012 19:20 hours

My dearly beloved daughter, My Love for My disciples, who have responded to My Messages, has swelled My Sacred Heart to such proportions that it will now burst forth with an abundance of Graces.

My Graces pour over you My beloved followers at this time.

They are being given to you to strengthen your resolve to spread My Holy Word.

My Messages from Heaven will nourish souls, including the most blackened, with the oxygen they need to survive the darkness poured out over the world by Satan.

His invisible, but powerful, influence weakens even the strongest of believers who begin to doubt their faith. When I give you these Graces I do so for a reason.

You, My disciples, are the anchor, from which all souls who wander aimlessly in confusion, will draw towards. Even if they will not listen to you in the beginning you must persevere.

Give them copies of My Messages and My Crusade Prayers and walk away silently.

They will be touched in some way by My Holy Spirit. If they do not accept them they will find it difficult to simply walk away and just forget them. No, they will come back for Me.

Some will come back reluctantly. Curiosity will get the better of them.

Some will come back with a view to try to dismiss these Messages and try to convince you to do the same.

Others will come back to argue with you, sneer at you and challenge you.

Others will tell you that these Words do not come from Me and this will break your hearts.

But, then there will be the converts. Those who will come running to you with pure joy in their hearts begging for more.

It will be these souls who will make it all worthwhile.

However, it is the dark souls for whom you must pray the most and it is because of them that I pour out My Graces upon you so that you will help salvage their souls. For without your help there is no hope for them.

This is the responsibility I give you, My Disciples, to convert the souls for whom I yearn the most.

Your Jesus

If you praise false gods and ask for great wealth, riches and other gifts, purely to satisfy your lusts, you will attract the Prince of Darkness
Tuesday, August 28, 2012 19:30 hours

My dearly beloved daughter, the world and the people who live in it are in denial.

They do not believe in the True God, My Eternal Father.

They, in their billions, run around in confusion and chase down blind alleys, seeking a god they can pay allegiance to.

The problem about the gods, the false gods they put on a pedestal, is that these idols are of their own making. Their own creation made to suit their interpretation of who God should be.

These gods, and My daughter, they have created hundreds of them, are formed out of their own imaginations.

These same gods only serve one purpose and that is to massage the expectations, borne out of self-love, as to what their ideal god should be.

The gods they create are elaborate. They appeal to their sense of the divine right of their souls. These souls believe that their self-made gods promote their rights to wondrous things.

To those of you who do not accept the Truth, the Existence of the one True God, know this.

Only the True Creator of humanity can give you free will.

My Father will never force you or command you to do anything for this is impossible.

When you ask false gods to give you riches, make you successful or when you seek favours, you are being selfish.

Only when you ask God to grant you gifts, according to His Holy Will, can you really communicate with the One True God.

If you praise false gods and ask for great wealth, riches and other gifts, purely to satisfy your lusts, you will attract the Prince of Darkness.

He is waiting for the moment when he will grant you such favours. Do not open the door to the King of Lies for it will come at a great price.

He will exchange such worldly gifts in return for your soul.

Your Jesus

Good versus evil is a battle between God, My Eternal Father and Satan. It is that simple
Wednesday, August 29, 2012 23:00 hours

My dearly beloved daughter, the battle begins now.

For every grievous law passed by nations, which oppose the Laws of God, the forces of punishment will lash down upon them by the Hand of My Father.

Every evil offense, carried out in defiance of the Laws of God, will be attacked and nations will suffer for their sins.

Just as the Mercy of God is great and will cover the widest possible breadth in order to salvage souls, so too, will the punishment of God be unleashed to stop the spread of evil.

Good versus evil is a battle between God, My Eternal Father, and Satan. It is that simple.

Those who follow the Laws of God will be upheld.

Those, for whom they pray and offer personal sacrifice in atonement for their sins, will be dealt with leniently.

Those who refuse to follow God, despite knowing the Truth, and who infest other souls through the wicked laws they lay down amongst their nations, will be punished.

There will be many storms, floods and earthquakes ahead.

For each insult against God will be met with fierce resistance so that, in time, the purification will be and can be fulfilled. Never forget, love for God must come from the heart.

Deny the Word of God and you will suffer for this.

Love for God must be pure. Fear of God is a natural part of the affinity for the Majesty of the Creator of all things and is part of this love.

Respect for God's Laws must be shown.

When the respect is absent and when man flouts the Laws of God, which corrupt humanity, the Anger of My Father will be unleashed.

Your Jesus

Virgin Mary: The awakening is coming soon
Thursday, August 30, 2012 18:15 hours

My child, the renewal of souls has already begun and the Era of Peace is not too far away.

As all of God's children are being blessed by the Gift of the Word of my beloved and precious Son, the Holy Spirit continues to spread across all nations.

There will be no stopping the Word of my Son, for this is by the command of My Father.

Conversion will ignite the hearts of humanity and many will feel the Love of God, their natural Father, grip them in such a way that it will surprise and shock them.

Once this Divine Love surges through them, they will feel an urge to shout for joy, for it is like no other love known to man.

The awakening is coming soon.

As the Spirit of God continues to fan out in Flames of Glory, evil will be diluted and Satan's army will be left bereft of its soldiers.

It will be left defenceless because many of his followers will be won over by God's Mercy, leaving Satan with only half an army.

Disillusioned with his empty promises, they will respond to the Light of my Son's Divine Mercy.

The battle has not only begun, but souls are now following my Son in their multitudes as they seek out the Truth of Eternal Life.

I bless you, my child.

Heaven rejoices because of the conversion of souls and the salvation of dark souls, which is being achieved through the prayers of those who love my Son.

Your beloved Mother
Mother of Salvation

No man knows the Truth of the real contents of the Book of Revelation. Only God knows
Friday, August 31, 2012 23:20 hours

My dearly beloved daughter, you are at the cusp of an explosion, which will see My Mercy pour out over the world in an event, which will change the face of the earth.

This Mission has been quick. You were called suddenly and with haste as I moved to ensure that the world was given the Truth.

So few people understand that this is how God calls on the prophets, unawares, leaving no time for preparation on the part of the prophet.

This means that the words flow without hesitation.

No man has the ability to write such Messages as these. To say that this is the case, is an insult to My Father and the Holy Spirit.

No man could, through human words, ignite the Flame of God's Love in the souls of His children like these Messages can.

Only God could produce such a result.

No man knows the Truth of the real contents of the Book of Revelation. Only God knows.

Only I, the Lamb of God, have the authority to reveal what they contain. I do this now through My messenger, Maria Divine Mercy, who will convey My Words, not hers, to a disbelieving world.

Heed My Word now, for it is being given to you to save you. To warn you. To prepare you. And to purify you.

Be ready when the time comes.

I come, through the Messages, to prepare you. You do not know the day or the hour; so therefore, you must prepare your soul, as if the time for Me to come is in the next day.

Always be ready. I ask that you keep a clear and open mind when reading My Messages for the first time, for this will probably be the only time you will witness My Voice from Heaven until the day you have all been waiting for arrives.

I bless you all.

I beckon you to come to Me.

When I ask you to pray I simply ask you to confide in Me, in your own simple words. In your own way. In your private thoughts. I hear everything. I see all. I feel what you feel. I am with each of you standing beside you, just waiting for the day when you will finally surrender to My Call.

You have nothing to fear from Me for My Love for you will overcome any darkness, which keeps you distant from Me.

Turn to Me and I will pour My Light over you.

Then I will give you the peace you crave. I am waiting. I am patient.

Come to Me when you are ready.

I love you. I bless you.

Your Saviour
Jesus Christ

This Mission is the last Gift of Prophecy sanctioned by My Father to save souls
Saturday, September 01, 2012 10:25 hours

My dearly beloved daughter, the speed at which My Messages are being given to humanity is indicative of the urgency of this Mission.

So many people in the world are lost. So many poor souls do not know who God, My Father, is. So many do not accept Me, His beloved Son, as the True Messiah.

This Mission is the last Gift of Prophecy sanctioned by My Father to save souls.

These Messages are for Christians, Jews, Muslims, atheists, agnostic and all those who seek solace in man-made religions.

All people, all souls, have the same desire to find meaning in their lives.

For most it is heart breaking if they do not believe in God, for they believe that all ends when their life on earth expires.

Oh if only they could see what happens when their souls come before Me. They see Me and are speechless, for they cannot believe that I am real. The joy in many such souls, is matched only by relief, if they die in a State of Grace.

However, the joy of those souls in darkness, when they see Me, is cut short and they drift away from Me, into the depths of Hell, in a state of shock and despair.

Those souls who know of God's Teachings, through His prophets and as a result of My own Mission on earth, and who reject Me, know this.

You have chosen to turn your back on the Truth. Because of My Love for you, I will do all I can to open your eyes.

I will bring gifts and because of My Great Mercy I will save you. I call on all of you, irrespective, as to which religion you follow, to listen to these Words now.

You all know what it is like to be part of a family.

Some of you are fortunate enough to have been born into a family full of love.

Others are not so blessed and may have suffered through difficulties and darkness within the family unit. Others are lost, bruised, angry, and cannot feel true love for their families.

Some are cast out into the wilderness to fend for themselves with no one to turn to.

Many simply need a crutch of some sort to lean on in order to feel hope. This is why many poor souls try to find religions, which provide that missing link.

Sadly this simply leads them into further despair. For these religions are based on a lie.

Lies hurt you, children. They give you a false sense of security. These religions have no substance because they do not follow the Truth, the path of the Lord.

Just know that We, the Holy Trinity, are your family. The New Heaven and Earth will be your true home.

Follow Me on the path of Truth so I can take you to your rightful home.

A home so full of love and joy that it is all you need strive for.

Please open your eyes because the time has come for the world to be finally presented with the Covenant of Truth.

My Death on the Cross was a Covenant to bring you salvation.

My Second Coming is also a Covenant, the final Covenant, to bring you home to God, the Creator of all things.

My Father, God the Most High, is now sending Me, soon, to bring Salvation to all of His children.

I can only do this and fulfil My Father's Promise if I can save every soul. Do not block My Path because of doubts. Do not reject My attempts to bring salvation to every soul. Do not forfeit the chance to live a fulfilled life full of love, joy and wonder, in peace and harmony, in the New Era of Peace.

Your Jesus

I call on all of you to set up centres where you can ensure that My Messages are spread
September, 03, 2012 10:08 hours

My dearly beloved daughter, the army has been formed and its ranks will spread across Christian countries as well as those run by Communists.

No country will be left untouched by My army, My Remnant Army.

There will be tiers within My army with ranks of every kind designed to ensure that My Mission to convert souls succeeds.

All those in My army, irrespective of the role they play, will have this in common with each other.

They will serve Me in humble servitude, and their love for Me, their Jesus, will stay alight throughout the Mission. The Torch of Flames, ignited by the Holy Spirit, will not flicker for this is a special Gift to strengthen My soldiers.

Remember this will be a war, a war to save the human race. A war, which My Father will ensure is won, in the Name of God.

I call on all of you to set up centres where you can to ensure that My Messages are spread in whatever way you can.

Prayer is an important part of such centres, because, when you set up prayer groups, you will strengthen the power of My army.

I will increase conversion, as more prayer groups are established in My Holy Name.

Call these prayer groups "Jesus to Mankind" and leave the rest to Me.

My Holy Spirit will cover you in such groups and guide you every step of the way. I will give you further instructions soon.

Be at peace. I am happy that you, My beloved disciples have responded to My Call with such love and trust.

Your Jesus

My Name is no longer revered. My Name is cursed
Tuesday, September 04, 2012 23:05 hours

My dearly beloved daughter, the pain of rejection and the hatred of humanity, is felt by Me, every moment of each day.

It never eases. My Crucifixion was only the beginning.

It may have heralded the salvation of mankind, but My pain will continue, until Satan is banished.

While he is present and reigns over the earth, which he does still at this time, My pain and torment is never ending.

The only relief is the joy I feel when I see real love present in the world of pure souls towards each other.

It is this love, which keeps the Light between night and day possible. For without My Light, darkness would prevail, twenty-four hours a day.

Imagine if you will, My pain.

For those among you, who suffer pain and hurt by the hands of those you love, you will know exactly what My pain is like.

When you are tormented cruelly, both mentally and physically, by someone you love, the pain is harder to bear.

Even if you know that the person who persecutes you is in terrible darkness, it does not ease your pain. If anything, it increases the intensity and severity of your suffering.

This is because you still care about your tormentors, but you know that they suffer and cannot help their behaviour.

So much darkness are they in, when you try to explain to them what they have to do in order to get rid of their darkness, they will not listen.

They don't want to listen.

Nor do they want to rejuvenate their spirit in order to see the light, the love and the joy they would feel, if only they would listen to you, the one person who truly loves them despite their faults, their one chance to reject this dangerous dark cloud, which covers their whole spirit, to set them free.

The pain of rejection is hard for Me, your Saviour, the Son of Man.

I suffered a terrible physical suffering, much of which was not given to the world in every detail; so horrible was the torture, for I did not want this kind of sympathy.

No, I just sought your loyalty, your faith, as well as, the joy and relief of your knowing that you were saved from eternal damnation.

But, does humanity really know of the Gift I have given them really?

Many to go Mass, or receive the wine at other Christian Churches to honour My Gift, but, they do not understand what this means.

I gave Myself completely in Body, Mind and Soul. When you receive Communion, you must consume My Body fully and not just say you honour Me.

For without My Body, My Real Presence, I cannot capture your souls. Don't you know this?

Why do you reject My genuine Gift in the way it was explained to My Apostles? That The Eucharist is indeed My Body?

You cannot imagine the graces, which have been lost to you, your families and generations because of your dismissal of the Power of such a Gift.

My pain never goes away. I weep. I suffer. I cry when I witness sin, so rampant in the world, that My Name is no longer revered. My Name is cursed. I feel intense pain.

You, My daughter, have been given this same pain for the last few months. I allowed this assault on you by the evil one to infiltrate you. This sacrifice, offered by you for Me, as a victim soul, was difficult, but you learned one simple lesson through it.

When you are the victim of such cruel suffering, at the hands of others, in My Name, you feel the very pain I am feeling at the same time.

Our pain is entwined, My daughter, in this mystical union. You accepted My Call to become a victim soul willingly, knowing the consequences, frightening though it was, in order to save souls.

Now that you bring conversion, you know that when suffering is required it is to match My own suffering, which is and can be very traumatic and hurtful.

Because of your human nature you will, from time to time, tend to struggle and fight against the horror being inflicted upon you especially when, even the pain of nails, being hammered into your wrists, would be preferable to the torment you have been asked to endure, in My Name.

My Graces helped you in your submission to these requests of suffering. They granted you a strength, which allowed you to rise, stand high and praise God. For these are graces to help you accept suffering as a Gift to God to save souls in mortal sin.

The next time someone torments you, treats you cruelly and mentally abuses you children if you could remember this then you will overcome your pain.

Say to Me this Crusade Prayer (75) I assign My Pain to You dear Jesus

Jesus, I assign my pain and suffering to that which You suffered during Your Agony on Calvary.

For every insult I endure I offer it to You.

For every abuse and verbal onslaught I suffer, I offer it in honour of Your Crowning of Thorns.

For every unfair criticism of me, I offer it in honour of Your humiliation in front of Pilate.

For every physical torment I endure at the hands of others, I offer it in honour of Your Scourging at the Pillar.

For every insult I endure, I offer it up in honour of the terrible physical torture You endured during the Crowning of Thorns, when they tore out Your Eye.

For every time I imitate You, impart Your Teachings and when I am sneered at in Your Name, let me help You on the road to Calvary.

Help me to be rid of pride and never to be afraid to admit that I love You, dear Jesus.

Then when all seems hopeless in my life, dear Jesus, help me to be brave by remembering how You willingly allowed Yourself to be Crucified in such a vile and cruel way.

Help me to stand up and be counted as a true Christian, a true soldier in Your army, humble and contrite in my heart, in remembrance of the Sacrifice You made for me.

Hold my hand, dear Jesus, and show me how my own suffering can inspire others to join Your army, with like-minded souls who love You.

Help me to accept suffering and to offer it up to You as a gift to save souls in the final battle against the tyranny of the evil one.

Amen.

Suffering, My daughter, difficult as it is, is a Gift, which I use by handing it over to those I trust in My Heart so that I can save souls.

You, My daughter, have eased My suffering greatly by your response. It will take some time, however, before I am free of the Cross.

This can only come about when I save every possible soul alive on the earth today.

Your Jesus